T0287975

# THESE RUGGED DAYS

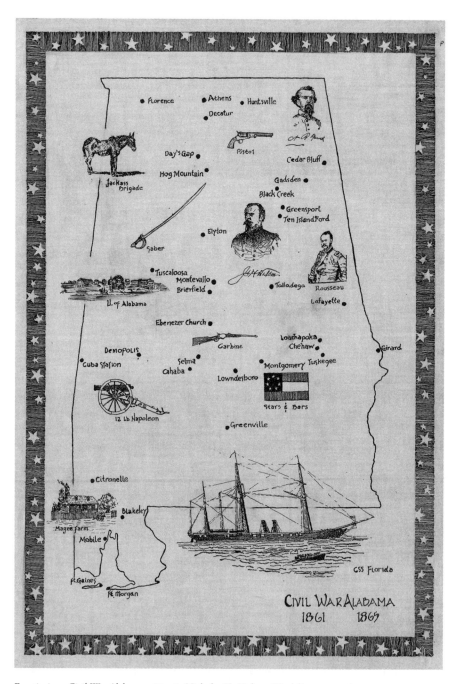

Frontispiece: Civil War Alabama, 1861–65. Nicholas H. Holmes III, delineator, 2016.

# THESE RUGGED DAYS

## Alabama in the Civil War

JOHN S. SLEDGE

The University of Alabama Press    Tuscaloosa

The University of Alabama Press
Tuscaloosa, Alabama 35487-0380
uapress.ua.edu

Copyright © 2017 by the University of Alabama Press
All rights reserved.

Frontispiece: Civil War Alabama map; copyright by Nicholas Holmes III

Inquiries about reproducing material from this work should be addressed to
the University of Alabama Press.

Typeface: Garamond and Futura

Manufactured in the United States of America
Cover image: *Wilson's Charge*; painting by Don Stivers; courtesy Stivers
Publishing
Cover design: Gary Gore

Cataloging-in-Publication data is available from the Library of Congress.
ISBN: 978-0-8173-1960-1
E-ISBN: 978-0-8173-9142-3

Publication of *These Rugged Days* is made possible in part through the
generosity of the A. S. Mitchell Foundation and the Alabama Bicentennial
Commission Foundation.

For the people of the great state of Alabama,
and in memory of Thomas Tyler Potterfield, friend of many years

Hereafter you shall recount to your children, with conscious pride, the story of these rugged days, and you will always greet a comrade of the old brigade with open arms.

—Brig. Gen. R. L. Gibson's farewell to his troops upon
their surrender after the Mobile campaign, May 8, 1865

# Contents

# Illustrations

**Plates**

# Acknowledgments

I must begin by thanking Joseph Meaher for his enduring interest in Alabama history in general and my work in particular. Joe encouraged me to seek the support of Mobile's A. S. Mitchell Foundation for this project, and the trustees happily agreed. Jay Lamar of the Alabama Bicentennial Commission was also an early advocate, and her enthusiasm throughout has meant a great deal. I am very proud that *These Rugged Days* is part of the state's official bicentennial observances.

One of the joys of doing any Alabama history project is the generous assistance of so many dedicated and talented professionals at libraries, archives, museums, historic sites, and universities. To begin with, profoundest gratitude goes to Robert Bradley, recently retired from the Alabama Department of Archives and History (ADAH); Mike Bunn of Blakeley State Park; and Mike Bailey of the Alabama Historical Commission (AHC) at Fort Morgan. These three gentlemen served as an indispensable Civil War brain trust, reviewing the manuscript and saving me from innumerable errors. Their expertise is astonishing, exceeded only by their good cheer. I consider it a privilege to have received so much of their time and attention. Numerous other individuals at various institutions provided help in small ways and large. Thanks go to Steven Murray, Scotty Kirkland, and Debbie Pendleton (recently retired) at ADAH; Jacqlyn Kirkland of the AHC; Charles Torrey and Nick Beeson of the History Museum of Mobile; Lauren Vanderbijl, Robert Allen, Melanie Thornton, and Bob Peck of the Historic Mobile Preservation Society; Cart Blackwell of the Mobile Historic Development Commission; Ned Harkins, Zennia Calhoun, and Pamela Major of the Mobile Municipal Archives; Jane Daugherty at the Mobile Public Library, Local History and Genealogy Division; Jo Ann Flirt of Blakeley State Park; Becky Nichols, Crystal Drye, and Stephen Posey at the Selma-Dallas County Public Library; Susanna Leberman of the Huntsville-Madison County Public Library; Judy Bolton at the LSU Libraries Special Collections; and the Rev. Danny Rasberry at Ebenezer Baptist Church in Stanton, Alabama. The following friends and colleagues provided important assistance at various points along the way: David Alsobrook, Dan

Brooks, Hardy Jackson, E. C. LeVert, Holly Jansen, Jacob Laurence, Sheila Flanagan, Mildred Orr, Roy Hoffman, Hudson McDonald, Stephen McNair, Tracy Stivers, Walter Edgar, Robert Gamble, Ken Niemeyer, Tom Root, Mike Mahan, Ken Noe, and Jim Day. At the University of Alabama Press, retired director Curtis Clark and acting director Dan Waterman expressed early and sincere interest in yet another Civil War book. Working with them and the press staff has been a distinct pleasure. Special thanks go to Nicholas H. Holmes III for the stunning map of Civil War Alabama. Nick is an old and dear friend, and this collaboration has been a delight.

Lastly, my family has been wonderful. My lovely wife, Lynn, edited the manuscript with her usual eagle eye for clarity and served as an invaluable sounding board. Our children, Matthew and Elena, both living upstate, have endured more than their share of historic site visits over the years with remarkable good humor. Their love and support buoys me. And then there's my mother, Jeanne Arceneaux Sledge, who read this book as I wrote it and offered helpful insight and encouragement. It is easy sometimes for a writer to get lost in the forest, but family always helps me regain the path.

There are no doubt errors herein, but they should be laid solely at my door.

# Prologue

*Chasing Wilson's Raiders with Aunt Octavia*

Virtually every southern boy of my generation has vivid memories of the Civil War Centennial. Reenactments, pageants, billboards, advertisements, full-page newspaper articles, and even restaurant menus celebrating the momentous anniversary were everywhere. Caught up in the excitement, my buddies and I refought the war throughout the woods and subdivisions of our little piece of the South. With high hearts, we nailed a Confederate battle flag to a wooden slat and hollered our juvenile Rebel yells as we overran the hated Yankees' positions. The enemy was imaginary, of course, since none of us wanted to be a Yankee, even in play.

Home was Montevallo in southern Shelby County, Alabama, a small college town of about 3,000 people then, thirty-three miles south of Birmingham. In fact, our community was just about as close to the geographical center of the state as it was possible to be, with a marble stone attesting to the fact off Highway 25, a little west of the city limit.[1] Downtown consisted of Main Street, a short commercial drag of one- and two-story Victorian-era buildings occupied by a bank, the post office, drug stores, a five-and-dime, clothiers, a book shop, a jeweler, and the Strand Theater. The charming Alabama College campus was only two blocks away. Designed by Frederick Law Olmsted's firm in 1896, the campus is still notable for its handsome red brick buildings and streets lined with graceful pecans and oaks. My family moved there in 1962 when Dad took a position as a biology professor at the school (rebranded the University of Montevallo seven years later).

Not content merely to study and act out the major Civil War battles like Antietam and Chickamauga that everybody had heard of, my buddies and I were eager to learn about the conflict in our own neck of the woods. And like any southern burg worth its salt, Montevallo could boast of a little fighting between the blue and the gray. For it was there, in the wet spring of 1865, that Union Maj. Gen. James Harrison Wilson's thunderbolt cavalry raid into the heart of the Deep South first encountered serious resistance. Somewhere along what is Highway 119 today, a smattering of Rebel cavalry under the command of Gen. Philip D. Roddey engaged the Yankees and was driven through downtown. Montevallo's capture was important to the Federals, even though it was little more than a dot on the map. It was there that the Alabama and Tennessee River Railroad connected from Talladega to the northwest and then bent south arrow-straight for Selma, Wilson's main objective. Montevallo was also the seat of a rich industrial district, and numerous foundries, rolling mills, and collieries were in the vicinity, perhaps none more critical than the Bibb Naval Furnace five miles away at Brierfield. Even as Union regiments fanned out to destroy these industrial assets, Roddey set up a skirmish line two miles south of Montevallo to try to check the advance. Undeterred, the Fifth Iowa made a mounted charge complete with blaring bugles, fluttering guidons, snorting horses, jangling spurs, flopping canteens, and flashing sabers. The Rebel line broke and a running fight commenced all the way to Selma. "I am satisfied that . . . [Wilson] drove us fifteen miles an hour a part of the time," one Southron later recalled. Confederate Gen. Nathan Bedford Forrest, the famed "Wizard of the Saddle," joined Roddey in the midst of this fracas, but even he and his legendary paladins couldn't quell the blue tide.[2]

For school-aged boys, this was heady stuff indeed, and we enthusiastically plunged into the fields and woods in a frenzied hunt for artifacts. The most promising territory was along Mahan Creek in Brierfield, where we knew from our history-minded fathers and our own reading that brisk skirmishing had occurred. Mahan Creek is a lovely stream that threads north and west through Bibb County's rolling farms and woodlands, eventually spilling into the Little Cahaba River. In her elegiac 1910 history, *The Story of Coal and Iron in Alabama*, Ethel Armes wrote that the "banks of Mahan's Creek droop with live oaks, cedar, and sycamore, yellow jessamine, and wild honeysuckle, yellow and red. Springs, at least forty in number, feed its course all along its way."[3] Needless to say, this was a boy's paradise, and since part of the land alongside the stream was owned by our family dentist, Dr. Mike Mahan, we had the run of it.

Chuck Hogue made the big find. If memory serves, he lived out that way himself, and one day while walking along a dirt road he spotted what looked like an iron pipe jutting out of the ground. As he told us later, he began digging around it, and as more of it was revealed, realized he had actually discovered a gun barrel. Excitedly pulling at it and digging farther down into the hard red clay, he eventually loosened the barrel enough to yank it free. My first glimpse of this find came when Chuck and his father brought it to Dad for identification. Dad was quite knowledgeable about the Civil War and had a fine collection of period guns and accoutrements he had acquired as a boy during the 1930s for laughable prices at surplus outfits. In truth Chuck's barrel wasn't much to look at, heavily rusted and the wooden stock long gone. Because there was a piece of quartz jammed in the breech, they thought it might be an old flintlock musket. But Dad knew immediately that it was a Spencer Carbine, a seven-shot repeater that had been standard issue for Wilson's troopers. Exhausted butternut cavalrymen armed with Colt pistols and homegrown militias of old men and boys toting 10-pound single-shot muzzle loaders didn't stand a chance against this ingenious weapon of war. Little wonder they'd dubbed it "the danged Yankee rifle you load on Sunday and shoot the rest of the week."[4]

I never will forget how it felt to actually hold a tangible piece of Civil War history. It spoke volumes that a valuable gun like that had been left behind. It was highly unlikely that a trooper would have simply lost it, as the consequences for such negligence were severe. No, my friends and I reflected in our discussions of this marvel, some Yankee had been shot out of the saddle by one of Roddey's men. Amid the dust and confusion of a full-on cavalry charge, the carbine was knocked into a ditch or covered by debris. Whatever the case, there it stayed for a century, until rain exposed it to the light again and a country boy happened to pass by. Gazing at that rusted Spencer, Wilson's Raid ceased to be an abstraction and became actual, even if still removed in time.

Happily, Chuck Hogue's archaeological triumph wasn't to be my only close brush with the historical reality of Wilson's Raid. As I soon learned, memories of the event were still within reach, albeit secondhand, through the magical storytelling ability of my great aunt Octavia Wynn, or Ta Ta (pronounced tay-tay) to the family. Ta Ta and my uncle, Charles Wooding Wynn, affectionately known as Pinkie for his bright, slightly rosy countenance, lived in Selma alongside the Jefferson Davis Highway (US Route 80). They were an extraordinary couple, married in 1911 when Ta Ta was barely twenty-one. Pinkie, a native Georgian, had a robust love for the outdoors. He even made his own fishing lures. He had followed a diverse career path, working as a traveling salesman, automobile garage proprietor, and bottling plant owner. To pre-

Figure 1. Aunt Octavia with her glue pot at the *Selma Times-Journal*, 1957. Author's collection.

serve his sanity during the Great Depression when there was no work to be had anywhere, he loaded a small motor craft and puttered down the Alabama River, living off catfish, blackberries, and the kindness of tugboat crews and black swampers. At the site of Fort Mims in Baldwin County, he kicked up a few artifacts, including gun flints and militia buttons, which I now keep in a little wooden box on my office shelf.

Fascinating as Pinkie was, Ta Ta intrigued me more. Physically she was unimpressive, very short with her gray hair in a bun and eyeglasses perched on her nose. But intellectually she was a powerhouse. She nourished a love for William Faulkner's novels, and her and Pinkie's little Cape Cod cottage was filled with books. She was an engaging conversationalist, even with a youngster, and a superb storyteller. Although mostly retired when I came to know her well, she had worked as a journalist for decades. Hired by the *Selma Times-Journal* as a social editor in 1914, she eventually became city editor and penned a popular column titled "Up and Down the Town." One of her renowned coworkers, Kathryn Tucker Windham, recalled that Ta Ta was a newsroom legend, "noted for her long, involved sentences." This was hardly surprising for a Faulkner fan. Ta Ta's proud record was 147 words, which almost certainly still stands and is impossible to imagine in today's world of dumbed-down newspapers. Years later, in going through some of Ta Ta's personal papers, I stumbled across a psychological evaluation conducted during the 1940s. It nailed her to a T. The test ranked her language capacity as "high" and noted "deep artistic appreciation," "tremendous detail capacity," "diagnostic ability," and good memory "as to events." Fittingly, the report concluded in part that she "should have been good in history."[5]

Of course, Ta Ta *was* good in history. Throughout her career at the *Times-Journal*, she had written stories about local history and architecture and had interviewed Confederate veterans, widows, ex-slaves, and civilians who perfectly recalled the Civil War. Ta Ta's years of trolling for stories and lore had supplied her with a virtually bottomless supply of material, all of it immediate, striking, and colorful. In relating these tales, Ta Ta was animated and eloquent. The personalities she conjured were vivid, the incidents rich, and the conclusions often tragic or poignant. Everything fell away except her voice, and it filled my imagination with wonder.[6]

I never will forget the most magisterial display of this native talent. When I was around ten, Dad drove the fifty miles down to Selma and brought Ta Ta back for a short visit. When it was time to take her home, we all piled into the family car for the trip. Dad pulled out of the driveway onto Pineview Road and then turned left on Highway 119, which took us down Main Street and across the bridge over Shoal Creek toward Wilton. And then, spontaneously, it began, Ta Ta on Wilson's Raid. As my mother later recalled, it was "a non-stop account from door to door."[7] Looking back on it now, I am immensely grateful for the privilege of that short hour. It was a defining moment for me, helping to cement my determination to be a historian and a writer.

Just across the bridge on the right were two large magnolia trees. Ta Ta said that General Wilson had tied his gray horse, Sheridan, to one of these and consulted with his officers about where the roads led, what to destroy, and how best to keep pressing the outnumbered Rebels. Dad laughed and said those trees would have been mere saplings in 1865, not likely to hold a spirited gelding. But Ta Ta was undeterred, and I wasn't interested in healthy skepticism. It was all about story, and Ta Ta was our narrator and guide.

Wilton didn't exist during the raid, but it was there that the railroad tracks appeared, paralleling our route along the west side and then at Ashby, south of Brierfield, gracefully curving across the highway and running along the east shoulder all the way to Selma. The proximity of those gleaming rails on creosote ties and chert rock lent even more immediacy to the tale. As it turned out, Ta Ta had known the engineer for General Forrest's ordnance train, who had desperately backed his cars just ahead of the bluecoats. She described his fevered efforts to keep up steam, frequent stops along with the troops, and pell-mell retreats as Yankee bullets clipped branches and banged into the iron locomotive.[8]

At the halfway mark we stopped at a claptrap gas station for Moon Pies and "cool drinks," as Dad called them. This was Stanton, a tiny rural hamlet anchored by Ebenezer Baptist Church, a white frame building on an elevated knoll right beside the highway. A historic marker in front commemorated the pitched battle fought there on April 1, 1865. As we gazed at this little country church, Ta Ta described how Forrest had finally managed to concentrate enough men to make a determined stand. The Confederates were thinly ranked behind primitive breastworks and a few cannon as Wilson's troopers thundered into view. But they were only 1,500 against 10,000, and Wilson smashed them and set them running for Selma again. Forrest himself was wounded by a young Indiana captain wielding a saber. He would have been a goner, Ta Ta averred, if the Yankee had used the point of his sword rather than the blade. Wiser in the ways of personal combat, the Wizard of the Saddle leveled a pistol and shot his assailant out of the saddle. The unfortunate Hoosier was buried behind the church, Ta Ta said, along with eleven of his comrades. I recall being very moved by this. Twelve young men, not too much older than me, killed far from kith and kin and laid to rest in an isolated and unfamiliar place.

South of Stanton the road dropped and rose across a series of wide hills before descending onto a fertile plain. During the war this would have been fine cavalry country, planted in corn and cotton and much less forested than now. Just ahead was Selma, the great industrial hub of the Confederacy and Wilson's desideratum. Here Ta Ta was in fine form, for she knew every inch of the place, from the soaring Edmund Pettus Bridge and decayed Saint James Hotel downtown out to the strip malls and motels along the Jefferson Davis Highway. Before we took her home, she had to show us the mansion that still displayed bullet holes from the battle, and then there was the obligatory

Figure 2. Ebenezer Baptist
Church, 2015. The original church
is long gone, but the current
building (ca. 1925) is suitably
plain. Courtesy Elena Sledge.

tour of Sturdivant Hall. Ta Ta worked as a docent there, and I thoroughly enjoyed the unfettered access this got me to every nook and cranny of the house.

Built in 1853 and occupied during the Battle of Selma by a local banker
named John McGee Parkman and his family, Sturdivant Hall is one of Alabama's best preserved Greek Revival mansions, a Corinthian-columned masterpiece of elegant proportions and exquisite interior plaster work. Ta Ta's love for
the home was infectious, and she possessed a bundle of stories about the house
and what had happened there during Wilson's Raid. Years later, her obituary
would note that she was as much "a part of Sturdivant Hall as the cupola on
its roof."[9] The cupola was always my favorite part of any ramble through the
house, and there were many over the years. Ta Ta loved to climb up to it just
as much as I did, and together we would ascend the tight spiral stair until we
emerged, exhilarated and she slightly out of breath, into the little square space
with its ample windows on all sides. Here, Ta Ta informed me, Parkman and
his family assembled to anxiously watch the battle. After Selma fell, booted

Yankee soldiers clomped into the house searching for Rebels and silver, and slashed a portrait with their bayonets. The painting of two little girls was later repaired, but the scars of that senseless vandalism remain evident.[10]

When we finally deposited Ta Ta back at her house, I think we were all a little dazzled. I know I was. Many years later, after I had completed my thesis in historic preservation, I traveled to the nursing home where Ta Ta then lived to share it with her. I had written about the little community of Summerfield, a Methodist enclave nine miles north of Selma that is rich in antebellum architecture. Ta Ta knew it well, of course. She greeted me warmly from her bed, and I pulled up a chair. After a hug, I showed her the thesis and pointed out the dedication, "To Octavia S. Wynn, who instilled in me a fascination of history when I was very young." She liked that, but sadly suffered from Alzheimer's disease and wasn't able to grasp much more. Ta Ta passed on July 22, 1986, and was laid to rest in Selma's New Live Oak Cemetery next to Pinkie, who had preceded her by a few years. Sui generis to the end, their stones are engraved with a few lines from the *Rubaiyat of Omar Khayyam*. Ta Ta's displays Canto XXVIII: "With them the seed of Wisdom did I sow, / And with mine own hand wrought to make it grow; / And this was all the Harvest that I reap'd— / I came like Water, and like Wind I go."[11]

Comes now Alabama's bicentennial, with all the attendant pageantry and scholarly reflection. Ta Ta would have loved it, no doubt, and I am profoundly sorry that the modern readers of the *Selma Times-Journal* will not benefit from her storytelling ability. But, moved by her spirit and love of good material, this book is offered for a popular audience. Of all the many important events in Alabama's two-hundred-year history as a state, the Civil War still looms as the most profound. There are, of course, already many good books about specific aspects of Alabama's war, from Wilson's Raid to the Battle of Mobile Bay, not to mention Ben Severance's *Portraits of Conflict* (2012), a fine photographic history, and Chris McIlwain's *Civil War Alabama* (2016), which focuses on politics and Unionism within the state. Despite this, the story of the shooting war in the Heart of Dixie proper is still underrepresented in broader histories. Most, including McIlwain, include only a paragraph on the Battle of Mobile Bay, but never fail to emphasize that Alabama was largely untouched by fighting until nearly war's end, and that what fighting did occur was minor and of little consequence.

While that is true from a grand strategic perspective, there is, as Ta Ta certainly understood, a great deal of story there nonetheless. Shots were fired in anger in thirty-one of Alabama's fifty-two wartime counties by uniformed opponents. Troops from every Confederate state plus Missouri and Kentucky fought against Union regiments from twenty-three different Northern states, including black troops and loyal units from Alabama, Louisiana, and Tennessee. The massive multivolume *War of the Rebellion*, a compilation of all the official army and navy correspondence and reports North and South, documents over three hundred military incidents within Alabama, variously defined as actions, attacks, battles, campaigns, engagements, evacuations, scouts, sieges, and skirmishes, from as early as January 4, 1861, days before the state seceded, to May 1, 1865, weeks after Robert E. Lee surrendered his Army of Northern Virginia at Appomattox Court House. Happily for the men involved, casualties were relatively low compared to the horrific bloodlettings at places like Shiloh and Gettysburg, but no one who fought in Alabama ever made light of the experience. Many of these men were hardened veterans who had "seen the elephant," as the baptism of fire was quaintly called then, in Virginia or Tennessee, and knew whereof they spoke when they described Selma as "a whirlwind of battle," the CSS *Florida*'s dash into Mobile Bay amid a rain of Federal shot and shell as "daring and gallant," and the skillful defense and evacuation of Spanish Fort as "one of the best achievements of the war." They, at least those men in blue and gray who had been there, as well as the civilians and slaves who had witnessed along with them, would never forget. Nor should we. In fact, what happened in Alabama not only affected the people who were there in important ways, itself worth relating, but also occasionally did indeed have important national consequences. One example was the sack of Athens, which led to a new federal policy endorsing the plundering of Confederate civilians, with infamous results later in Georgia. Another was the Union victory at Mobile Bay, which enhanced President Lincoln's reelection chances and further demoralized the beleaguered South. Here then, from the Tennessee Valley to the Gulf beaches and so many places in between—Auburn, Blue Mountain, Elyton, Eufaula, Greensboro, Lowndesboro, Montgomery, Montevallo, Selma, Stanton, Talladega, Ten Island Ford, Tuscaloosa, Tuskegee, and Whistler, the story of those rugged days.[12]

# THESE RUGGED DAYS

# Introduction

*Alabama, 1860*

Abraham Lincoln was elected president of the United States on November 6, 1860. After decades of sectional wrangling over the issue of chattel slavery, most Southerners considered this the last straw. Only weeks later, on December 20, South Carolina became the first state to secede from the Union. The momentous news clacked into the Montgomery telegraph office that afternoon, and by evening citizens had transformed the streets of Alabama's capital city into a huge, impromptu carnival of celebration and support. The *Montgomery Weekly Advertiser* enthusiastically reported bonfires, flags, marching citizen-soldiers banging drums, "volleys of musketry, the firing of cannons and ringing of bells," all mixed with the unrestrained shouts of men and boys and smiling female approval. Down in Mobile, a young woman named Kate Cumming witnessed a similar outpouring. "The city was one blaze of light from the illuminations," she later wrote, "scarcely a window in the whole city was not lit. The noise from the fireworks and firearms was deafening. Speeches were made, processions paraded the streets with banners flying and drums beating, and in fact everything was done to prove that Mobile at least approved of what South Carolina had done." Would Alabama follow suit?

Sentiment was divided among straight-outs, cooperationists, and Unionists, but anxious residents wouldn't have long to wait for an answer. Governor Andrew B. Moore had called a state convention in Montgomery for January 7 to decide.[1]

If Alabama indeed cast her lot with the Palmetto State, she would be a welcome ally in any armed confrontation with the powerful North. On the eve of the American Civil War, the Heart of Dixie was widely regarded as a wealthy and rapidly developing place of great beauty and promise. Then, as now, the state's physical dimensions were impressive—336 miles from the Tennessee line to the Gulf of Mexico's sparkling waters and 150–200 miles wide between Mississippi and Georgia, with a 60-mile coastal stretch between Mississippi and the Florida panhandle, the whole encompassing over 50,000 square miles, or in the terms of Alabama's many farmers, 32,462,080 acres. Within these borders is a breathtaking geographical diversity. Immediately noticeable to anyone studying a topographical map are the parallel ridges and valleys that finger northeast to southwest and the state's plurality of rivers and streams. The ridges mark the termination of the Appalachian Mountain chain. Flat-topped and generally below 2,000 feet, they have always been considered agriculturally viable. According to *A New and Complete Gazetteer of the United States*, published in 1854, Alabama's mountains feature "fine grazing lands, while the flats between them are very rich in soil."[2] Where not planted in corn or trod by cattle, the ridges were mantled in bountiful woods of oak, black gum, poplar, hickory, chestnut, and mulberry, green in summer, gold and red in autumn.

The north central counties of the state—Jefferson, Tuscaloosa, Shelby, and Bibb—were known very early on for their "mineral treasures," including iron, coal, red ocher, and lead. In 1855, *DeBow's Review*, a magazine devoted to agricultural, commercial, and industrial matters, predicted that Alabama would soon be a "seat of manufacturing empire." "A liberal hand has stored, side by side with the plentiful ore of iron, inexhaustible quantities of flux and fuel for its reduction," the magazine continued, "to be in future a source of incalculable social wealth and industrial power." Just how liberal was revealed during an 1862 survey of the Cahaba Valley by Willis Brewer. Tramping over the wooded hills and intermittent fields, Brewer calculated "seventy billions of tons" of coal bedded beneath the soil and "five hundred billions of tons" of iron ore locked in Red Mountain. These riches had only begun to be exploited, however, mostly in Shelby County. An engineer who rode his horse along Red Mountain in 1858 looked out over the future site of Birmingham and saw only a lightly settled and cultivated valley. "It was one vast garden as far as the eye could reach," he wrote. Bibb County was even less peopled. A correspondent for a Mobile newspaper visited there in 1859 and reported "some of the wildest and grandest scenery" he had ever encountered.[3]

The state's finest farmland was located in two fertile crescents north and south—the Tennessee River Valley and the Black Belt. As early as 1817, a traveler named Anne Newport Royall was astonished by the extent of picked-over cotton fields near Huntsville. "Fancy is inadequate to perceive a prospect more grand," she exclaimed. "Although the land is level you cannot see the end of the fields either way. To a stranger, coming suddenly amongst these fields, it has the appearance of magic." The Black Belt, the tier of counties along and just below the fall line—Greene, Marengo, Perry, Dallas, Lowndes, Montgomery, Macon, and Russell—was even more productive. Once forming the shoreline of an ancient shallow sea, these counties are noted for their sticky, black, gumbo soil that before the Civil War delivered legendary cotton yields. In 1859, Marengo County produced 62,428 bales and Dallas a thousand more than that. The British naturalist Philip Henry Gosse, who taught at a plantation school in Dallas County, thought the crop beautiful when the bolls burst. "The fine, dark-green foliage is relieved by the bunches of downy cotton of the purest white," he wrote, "bearing a curious resemblance to a meadow on which a light shower of snow has just fallen."[4]

North Alabama's hill counties and south Alabama's vast coastal plain boasted neither iron nor cotton. Poor whites and hardscrabble farmers were the rule in these areas. The people were unsympathetic to the dreams and schemes of the state's plantocracy but shared a horror of abolition. The economic prospects in the south were a little brighter given its timber resources. As *DeBow's Review* explained in an 1855 article, "The pine, the white-oak, the live-oak, the cypress, and some others, are in very great abundance, and to some extent quite accessible to our commercial port."[5]

Getting Alabama's cotton and other products to market depended on the rivers. *A New and Complete Gazetteer* noted "more than 1500 miles of steamboat navigation" on the state's waterways, "giving an outlet not only to her own productions, but also to some of those of Mississippi and Georgia."[6] Alabama has always been justifiably famous for its rivers and creeks, which cut and thread their way through rock and loam alike. In the north, the shining Tennessee loops through the state in a great bend, flowing perversely west and north toward its union with the Ohio River in Kentucky. More logically, the rest of the state's big rivers aim directly for the emerald Gulf. On the east, the Chattahoochee traces the Georgia line and flows through the Florida panhandle, where it finds an outlet at Apalachicola. From the northeast the Coosa tumbles southwest through the ridge and valley country and prior to the twentieth century was noted for its many shoals, rapids, and falls. It unites with the Tallapoosa above Montgomery to form the mighty Alabama. After absorbing the Cahaba west of Selma, that muddy stream sweeps through graceful curves and tight bends west and south. From the northwest, the storied Tombigbee comes out of Mississippi, entering Alabama at the Pickens County line. It is joined by the Black Warrior and Sipsey, as well as numberless smaller watercourses, before it unites with the Alabama 50 miles north of Mobile to form the Mobile River Delta. After filtering through this 300-square-mile natural wonderland of forest, swamp, and marsh, millions of gallons of water finally empty into Mobile Bay through five river mouths—the Mobile, Spanish, Tensaw, Apalachee, and Blakeley.

During the Civil War, the Tennessee was navigable from east to west all the way to the Muscle Shoals, 10 miles below Decatur. In those predam days, the rocky shoals disrupted the river for a 38-mile stretch to Florence and made through steamboat travel impossible. By contrast, the Alabama was navigable from Mobile to Montgomery and the Tombigbee to Aberdeen, Mississippi. Mobile Bay provided the state's outlet to the wider world. The bay itself is a large sheet of shallow, brackish water averaging 10 feet in depth except for the ship channel leading into the Gulf, first dredged during the 1830s. Shaped like a gunstock, Mobile Bay has been favored for its shrimp, oysters, flounder, trout, and crab since Indian days. Its three-mile-wide mouth is flanked to the west by Dauphin Island and to the east a long peninsula, on the western tip of which sit the brooding ramparts of Fort Morgan, already the site of much history by 1860.

Before the war, most Alabamians were spread along these vitally important rivers. That left nearly half the state's land—rocky uplands, sandy pine barrens, thickets and swamps everywhere—in the public domain. Forty years beyond statehood, less than a million people lived in Alabama, and almost half of them were slaves. Fewer than 50,000, white or black, resided in towns. In fact, only seven cities were listed in the 1860 census—Florence, Huntsville, Jacksonville, Marion, Montgomery, Selma, and Mobile. By far, Alabamians were a rural people, their world the plantation and farm. Most white males worked the land, with a smattering of lawyers, doctors, store clerks, merchants, brickmasons, mill hands, carpenters, blacksmiths, and iron founders in the towns. Illiteracy was high, but virtually everyone knew their King James Bible, and some country people spoke a charming hillbilly Shakespeare. For the educated there were almost a hundred newspapers in the state and 361 public libraries containing 123,000 volumes. Schooling was irregular but improving. Roughly half of all white children attended school at least part of the year. Female academies were common, and at Tuscaloosa the University of Alabama, founded in 1831, boasted a 7,000-volume library, laboratories, classrooms, dormitories, and an observatory sheltering an 8-inch refracting telescope underneath its 18-foot dome. Well-bred white women were generally confined to the domestic sphere. Cooking, sewing, child-rearing, doctoring, and holding the spiritual and emotional centers of their families occupied them, as did a hundred other tasks whether in pillared mansion or urban town house.[7]

For the slaves, male or female, mind-numbing labor in field, stable, or kitchen was their general lot, and everything to do with their lives was strictly regulated by draconian law and custom. The 1852 *Code of Alabama* listed a blizzard of rules and infractions along with the required punishments. Movement was tightly controlled. No slave was allowed to "go beyond the limits of the plantation on which he resides, without a pass." The penalty for doing so was up to "twenty stripes, at the discretion of any justice before whom he may be taken." Slaves could not enter a white person's house without permission and were forbidden to carry guns or own a dog or, for that matter, any kind of property. Rebellion, including "seditious speeches," was punishable by up to 100 lashes or even death. Education was prohibited, and families could be separated by a sale. Manumission was occasionally granted but was only a distant dream for most.[8]

Slaves could be found in every corner of the state, but unsurprisingly their numbers were concentrated on the best farmland. North Alabama's slave population stood at 63,000 in 1860, the majority of these flanking the Tennessee River. Even there, however, blacks outnumbered whites, and that barely, only in Madison and Limestone Counties. Slave numbers in the hill counties to the south like St. Clair and Winston, were tiny—an infinitesimal 3.4 percent in the latter. Black Belt totals were staggering by comparison. Dallas, Marengo, and Greene Counties all counted significant slave majorities, approaching 80 percent. Isolated Alabama River planters and their families lived in a sea of black humanity and, as secession loomed, keenly felt their vulnerability. Slave numbers were correspondingly low in the coastal plain, with a large cluster in Mobile County. Most of Alabama's few thousand free blacks also lived there, many of them Creoles, an exotic legacy of colonial rule. These mixed-race descendants of French or Spanish planters and their black concubines were protected by international treaty and could attend school, go out at night, and own property, including slaves.[9]

While a few Creoles held slaves, like Zeno Chastang, who owned twenty-nine in 1860, most did not. Nor, for that matter, did most white Alabamians. Among the 35 percent who did, some were modest farmers who hoed their cotton and beans alongside two or three chattel or maybe kept a slave woman for housework. Others were small-town merchants who had a few slaves about their stores or for blacksmiths who needed a little extra help at their forges. Technically those owning at least twenty slaves were the planters, the least prosperous of whom were mortgaged to the hilt and dependent on a good harvest and high cotton prices. Frederick Law Olmsted, the journalist and landscape architect, met several planters during an 1850s trip through Alabama and was unimpressed. "Not sociable," he later wrote of them, "except when the topics of cotton, land, and negroes, were started; interested, however, in talk about theatres and the turf; very profane; often showing the handles of concealed weapons about their persons, but not quarrelsome . . . very ill-informed, except on plantation business; their language very ungrammatical, idiomatic, and extravagant." Distinctly in the minority, but together owning thousands of slaves and wielding considerable influence and political power, were the wealthiest planter aristocrats. They were generally better educated and more cultivated than the rustics Olmsted had encountered. Among their number was Nathan Bryan Whitfield of Demopolis, who managed his 7,000 acres and 200 slaves even as he converted his two-room log house into a sophisticated Greek Revival masterpiece known as Gaineswood.[10]

Like its master, Gaineswood was an exceptional example. Alabama's plantation houses differed widely. Some were plain log dwellings that acquired clapboarding and a portico if the owner prospered. Others were the full-blown creations of itinerant builder/architects with copies of the *Antiquities of Athens* and the *American Builder's Companion* tucked in their baggage. One Tallapoosa River plantation of the 1850s, McKenzie Mill Place, was anchored by a large one-story, hipped-roof Greek Revival house with flanking wings.

Figure 3. Gaineswood, Alabama's finest antebellum mansion, evolved from a simple log cabin. Courtesy Alabama Historical Commission.

As later recalled by a family member, it "had the standard forty-foot central hall, with double parlors to its left, a dining room behind, and with four bedrooms to the right." Furniture included a large parlor mirror, a classical sofa, three rugs, two lounges, cane-bottomed rocking chairs, and a long mahogany dining table. The grounds were enlivened by a cape-jessamine-lined walkway and flower beds of "pansies, hyacinths and johnny-jump-ups." During the summer of 1860, a correspondent for the *New York Spirit of the Times* visited Oak Grove, the Coosa River plantation of US senator Benjamin Fitzpatrick of Montgomery. Fitzpatrick's 6,000-acre farm spread along the river two and a half miles. The wooden mansion was "pleasantly situated on an eminence, overlooking an extensive tract of bottom land" and sported "piazzas and projecting eaves." But the big house was only the beginning. The farm included a dairy, a smokehouse stuffed with 30,000 pounds of bacon, a barn, corn cribs, and "a row of frame houses, one story and attic high, tenanted by the negroes, and presenting all the appearance of a little village." Among the slaves the writer met Mary, "the doctress and nurse"; Willis, "the gardener and steward"; Willis's wife, Susan, "detailed for general housework"; Ephraim, at seventy limited to light tasks like making mats and watering the horses; March, a seventeen-year-old mulatto field hand; Aham, the carpenter and "machinist genius"; and Austin, the blacksmith. Livestock included five horses, thirty mules, fifteen oxen, ninety head of cattle, eighty sheep, and four hundred swine. Fitzpatrick's plantation was clearly a model operation, and it earned him $5,000 a year from cotton alone.[11]

Fitzpatrick's slaves certainly had it better than many, given that their master was wealthy and benevolent. More typical was the experience of Jenny Proctor, born in 1850. She recounted her life in bondage decades later. "I's hear tell of them good slave days," she told her interlocutor, "but I ain't never seen no good times then." Proctor's mother was a cook who had to rise at 3:00 a.m. to get breakfast for the field hands. "We had old ragged huts," she recalled, "made out of poles and some of the cracks chinked up with mud and moss and some of them wasn't. We didn't have no good beds, just scaffolds nailed up to the wall out of poles and the old ragged bedding throwed on them." Proctor tended children and cleaned the master's log house. Once, after snatching a biscuit, she was beaten by the mistress with a broom and soon relegated to "that cotton patch." In Dallas County, British naturalist Gosse lamented the sight of female slaves wrestling "rude and ineffective" plows, their "sordid rags" flapping forlornly about their hardened brown bodies as they staggered down the rows. Unfortunately for slave women, besides backbreaking work, sexual predation by overseers, masters, and their adolescent sons was an all too real possibility, and any children born of such exploitation were likewise chattel. One of the most chilling incidents on record concerns some University of Alabama students who compelled a professor's slave to pimp them a young slave girl named Luna. The school president was appalled when he learned of it, reporting the students had raped the girl "in great numbers nightly."[12]

Even the poorest whites lived better than most slaves. Their small farms were attractive to some travelers, but their lives were full of toil and struggle. During his southern tour, Olmsted passed through a north Alabama valley "of thin, sandy soil, thickly populated by poor farmers." Most of the houses were one-room log cabins, occasionally "neat, new," each with a well "and a garden inclosed with palings." Cows, goats, mules, pigs, and fowl were everywhere. Olmsted found the people friendly but "very ignorant; the agriculture is wretched and the work hard." White women were in the fields with the men wielding hoes or ensconced in the little cabins spinning yarn at the wheel.[13]

The productivity of Alabama's many plantations and farms was staggering. In 1860, the state's aggregate agricultural wealth ranked fifth in the nation. The corn crop was more than thirty-three million bushels, potatoes five million, wheat over a million, and oats over 600,000. Better than six million pounds of butter was produced, as were some 140,000 gallons of molasses and 47,000 pounds of honey. But cotton was the money crop. Large plantations could produce hundreds of bales in a year, whereas small farmers might only manage a few, but an absolute mania for growing it prevailed. And little wonder. Cotton was white gold, worth over 10 cents a pound, a value bound to go higher if there was war and foreign markets became starved. Over five million acres were devoted to its cultivation, and almost a million bales—each weighing around 400 pounds—were shipped out to the spinning mills of New England and England. Most Alabama cotton was carried downstream by side-wheeler steamboats with colorful names like the *Eliza Battle*, the *Illinois Belle*, and the *Forest Monarch*, and exported through Mobile. The route to market was different for the Tennessee Valley, however. Its product went by river to the Ohio and then down the Mississippi to New Orleans or by rail on the Memphis and Charleston Railroad to the Atlantic Seaboard. This accounted for a powerful disconnect between north and south Alabama, as noted by *DeBow's Review* in 1855. "One seventh part of the State on the north is commercially, and therefore socially and politically disunited from the remainder," it wrote. The *Review* considered this fact an "unfortunate distinction," and it would play its role in the great events to come.[14]

Not to be dismissed was the state's livestock wealth. In 1860 there were over 125,000 horses and nearly as many mules. There were better than 200,000 head of cattle, which enjoyed more freedom than the slaves. The 1852 *Code* allowed Alabama's cows and bulls to wander anywhere that was unfenced, if earmarked or branded. Cows could be sold for up to $10 a head, but small farmers valued them more for their steady milk production. Hogs outnumbered every other farm animal in the state, with almost two million rooting around. Sheep were common, with over 300,000 grazing the green fields. Taken in toto, Alabama's livestock was valued at more than $43 million. With this kind of agricultural bounty, it did not take a genius to know that if protected, the Heart of Dixie could be a breadbasket to a people or an army.[15]

Considerably less impressive was the state's industrial development. On the

Figure 4. *Slaves Shipping Cotton by Torchlight—River Alabama*. The heavy bales were sent down a long wooden slide to the landing. Courtesy Alabama Department of Archives and History.

eve of war, the census enumerated 1,459 manufacturing establishments, far behind most Northern states. They included 110 brick kilns, three cigar factories, 236 grist mills, thirty furniture-making outfits, 336 sawmills, ten marble works, five gun makers, eleven potteries, and, ironically in such coal- and iron-rich territory, only four collieries and a handful of foundries. Fewer than 8,000 Alabamians were employed by industry, and their annual output was little more than an anemic $10 million. Despite the small numbers of mills, factories, and foundries, some were model operations and the subject of admiring newspaper and magazine attention. In 1858, *Hunt's Merchants' Magazine* noted the Bell Factory, a cotton mill near Huntsville, "which has for many years been paying large profits from the manufacture of various kinds of plaids, checks, tickings, & etc." The mill's labor force consisted entirely of slaves owned by the company. But most impressive of all was transplanted New Englander Daniel Pratt's "thrifty and handsomely situated manufacturing village" of Prattville, perched on the Alabama River 14 miles outside Montgomery. A writer for the *American Cotton Planter* magazine toured in the spring of 1857 and penned a full account. "We arrived at Prattville as the sun was going down," he wrote, "when every thing inanimate, with the operatives in the various factory departments, were, in the setting sun, closing the performances of the day." The writer spent a relaxing and delightful evening with Pratt and his family and marveled at the industrialist's "Gallery of Paintings," probably one of the finest private art collections in the South, consisting of "scenes of passed grandeur and greatness." But what signified for the reporter, and his readers, were the three-story brick buildings that were at the heart of Pratt's endeavor. These included the Gin Factory, with a 250-by-50-foot room filled with over "seventy drums for driving the various machines used in the manufacture of gins." The finished products were hoisted in an elevator to the second floor, where they were tested and any problems corrected. "No gin is allowed to leave the shop until it performs satisfactorily," the reporter approvingly noted. The machines were painted and varnished on the third floor "and put in order for boxing and shipping." In addition to its elevator, the Gin Factory boasted a large cistern in the attic, which was kept full of water by a pump feeding into a spring underneath the building. The lumber to build the gins came from a nearby warehouse connected by a little railway. There was also an iron foundry alongside. As if all of that wasn't enough, Pratt's establishment featured a sash, door, and blind factory; a grist mill; a machine shop, and a carriage shop, "all furnished with suitable machinery for these various branches of business." Then there was the Cotton Factory, with 2,800 spindles and 100 looms, manned by 150 workers, some of them slaves. Pratt was clearly a showman and ended the tour with a flourish, walking the reporter through "his garden, orchard, and vineyard." Here were "fine, large fruit trees," including apple, peach, pear, plum, and fig, "all healthful and thrifty," and to top it all off, a five-acre terraced plot of "scuppernongs and catawbas," the vines held aloft by cast iron posts.[16]

Pratt's workers were fortunate to have the use of a bit of railway. The majority of Alabamians weren't so lucky. Despite over a decade of effort and development, by the fall of 1860 the state had less than 800 railroad miles, woefully behind its northern sisters. There were only 117 depots and junctions, and fewer than 40 percent of Alabamians lived within 15 miles of one. Despite the dearth of track, some good lines did exist, and more were underway. All would play critical roles in the conflict to come. In the north, the Memphis and Charleston Railroad looped across the state, generally following the course of the Tennessee River. In the center of the state, the Alabama and Tennessee River Railroad ran between Selma and Blue Mountain (modern Anniston), and work was ongoing to extend track west to Meridian, Mississippi. To the south, the Mobile and Ohio Railroad ran from the Port City all the way to Columbus, Kentucky. Under construction was the Mobile and Great Northern Railroad, which was projected to run from Tensaw, a landing on the eastern side of the Mobile River Delta, to Pollard, hard by the Florida line, where it would link with the existing Alabama and Florida Railroad. That line ran from Pensacola to Montgomery, where it joined the Montgomery and West Point and completed track all the way to Atlanta.[17]

By modern standards, antebellum train travel was inefficient, uncomfortable, and occasionally dangerous. The locomotives were ungainly, 30-ton, wood-fed iron monsters with exaggerated cowcatchers and funnel smokestacks that belched black smoke and chuffed loudly. At best they could reach speeds of 25 miles an hour, far less with heavy loads. Cars swayed crazily and creaked when in motion, and derailments were common. This was little wonder since most rails were lightweight iron, perhaps weighing 60 pounds to each yard of track, and in some cases, wooden with strap iron fixed atop. The latter arrangement was unable to handle significant weight, and the straps had a tendency to break loose and spring up where they had been joined, creating vicious "snakeheads" that could rip out the wooden flooring of the passenger cars. Furthermore, railroad gauges (the widths between the tracks) were not standardized, occasioning time-consuming transfers at the change points, such as at the Georgia line on the Montgomery and West Point road. In 1846, the English geologist Sir Charles Lyell rode a train out of Montgomery. His car was "a long apartment, with cross benches and a middle passage." Among the passengers was "one rustic, evidently in liquor, who put both of his feet on one of the cushioned benches, and began to sing." The drunkard was kicked off for his behavior, but vocal "news boys" and "others who sell apples and biscuits" kept the car animated. In 1854, the *Huntsville Democrat* helpfully published "Rules for Safe Travel." Among them: "Never sit in an unusual place or posture," "beware of yielding to the sudden impulse to spring from the carriage to recover your hat," and "travel by day, if possible, not in foggy weather."[18]

Alabama's most important cities and towns all had rail connections by 1860.

Even so, they were little more than wide places in the road or clearings in the wilderness. Olmsted observed, "Towns, frequently referred to as important points in the stages of your journey, when you reach them, you are surprised to find consist of not more than three or four cabins, a tavern, or grocery, a blacksmith's shop, and a stable." Talladega, population 800 and situated alongside the Alabama and Tennessee River Railroad, was fairly typical. It had a depot, and the three-story courthouse centered in the square was surrounded by a hotel, a pharmacy, dry goods stores, and several smithies. Marion, near Selma, was a little bigger, with two grocery stores, two shoemaker's shops, a gin factory, a telegraph office, an Odd Fellows Lodge, and doctor and dentist offices. Residents were usually proud of their growing communities but were just as apt as visitors to comment on their isolation and natural surrounds as they were the streets or the buildings. Mrs. Clement C. Clay, wife of a US senator and a resident of Huntsville, population 4,000 free and slave, waxed eloquent in a postwar memoir. "Situate among the low hills that separate the higher points of the Cumberland range," she wrote, "Huntsville smiles up at the sky from a rare amphitheater, hollowed in the cedar-covered mountains." Nearby, she continued, was the Tennessee, rolling "on its romantic way," and a carriage ride "wherever one will" presented vistas of hazy mountain tops "disappearing in the blue ether, and intervening valleys yellow with corn or white with cotton, or green with the just risen grain." As for Huntsville itself, it was crisscrossed by floral-scented "shady avenues, along which are seen, beyond the gardens and magnolia trees, the commodious town houses of the prosperous planters." Similarly, a writer described Eufaula alongside the Chattahoochee River as surrounded by "a magnificent savannah of hundreds of acres, stretching far to the east and southeast." And in Montgomery, Olmsted was practically overwhelmed by the city's physical insignificance: "Even from the State-house . . . the eye falls in every direction upon a dense forest, boundless as the sea, and producing in the mind the same solemn sensation."[19]

There was, of course, more to Alabama's capital city than a few government buildings surrounded by woods. In a short magazine article about Montgomery, a correspondent admitted that he would not have formed a "correct idea" of the place if he hadn't been "buggied round by a friend." He noted "many fine mansions, and tastefully built cottage-residences, which extended in every direction from Market and Commerce streets, for a mile or two."

T. C. Cooper De Leon, a Confederate functionary who arrived in Montgomery early in 1861, wrote, "As in most southern inland towns, its one great artery, Main street [actually Market Street], runs from the river bluffs to the Capitol, perched on a high hill a full mile away." The street was "wide and sandy," De Leon continued, and though the capitol was not especially a "stately pile," it still "dominated the lesser structures, as it stared down the street with quite a Roman rigor." William Howard Russell, a *London Times* correspondent who witnessed the formation of the Confederate government, nonetheless found the city decidedly lacking. "Montgomery has little claims to be called a capital," he declared. "The streets are very hot, unpleasant, and uninteresting. I have rarely seen a more dull, lifeless place; it looks like a small Russian town of the interior."[20]

Cosmopolitan Mobile was different. The state's largest city and only seaport, it had 30,000 residents, roughly a third of them slaves. By nineteenth-century standards it was a good-sized town, second only to New Orleans on the Gulf. Its colonial Latin heritage had bequeathed a strong dash of Catholic culture, unusual in overwhelmingly Protestant Alabama and, combined with the presence of bustling steamboats and oceangoing commerce, lent it an air of foreignness, excitement, and possibility. All of those tens of thousands of bales of Black Belt cotton were unloaded at the city's wharves, stored, compressed, and then reloaded onto sailing ships, making Mobile the nation's third-busiest port. When the crop was in season, the waterfront was crowded with impatient horses, stamping mules, rattling wagons, rumbling drays, shouting stevedores, and hurrying river men. Everywhere were people such as few upstate Alabamians had ever encountered. "Here is a sailor just on shore with a pocket full of rocks ready for devilment of any kind," one visitor wrote, "and there is a beggar in rags. Pretty Creoles, pale faced sewing girls, painted vice, big headed & little headed men, tall anatomies & short Falstaffs." Russell commented on "mulattoes, quadroons, and mestizos of all sorts, Spanish, Italian, and French, speaking their own tongues, or a quaint lingua franca, and dressed in very pretty and striking costumes." Straw-hatted planters accompanied by well-dressed wives and children took it all in as they gingerly picked their way past the smelly piles of animal droppings, oyster shells, and cordage toward top-hatted black carriage drivers loudly soliciting fares. There were so many cotton bales stacked in teetering rows just back of the wharves that women sometimes had trouble getting their hoop skirts between them. "Mobile is a city of cotton," one visitor wrote. "It is to be found in the quay warehouses, sidewalks, everywhere." A correspondent for the *Georgia Courier* found the commodity ubiquitous, even in conversation. "This place is a receptacle monstrous for the article," he declared. "Look which way you will see it; and see it moving; keel boats, steam boats, ships, brigs, schooners, wharves, stores, and press-houses, all appeared to be full." During his three-day visit the reporter boarded with cotton factors, cotton merchants, and cotton planters. "I must have heard the word cotton pronounced more than 3000 times," he wearily concluded.[21]

Once past the wharves, Mobile presented a more pleasing aspect. Three-story brick stores and coffee saloons sported elegant cast iron balconies, and crowds of young clerks spilled onto the sidewalks in the afternoons. Government Street cut west through the middle of town, a sandy thoroughfare crowded with carriages and horses whispering along at an astonishing 15 miles an hour. Its wide borders featured shady live oaks, blue-gray slate sidewalks, and finely proportioned Greek Revival buildings like the Presbyterian Church and Barton Academy with its columned drum floating above the tree line. One traveler gushed, "Columns, porticos, rich cornices, handsome verandahs meet the eye everywhere; it is a city of villas, the upper part standing in their own small gardens." Resident Kate Cumming loved to take visitors down the Bay Shell Road south of town. To the right were "charming villas nesting among magnolia and orange groves," she explained, and to the left "the broad expanse of the bay," dotted by the "white sails of the ships of all nationalities."[22]

Such was the twenty-second state in the Union and its people at the end of the Year of Our Lord eighteen hundred and sixty. Growing, full of promise, agriculturally rich, industrially underdeveloped, religious, family-centered, burdened by slavery, but determined not to be reformed, intimidated, or dominated. Excited Alabamians were still celebrating South Carolina's secession when the 545-ton, 13-gun screw steamer USS *Crusader*, the Stars and Stripes fluttering from her mast, hove into Mobile Bay and dropped anchor off the Dog River Bar with a splash.

# I

# Secession

The people of Alabama *will not submit.*
—Resolution of Resistance

Governor Moore learned of the *Crusader's* arrival by telegraph the afternoon of January 2, 1861. His immediate thought was that she had been sent to reinforce Fort Morgan. Constructed during the early nineteenth century by the US Army, Fort Morgan was a pentagonal brick structure armed with heavy cannons pointed at the ship channel immediately opposite. It was by far the most formidable of the three Federal installations in the Mobile area, for whoever controlled it controlled the bay. Also under Federal authority were Fort Gaines, a smaller masonry construction on the eastern tip of Dauphin Island, and the Mount Vernon arsenal, a 35-acre post with numerous two- and three-story brick buildings and a horseshoe-shaped, 10-foot-high brick wall, situated on the western bank of the Mobile River, 30 miles north of the Port City.[1]

Nothing in his career or actions theretofore suggested that Moore would be anything less than decisive upon receipt of this news. A native South Carolinian who had moved to the Black Belt during the 1820s, where he worked as a lawyer and served in the state House of Representatives, Moore had been elected governor in 1857 and was now serving his second term. He was a Democrat and pro states' rights, but measured on secession. Six feet tall with big ears, a resolute mouth, an aquiline nose, a broad forehead, and a healthy crop of white hair, he was easy to spot in a crowd. One legislator described him as "a clever fellow but scary," with "a good opinion of himself." Fully cognizant of the titanic forces tearing at the nation, Moore had already taken steps to prepare his state for conflict, organizing and funding the Alabama Volun-

Figure 5. Governor Andrew Moore ordered Federal installations seized before his state had formally seceded. Courtesy Library of Congress.

teer Corps, made up of preexisting militia companies; hurrying forward construction on the Alabama and Tennessee River Railroad; promoting industrial development; sending agents North to buy arms; and asking banks to hold specie for the state. Lastly, thanks to the example and urging of Governor Joseph E. Brown of Georgia, who had just seized Federal installations in that state, Moore was considering the same when the *Crusader* appeared in Alabama waters. Clearly, it was time to act, and on January 3 he ordered the state militia to take the forts and arsenal.[2]

Ironically, despite the agitated political climate, the *Crusader*'s mission was routine. For the past several months, she had been apprehending slave ships in the Caribbean, and her commander, Lt. John Newland Maffitt, had been instructed to cash the prize-money check in Mobile. At forty-one, Maffitt cut a dashing figure. His pleasant countenance was framed by a dark chin beard and wavy black hair habitually topped by an angled captain's cap. He had been born at sea—his wife said he considered himself "a son of old Neptune"— and had spent most of his life ever since on a rolling deck. He joined the US

Navy as a midshipman at age thirteen, and his prior service included a stint on the famous *Constitution* and decades with the US Coast Survey. He knew the South well, especially North Carolina where he spent his childhood, but he was also serious about his professional responsibilities. Shortly after arriving in Mobile Bay he got word that a band of secessionist hotheads was planning to seize his ship. Maffitt immediately prepared for action and called on the editor of the *Mobile Register*, informing him that if any boats threatened he would "open my broadsides and sink them in fifteen minutes with every desperado on board of them." That effectively cooled their ardor. Determined to get back into the Gulf where it was safer, Maffitt cashed his check and departed. He would return to Mobile Bay sooner than he realized, and to a very different kind of welcome.[3]

False alarm though the *Crusader* had been, the die was cast, and troops were on the move. During the wee hours of January 4, men from the Mobile Rifles, the Washington Light Infantry, the German Fusiliers, and Gardes Lafayette silently trotted toward the walls of the Mount Vernon arsenal with scaling ladders held over their heads. They looked more like Napoleonic troops on parade than Southern soldiers on a secret and dangerous mission. The Rifles sported dark green coats and white-plumed shakos, while the Washington Light Infantry was resplendent in scarlet. Despite their extravagant dress and high spirits, these lads were in earnest and quickly mounted the walls, dropped inside, opened the gate, and surrounded the armory.[4]

The garrison had not even bothered to post a sentry and was caught completely off guard. Seventeen Federal troops under the command of Capt. Jesse L. Reno stumbled sleepily and sheepishly into the gloom and gave themselves up to the grinning militia without a fight. With no more trouble than that, Governor Moore and the state of Alabama were in possession of a first-class military facility, 20,000 stand of arms, 150,000 pounds of gunpowder, 300,000 cartridges, and much else besides. For his part, Reno tried to justify his action, or rather nonaction, to his superior. "I did not make, nor could I have made, any resistance," he whined, "as they had scaled the walls and taken possession before I knew anything about the movement." Surely, he begged, "the Department will not hold me responsible for this unexpected catastrophe." The pattern was repeated at Forts Morgan and Gaines, which fell with equal ease. The state's take at Morgan was especially impressive, including almost 100 heavy guns, over half of them massive 32-pounders, so designated for the weight of their projectile, as well as robust quantities of shot and shell.[5]

Contemplating the fall of these posts, as well as those in other Southern states, the *New York Times* expressed incredulity and outrage. "The military history of this second American revolution is not likely to invest the national Government with glory," it gloomily opined. "Its military and naval officers, either through cowardice or in sympathy with treason, have offered no resistance to the capture of Federal property; at the first summons of an incompetent and undisciplined rabble in uniform, they have hauled down the flag every American soldier is bound in honor to save from dishonor with his life; and have surrendered their trust to treason." But Captain Reno and his compatriots weren't the only ones who had some explaining to do. Governor Moore was faced with the delicate dilemma of having seized federal property before his state had formally seceded from the Union. In a letter to lame-duck president James Buchanan he attempted to justify his course. "Sir," he began, "In a spirit of frankness I hasten to inform you by letter that by my order Fort Morgan and Fort Gaines, and the United States Arsenal at Mount Vernon were . . . peacefully occupied, and are now held by the troops of the State of Alabama." He had been compelled to do this, he continued, because he had received word that the federal government was about to reinforce the garrisons. "Having that information," he continued, "it was but an act of self-defense, and the plainest dictate of prudence, to anticipate and guard against the contemplated movement of the authorities of the General Government." All eyes now turned to Montgomery to see whether or not the State Secession Convention would indeed take Alabama out and redeem Moore's audacious gamble.[6]

The momentous issue was to be decided not by popular referendum, but by one hundred previously elected delegates from around the state. Of these, fifty-four were known secessionists, and forty-six were cooperationists. Their preferences were dictated by their geography. The secessionists were predominantly from the Black Belt and south Alabama, while the cooperationists were north Alabamians. This division illustrated the economic split noted by *DeBow's Review* during the 1850s. North Alabama's interests were more closely allied to those of Tennessee, and since that state was yet doubtful about secession, most north Alabamians, whether from the hill counties or the Tennessee Val-

Figure 6. The Selma Independent Blues pose before heading downriver to seize Fort Morgan in January 1861. Courtesy the History Museum of Mobile.

ley, took their cue from there. The delegates convened on January 7 at the capitol. Initially, citizens were allowed inside to witness the debate, but their continual applause caused the delegates to go into closed-door sessions.[7]

The secessionists were led by Montgomery lawyer William Lowndes Yancey, the proverbial fire-eater who had long agitated for separation. Among the co-operationists was Jeremiah Clemens of Huntsville, a novelist, lawyer, former US senator, and second cousin to Samuel Langhorne Clemens (Mark Twain). An early resolution floated by the secessionists declared that the federal government's antislavery "*acts* and *designs*" absolved Alabama from any obligation to "support a Government of the United States, to be administered upon such principals, and that the people of Alabama *will not submit* to be parties to the *inauguration and administration of* Abraham Lincoln as President, and Hannibal Hamlin as Vice President of the United States." The cooperationists objected to this. They, too, viewed the incoming Federal administration with distaste, but still believed moderation was preferable to outright withdrawal as suggested by the resolution. Yancey pushed hard for the resolution, Clemens resisted, and ultimately a joint Committee of Thirteen, consisting of seven secessionists and six cooperationists, was appointed to chart a course of action.[8]

Meanwhile, outside the House chamber events accelerated. Mississippi, Florida, and Georgia were all holding similar conventions, and reports indicated their imminent separation. Recognizing that a group of small, independent republics was bound to fare ill against the might and resources of the federal government, South Carolina invited her slaveholding Southern sisters to join in the formation of a confederacy. Even as the Alabama delegates tried to absorb all of this, Florida governor Madison Perry telegraphed Moore asking for troops to help seize the US Navy yard and forts at Pensacola. Situated in the panhandle, Pensacola was only 50 miles from Mobile and had a direct rail connection to Montgomery, representing a critical strategic threat to Alabama's underbelly. Secessionist delegates gave Moore the nod, and on January 9, the Montgomery True Blues, Metropolitan Guards, and Independent Rifles, better than two hundred men total, enthusiastically boarded a train south. Once arrived, the Alabamians helped bloodlessly seize the naval yard, a hospital, and two of the forts, but Fort Pickens, a brick installation on the western tip of Santa Rosa Island commanding Pensacola Bay, held out. Similarly, almost 600 miles to the east, Federal troops hunkered down at Fort Sumter, in the middle of Charleston harbor, refusing to surrender or evacuate. A shooting war looked more likely by the day.[9]

On January 10, the Committee of Thirteen, led by Yancey, proposed an Ordinance of Secession. The document stated that because the incoming Lincoln administration was "avowedly hostile to the domestic institutions and to the peace and security of the people of the State of Alabama," separation was justified. "*Be it declared and ordained by the people of the State of Alabama in Convention assembled*," it boldly continued, "That the State of Alabama now withdraws, and is hereby withdrawn from the Union known as 'the United States of America,' and henceforth ceases to be one of said United States, and is, and of right ought to be a SOVEREIGN, and INDEPENDENT STATE." A vote the next day decided the matter for all. The margin was close, 61 ayes to 39 nays. It might have been closer had not a handful of cooperationists, including Clemens, crossed over at the last minute. Writing to a childhood friend in Huntsville, he explained his turn: "I resisted the passage of the Ordinance to the last moment in every form, and then, when no more was to be accomplished, I did what I had pledged myself to do on every stump, and openly placed myself on the side of the State." Clemens was sober about the future: "God knows where all this is to end. I see very plainly the storms that are gathering."[10]

For the people awaiting a decision outside the locked chamber, the yea vote meant only jubilation. William Henry Mitchell, a Presbyterian minister, wrote to his wife in Florence about what happened after the doors were thrown open and the vote announced. "The scene that followed was perfectly thrilling," he exulted. "The galleries were crowded with ladies and gentlemen." Yancey, attired "in homespun," presented a handsome new flag on "behalf of the ladies of Montgomery" for the nascent Republic of Alabama. The blue banner featured a goddess of liberty on one side, and on the other the phrase "Noli me tangere" ("Touch me not") above a cotton plant and a coiled rattle-snake, which, Mitchell quoted Yancey as saying, is "peaceful and harmless until disturbed." Waves of applause circulated the chamber, and a Tuscaloosa delegate marveled that men "mounted the tables and desks, held up the floating end, the better thus to display its figures. The cheering was now deafening for some moments."[11]

The *Montgomery Weekly Advertiser* announced the decision in its pages the following morning. "Alabama Out of the Union!" the headline shouted. "A glorious day!!" Below, a short article related that citizens were hailing the "new era with demonstrations of profoundest emotion. The Capitol grounds and streets are alive with the moving mass of the cheering throng. Cannons are booming and bells ringing." In Mobile, the reaction was equally effusive. "Immediately on the receipt of the news," one observer reported, "an immense crowd assembled at the 'secession pole' at the foot of Government Street, to witness the spreading of the Southern flag, and it was run up amid the shouts of the multitude and thunders of cannon." A lone-star flag flew over the Custom House, and the balconies of the Battle House Hotel opposite as well as the street below were packed with excited citizens and marching cadets. That night, burning tar barrels illumined the intersections along Government Street while "rockets blazed, crackers popped, and the people hurrahed and shouted as they never had before." The mayor called for "a thousand laborers" to help prepare the city's defenses—"these were at once supplied"—and the Common Council passed an ordinance changing the names of Maine, Massachusetts, New Hampshire, and New York Streets to Palmetto, Charleston, Augusta, and Elmira respectively. Augusta Jane Evans, a successful novelist at only twenty-six who lived in a cottage just outside of town, declared that she and her fellow Alabamians would rather "drain our veins than yield to the ignominious rule of Black Republicanism." Not surprisingly, reaction was mixed in north Alabama, where many had preferred a popular referendum on the issue. Newspapers expressed their support now that the matter was decided and asked the public to do the same. Nonetheless, the United States flag purportedly remained over the courthouses at Huntsville and Athens a bit longer than many south Alabamians thought proper. As for slave reaction around the state, it was muted and cautious. Gus Askew, born into bondage in Henry County, was a child at the time and later recalled, "dat was one time when de ban' was playin' and flags was flyin' dat us lil' niggers didn't get no joy outen it."[12]

The independent Republic of Alabama was a short-lived creation. On February 4, per South Carolina's recommendation, delegates from the six seceded states— South Carolina, Mississippi, Florida, Alabama, Georgia, and Louisiana—met in Montgomery to establish the Confederate States of America. Alabama's capital city was chosen for its central location, for its rail and river connections, and for its symbolic value as Yancey's home. During the coming weeks, the city's population would double as officials, military men, clerks, office seekers, reporters, opportunistic merchants, militia, hangers on, and curiosity seekers flooded into town. Included in the Georgia delegation was T. R. R. Cobb, a lawyer and ardent secessionist, who wrote frequent letters to his wife about the deliberations. According to Cobb, the convention's first day consisted of routine business, like settling into place and electing convention officers. Cobb was surprised at the "very much divided" Alabama delegation. "The truth is there is a very bad state of things in this State," he informed his wife, "the minority are sullen in their opposition and not disposed to yield to the fact of secession." The following day the convention went into closed-door sessions, to the vocal disappointment of onlookers, especially women, "who were out in large numbers."[13]

Despite some differences and petty wrangling, the delegates got on with the business of making a new government remarkably quick. On February 9, they unanimously adopted a constitution. This was essentially a copy of the

United States Constitution with minor tweaking to, among a few other things, recognize slavery. Jefferson Davis, a native Kentuckian but Mississippi-reared, was elected president and Alexander Stephens of Georgia, vice president. Davis had not yet arrived at Montgomery, but his choice was generally popular with both delegates and the people. A tall, spare man with "beautiful blue eyes," he was a West Point graduate, a Mexican War hero, former US senator and secretary of war, lawyer, and planter. He preferred military service to politics but accepted his nomination with a strong sense of duty and honor. The inauguration was set for February 18.[14]

Davis arrived in Montgomery late at night on the sixteenth. He was exhausted by the circuitous route he had been forced to take from Mississippi, through Chattanooga and Atlanta, making speeches at every stop, but any hopes of going straight to his hotel were dashed by the expectant crowd that awaited him. An artillery salvo boomed a salute at the depot, and a special committee steered him through the throng toward the Exchange Hotel. This was Montgomery's largest public accommodation, and during the coming weeks it would become the Confederacy's administrative hub. But for a man as polished and well-traveled as Davis it can't have been very impressive—a four-story, flat-roofed rectangular block with paired monumental classical columns set into each elevation, a bit of Greek Revival flair known as distyle in antis. Shops occupied the first floor, and a broad staircase led up to the lobby and bar on the second level. Before he took to bed, Davis graciously accommodated the crowd and made a few brief remarks from the balcony. Saying he was very fatigued from his travels, he thanked the people for their warm welcome and assured them, "I will devote to the duties of the high office to which I have been called, all I have of heart, of head, of hand." Yancey, standing at his elbow, was more alert to the historical moment, and he followed with a short but far more memorable speech of his own. He extolled Davis as a statesman, soldier, and patriot, "upright and incorruptible." Gesturing to the dignified president-elect he announced, "The man and the hour have met. We may now hope that prosperity, honor and victory await his administration."[15]

Inauguration day dawned bright, sunny, and mild with a light wind out of the southwest. Providence appeared to be smiling on the Southern cause. According to one witness, the "stately capitol building" had been transformed into "a grand amphitheater, whose huge columns were wreathed with festoons of laurel and of magnolia." At an early hour thousands of people, white and black, began staking out spots along the Market Street parade route, including on rooftops and in second- and third-story windows. Market Street, now known as Dexter Avenue, began near the river, where its intersection with Court and Commerce Streets was marked by an artesian well with a catch basin encircled by a cast iron fence. From there it steadily ascended between brick commercial buildings toward the capitol. At 10:00 a.m. the parade marshal called for Davis at the hotel, and the procession formed up along Montgomery Street, which led the short distance to Market. Herman Arnold's Band was in front, where it struck up the popular new tune "Dixie," set to band music for the first time for the occasion. Next was the military escort, which included the Eufaula Rifles, German Fusiliers, and, dazzling in their sky-blue pants and red coats, the Columbus Guards holding aloft a banner with the Georgia coat of arms. Following the troops came various committees from the Secession Convention, the Alabama State Legislature, and the Montgomery City Council in open carriages, and then Davis, Stephens, a clergyman, and an army officer in an open carriage with a spotless saffron and white interior, drawn by six gray horses. Behind them trailed members of the Provisional Congress, several governors, distinguished citizens, civic societies, and a long tail of enthusiastic civilians on horseback and afoot.[16]

Arrived at the capitol, Davis was escorted inside to the strains of "The Marseillaise," where he was formally presented to the Congress. He then took his place on the portico—famously marked today by an inlaid gold star—and amid a sea of broadcloth and homespun gave his inaugural address in clear, determined tones to the hushed crowd. "We have entered upon the career of independence," he said, "and it must be inflexibly pursued." After noting the "many years of controversy" with the Northern states, he insisted that separation was "a necessity, not a choice." He invoked God's blessing and concluded that the Southern government and people might "hopefully look forward to success, to peace, and to prosperity." He then took the oath of office. According to one witness, "In uttering the words, 'So help me God,' Mr. Davis, turning his eyes towards the heavens, in a most impressive manner repeated the words, '*So help me God*,' in a tone of voice so loud and distinct that he could have been heard to the extreme outskirts of the immense assembly." He then kissed the Bible, and the crowd erupted into cheers and whoops. Among the people up close was Ellen Jackson, a Bostonian married to a local lawyer. Her two daughters were exhausted by the waiting, the jostling, and the cheering, but Jackson "fared better." She was extremely proud of having helped prepare a wreath of arborvitae, box, japonica, and hyacinths, which the president "slipped on his arm." On the balcony above, ladies tossed flowers by the basketful onto Davis's head. Down in Conecuh County, where she was visiting family, Mary Boykin Chesnut was more reserved. A native South Carolinian and the wife of former US senator James Chesnut, in Montgomery as a member of that state's delegation, Mrs. Chesnut was well-read, poised, and keenly observant. That night while fireworks, street demonstrations, and dress balls enlivened Alabama's capital city, she listened to crickets and began what was to become her famous diary. "I do not allow myself vain regrets or sad foreboding," she mused. "This southern Confederacy must be supported now by calm determination—& cool brains. We have risked all, & we must play our best for the stake is life or death."[17]

As the new Confederate government got down to business, the effort to "select a proper flag" was proving more difficult than anticipated. The committee so charged, chaired by William Porcher Miles of South Carolina, solicited designs from the public and over one hundred were submitted, some beautifully sewn silk, others crudely painted paper, and a few awkwardly assembled bits of colored pasteboard. The submissions fell into "two great classes," according to the committee's report to Congress. In the first were those that mimicked the United States flag too closely, and in the second were "those which are very elaborate, complicated, or fantastical." The problem was resolved when the exasperated committee submitted four of its own designs to the Congress for approval. The one chosen became the famous Stars and Bars. Similar to the national flag of Austria, it consisted of two red stripes sandwiching one of white, with a blue field bearing seven white stars (Texas had since seceded) in the upper left-hand corner. The oft-repeated story that Prussian émigré and Marion resident Nicola Marschall designed the Stars and Bars dates to 1905, and is not supported by the evidence, though he did subsequently design several flags for Alabama military companies.[18]

Racing the clock, two men rushed the approved design to a nearby dry goods store that stocked the Wheeler and Wilson sewing machine. This state-of-the-art device featured a rotating hook and four-motion feed driven by foot

Figure 7. The inauguration of President Jefferson Davis at Montgomery. From *Official and Illustrated War Record*. Washington, DC, Edward J. Stanley, 1898.

pedals. Here, according to Miles, "fair and nimble fingers" took over, and the first full-size example of the design was made of merino wool, "there being no bunting at hand." The new banner was unfurled for everyone to see the afternoon of March 4, the very day of Lincoln's inauguration in far-off Washington. In a rapt account, the *Montgomery Weekly Advertiser* described the event: "A large concourse of spectators had assembled on Capitol Hill," the paper reported. The honor of raising the flag went to Miss Letitia Christian Tyler, a granddaughter of President John Tyler. Fifty-five years later, she described the experience to Alabama's archivist Marie Bankhead Owen: "I clearly remember ascending the stairs that led to the dome of the building and that I was escorted by Hon. Alex B. Clitherall, one of the Confederate officials." From her dizzying perch, Tyler could see "throngs of people" below, "watching and waiting." The cord was handed her, and she promptly hauled away, releasing the banner. The *Advertiser* thrilled that it "seemed to wave defiance to the *Northern wind* that came rushing down from the Potomac laden with threats of Abolition coercion." An artillery salute thundered, and "the vast assemblage rent the air with shouts of welcome." Then occurred an unusual atmospheric phenomenon, which the newspaper interpreted as "a Providential omen." A great blue vapor ring lifted gently over "the assemblage of Southern spirits . . . rested for many seconds on a level with the Flag of the Confederate States, then gradually ascended until lost to the gaze of the multitude."[19]

Despite much latter-day argument, there was no doubt at the time as to what the Confederacy and its various flags stood for. Independence and liberty, yes, but mostly from Northern meddling on the slavery question. Even though the majority of white Southerners were not slave owners, they shared a dread of abolition and a bedrock conviction that it would be the ruination of their economy and social structure. Vice President Stephens's notorious "Cornerstone" speech was perhaps the starkest demonstration of this fact. Given in Savannah just over a month after the inauguration, Stephens said that the Confederate government's "foundations are laid, its cornerstone rests, upon the great truth that the negro is not equal to the white man; that slavery, subordination to the superior race, is his natural and normal condition." There were other similar statements from individuals and institutions in Alabama. To take only one example, in January 1861, the Alabama Methodist Episcopal Church stated that "African slavery as it exists in the South is wise, humane, and righteous, and approved by God and any measure looking to its overthrow can be dictated only by blind fanaticism." Certainly Confederate officials and Montgomery's town fathers made no effort to conceal chattel slavery's disagreeable aspects from the many outsiders swarming the new capital. In May, Russell, the *London Times* correspondent, was disgusted by the sight of a small slave auction in front of the artesian well. "Three or four idle men in rough homespun, makeshift uniforms, leaned against the iron rails," he wrote. A few men on horseback, some Irish laborers, a fellow with "a lack luster eye" on a small cart, and "six other men, in long black coats and high hats, some whittling sticks and chewing tobacco, and discharging streams of discolored saliva, completed the group." Next to the auctioneer stood a young black man with a sad countenance, wearing a greasy blue jacket, "a coarse cotton shirt, loose and rather ragged trowsers, and broken shoes." Russell was troubled by his excitement that for $975 he could become "as absolutely the owner of that mass of blood, bones, sinew, flesh, and brains as of the horse which stood by my side." He had seen slave markets in the Orient, but those exuded a glow of colorful dress and exoticism. In Montgomery, he found it painful "to see decent-looking men in European garb engaged in the work before me." Even native Southerners could be unsettled by such scenes. Mary Chesnut stumbled upon an auction downtown, where a young woman stood upon the block. "She was magnificently gotten up in silks and satins," Chesnut recorded in her diary later. "She seemed delighted with it all—sometimes ogling the bidders, sometimes looking quite coy and modest, but her mouth never relaxed from its expanded grin of excitement." Here was a side of slavery that planters' wives knew all too well but rarely dared to discuss. Their husbands could and many did sexually use female salves, while any hint of black male desire for a white woman resulted in vicious reprisals.[20]

Montgomery served as the Confederate capital until May, when it was moved to Richmond, Virginia. During that brief period, the city and its people experienced enough excitement for a lifetime. At the noisy Exchange Hotel Russell encountered "congressmen, politicians, colonels, and place-men with or without places, and a vast number of speculators, contractors, and the like, attracted by the embryo government." Embryo was the right word. The Confederacy had a constitution, a president, a vice president, cabinet officers, a congress, a flag, and a stirring tune, but little else. The secretary of the Treasury's private secretary, Henry D. Capers, sought out his new office at the Government Building, a plain, three-story, brick warehouse-like structure a block from the Exchange Hotel. A card affixed to one of the interior doors identified the Treasury office. When Capers unlocked the door, "I found it without furniture of any kind." Expecting Treasury Secretary C. G. Memminger within the hour, he hastened to a furniture store to put things to rights. Soon enough he had procured "a neat walnut table, a small desk, and a set of office chairs." But when a "tall, soldierly-looking person" rapped at the door and presented an order for one hundred blankets and rations, Capers humorously opened his wallet and remarked, "This, Captain, is all the money that I will certify as being in the Confederate Treasury at this moment." At first irritated, the captain quickly appreciated the situation, and they shared a good laugh. Diligent official that he meant to be, Capers promptly tracked down Memminger at the capitol, secured a note to open a line of credit at the Central Bank of Alabama, and took care of the captain's order.[21]

Davis was pressed on every side. John Beauchamp Jones, a successful novelist and journalist turned war clerk, called upon the chief executive and found him "overwhelmed with papers." Military men who had recently resigned from the US Army and Navy prowled hotel and office corridors seeking interviews and appointments. Among these hopefuls were P. G. T. Beauregard, "the Little Creole"; Joseph E. Johnston, a veteran of both the Mexican and Seminole Wars; the dashingly handsome and romantic Indian fighter Earl Van Dorn; and naval men like the extravagantly mustachioed Raphael Semmes and John Newland Maffitt, the very same who had so recently cashed his check in Mobile and stood down secessionist rowdies. Maffitt secured an interview with Davis in early May, and, like everyone else, offered his services to the Confederacy. As he later wrote, Davis "informed me that the South did not contemplate creating a Navy." When the astonished Maffitt asked why not, Davis answered, "Our friends at the North assure us that there will be no war." Told that he could join the army instead, the disgruntled Maffitt returned to his hotel room "to pack my trunk for Europe." Within minutes his door burst open and a gaggle of officials rushed in "direct from seeing Mr. Davis, and who insisted that I reconsider my determination, and assured me that the Confederacy could not afford to lose my services." Davis's lack of foresight and imagination had nearly deprived the South of one of its most effective naval officers, a man destined to cost the Union government millions on the high seas.[22]

The social scene was just as frenetic as the political and military ones. The city's elite families staged frequent parties, balls, and dinners for the various dignitaries, while the hoi polloi jammed barrooms, street corners, and raucous hotel dining rooms. At one crowded upper-crust dinner, the guests made much over the ambrosia, but T. R. R. Cobb quipped that it was "nothing but sliced oranges and grated coconut." Other dinner table fare included oysters, ham, turkey, and beef, all washed down with copious drafts of tea, coffee, wine, or brandy. Some government figures reveled in getting away from somnolent meetings and endless paperwork. Stephen Mallory, who despite Davis's lack of interest in marine matters had been appointed secretary of the navy, was completely charmed by an evening in Mary Chesnut's company. When a courier interrupted and asked Mallory to obtain some papers for the

Figure 8. Varina Howell Davis, First Lady of the Confederacy, enlivened Montgomery's social scene. Courtesy Alabama Department of Archives and History.

congress, he snapped, "Do you think I am going to leave Mrs. Chesnut for *that*? I came in here to talk to her & be invigorated & exhilarated." The president's wife, Varina Howell, arrived in early March and instantly became the center of admiring local attention. Mrs. Davis was dark-haired and beautiful, with impeccable manners and dress. She was graciousness personified to one and all she encountered, high or low, hardly surprising for a Natchez planter's daughter and former US senator's wife. Russell met her at a small gathering and was favorably impressed, calling her "ladylike, and clever." She and Davis rented a modest white Italianate cottage in the center of town, where she hosted frequent dinners.[23]

Talk of war ran hot and cold, but in early April events took a decided turn when Lincoln announced that the isolated and beleaguered garrison at Fort Sumter would be resupplied. Determined to prevent this, Davis and his cabinet decided to take action. On April 10, LeRoy Pope Walker, the Confederate secretary of war, sent a telegraph out of Montgomery to General Beauregard in Charleston. "If you have no doubt of the authorized character of the agent who communicated to you the intention of the Washington Government, to supply Fort Sumter by force," it read, "you will at once demand its evacuation, and if this is refused, proceed in such a manner as you may determine to reduce it." In the early hours of April 12, the batteries at Charleston opened fire. Mrs. Chesnut, who was back in the Holy City, was awakened by the booming and rushed to the rooftop with her sisters. Clutching one another, praying, and crying, they looked out over the harbor at "the shells bursting." The Federal garrison surrendered two days later, and Lincoln responded by calling for 75,000 volunteers and a blockade of Southern ports to quash the rebellion. In the days and weeks following, the mid-South states of Virginia, North Carolina, Arkansas, and Tennessee finally cast their lot with the Confederacy. Nationally, the battle lines were now fully drawn, eleven states against twenty-three.[24]

As spring advanced, Montgomery's disadvantages as a national capital became increasingly evident. Temperatures steadily climbed, swarming mosquitoes bedeviled everyone, and the overcrowded, dirty hotels were more and more an embarrassment. Talk of moving the capital to Richmond, long in the air, circulated more freely. Located only 100 miles from Washington, Virginia's capital city was closer to the expected major theater of operations, and it was logical for the Confederate government to be nearby. Richmond was also four times larger than Montgomery and offered better hotels, restaurants, and entertainment, further incentive for overfed politicians and their culture-starved wives. The relocation was approved, and on May 21 Congress held its final meeting in Montgomery. Despite its many inconveniences and irritations, Alabama's little capital city had managed capably enough in birthing the new government, and has ever afterward been known as the Cradle of the Confederacy.[25]

While local boosters mourned the move, the martial spirit was triumphant all over Alabama. Throughout early 1861, men, women, and children remained caught up in an optimistic, bellicose fervor. Lovingly stitched flags were formally presented to outfits like the Magnolia Cadets in Selma. "It was a beautiful sight!" declared one woman at the ceremony. "Wealthy, cultured young gentlemen voluntarily turning their backs upon the luxuries and endearments of affluent homes, and accepting in lieu the privations and hardships of warfare." One observer noted that Selma's "unmarried ladies were so patriotic, that every able-bodied young man was constrained to enlist." When one vacillated, his sweetheart sent him a package that contained "a lady's skirt and crinoline, and the note with these terse words: 'Wear these or volunteer.'" Most men needed no such prodding, however. Even young boys wanted to participate. At Demopolis, over a dozen, aged eight to fourteen, formed themselves into the Canebrake Cadets and offered their services to Governor Moore. "We are too young to take the field with regular troops," they wrote, "but if you can furnish us with suitable arms we think we can do some service in case our country is invaded." Enthusiasm was equally fervent in north Alabama. "Parties were out drumming up companies," a volunteer wrote. "There were no examinations by Surgeons as to physical condition, nor were youth or old age a bar to eligibility, every man or boy capable of carrying a gun was gladly received, and no questions asked." Eager to present an intimidating appearance, many soldiers obtained fearsome, long-bladed Bowie knives. These were so popular that "the ring of the blacksmith's hammer could be heard in every shop," as any kind of old iron was refashioned to "exterminate all the Yankees who should be so foolish as to attempt to come up the Tennessee River." Many an Alabamian posed for his portrait with one of these frightful things, which proved virtually useless in combat.[26]

Men who were to become legendary on the battlefield resigned US Army commissions and returned home to wear the gray. Among them was John Pelham of Jacksonville, who, along with a friend, dropped out of West Point and dodged Union patrols and overly inquisitive Northern civilians to get back. Pelham's overjoyed parents threw an outdoor barbecue with an entire pig on the grill. Beaming neighbors asked the young officer candidate to demonstrate his military skills with a company of the local militia. While citizens crowded in to watch, Pelham took command over a slouched crew of gangly country boys and attempted to put them through a series of drills. As his brother, Charles, recalled it later, "I remember John had an awful time, trying to get them to 'assume the position of a soldier.'" The boys cut up, joked, and chewed tobacco in the ranks. Pelham was furious, red-faced, and shouting, but there was nothing for it. The exercise mercifully ended when the dinner bell clanged. Charles remarked: "I could see the neighbors thought that the money spent upon John's military was as good as thrown away. At least a dozen of them took dinner with us but my mother was not as proud of her boy as she expected to be." That would change soon.[27]

War begun, the time for flag presentations, dress parades, celebratory barbecues, and fire-breathing stump rhetoric was past, to be replaced by tearful departures, excitement, hardship, anxiety, and loneliness. Many young men were leaving home for the first time. On April 24, the *Mobile Daily Advertiser* reported the departure of the Mobile Cadets and Washington Light Infantry, bound for Montgomery and points farther north. "The concourse which assembled to bid adieu to the flower of our youth was the greatest ever seen in Mobile," the paper wrote. "The wharves, the balconies on Front street, the boat which was to carry the soldiers away and those lying adjacent were densely crowded." Family members hugged, kissed, clasped hands, and waved handkerchiefs as they bid their boys farewell. Amid cheering and well wishes, the vessel backed from the wharf, accompanied by an artillery salute and ships' bells ringing throughout the harbor. Among the troops was Henry Hotze, a twenty-six-year-old Swiss immigrant and journalist for the *Mobile Register* who kept a record of the war's early months. After the excitement of the departure, Hotze and his comrades found they had to sleep wherever they could claim a spot. "Here on the floor of the vast saloon lie some 300 men, so closely packed that it is actually impossible to tread through or between them," he wrote of their first night afloat. But optimistic young men can endure no end of inconvenience, and Hotze declared, "Fun and merriment run riot in the saloon, for 'taps' has not beat yet." The men guzzled so much liquor that the officers "threatened to shut up the steamboat bar," but the troops remained good-humored, engaging in practical jokes and sham fights. Daylight brought drills on the upper deck under a punishing sun. Hotze reported that some men were so eager to excel at their new craft that they practiced after taps, earning gentle reprimand. The troops arrived at Montgomery late in the evening after two full days on the river. Expecting a big welcome, they instead found the place "dark and silent." Disappointed, they filed ashore, marched to the fairgrounds, and lay down on the "rough plank floor of the Exhibition Building." As Hotze wrapped himself in his blanket, he reflected on "the first lesson learned," "that in leaving home we had also left behind the individual and collective importance our youthful vanity had tempted us to ascribe ourselves."[28]

Likewise, the glamour of military service wore thin quickly for one Henry

County recruit. "A soldier is worse than any negro on the Chattahoochee River," he grumbled after only a few days off the farm. "He has no privileges whatever. He is under worse task-masters than any negro. He is not treated with any respect whatever. His officers may insult him and he has no right to open his mouth and dare not do it." Marcus A. Worthington, a prosperous Jefferson County landholder, awaited orders with the Tenth Alabama at Montgomery, battling bad food and boredom. "I am of the opinion that if some of the boys were at home they would not volunteer soon again," he wrote his sister. But, he hastened to reassure her, "I don't regret the step I took in going to the war & should do it again if I was called on." For still others, the war's earliest days meant the stimulation of an exotic new locale. Mississippian William Cowper Nelson was stationed at Mobile, where he was fascinated by the architecture, the fragrant gardens, and the harbor. He scarfed oysters daily and frequented the city wharves where "ships, brigs, schooners, sloops, steam boats" were moored. He boarded a Spanish vessel that had no cargo, only "doubloons, with which to buy cotton and return." He went to a play—"only tolerable"—and attended Easter mass at the cathedral. "The house was densely crowded," he wrote to his mother. Like most Protestant upcountry boys he had never seen a bona fide bishop or a priest, and he marveled at the "innumerable wax candles burning (some of them seven or eight feet long), it was to me a scene altogether novel."[29]

For the women left behind, a new reality set in, defined by worry, loneliness, and the necessity of performing theretofore unfamiliar tasks and duties. On September 1, Emily Beck Moxley of Pike County wrote to her husband, William, not long after he had gone to Montgomery with the Pike Guards. "You know not my feelings this morning. Oh, if I could just see you I would be so happy, but I shall have to submit to my fate." Two days later she penned him another letter. "It is so lonsome. If you could be with me tonight, how different I would feel but that can not be." She remembered that he had told her to comb her hair "ever time I thought of you." But she feared it would not help, "for I would do nothing but comb it, for there is not one minute in the day but what I think of you." Everywhere she looked she was reminded of him, and she took comfort in his old jackets and hat. Plantation wives experienced considerable nervousness at the dearth of white male authority in their counties. In the spring of 1862, Mrs. P. E. Collins of Cahaba, on the Alabama River, wrote to the governor "on behalf of the ladies of the neighborhood." She explained that they were surrounded by large farms "entirely without overseers." One woman lived on a farm with fifty slaves; another was the sole white person among one hundred slaves. She feared for the defenseless white women, children, and elderly, and begged the governor to excuse one of the more particularly effective overseers from military service, in the belief that the man could help control the field hands.[30]

While the majority of Alabama's young white men rode the rails into Virginia or Tennessee, a few remained stationed within the state. Mobile in particular was vulnerable, with only the outdated brick bay forts as protection. "The city was in a most defenseless state," wrote Kate Cumming during the war's first summer, "and could have easily been captured, and no doubt would have been had the fact been known to the enemy." And the enemy was very much in evidence. On clear days down at Forts Morgan and Gaines, Rebel soldiers could easily make out the Union blockaders' masts standing several miles off the Mobile bar. The USS *Mississippi* and the USS *St. Louis* rode at anchor, their lookouts scanning the horizon for ships heading into or out of Mobile Bay. During the war's earliest days no one was quite sure how the blockade would actually work. The first test came in early June, when a large British bark named the *Amstel* carrying building materials and a fine brass bell cast in Troy, New York, ran aground at the mouth of the bay. The *Amstel* had hoped to dart into Mobile and pick up a valuable load of cotton before the blockade went into effect, but hers was an ill-starred gamble. Aboard the USS *Niagara*, Capt. William McKean squinted through his spyglass as a strange vessel rocked alongside the bark. "A schooner, supposed to be armed, and having a number of men on her deck, has been seen for a number of days past beating about the harbor of Mobile, just within the bar," he wrote in the ship's log. Careful inspection revealed that the crews of the schooner, named the *Aid*, and the bark were salvaging cargo from the latter vessel. On the night of June 5, McKean dispatched the wooden screw steamer *Mount Vernon*, armed with a single 32-pounder, and three small boats to cut out, or capture, the schooner. Union jack tars scrambled aboard the *Aid* flashing revolvers and cutlasses to the protests of the crew, seized her, and sailed her out toward the blockading fleet as a prize. Her crew was put aboard small boats and sent to Fort Morgan. "She is not armed," McKean reported, "but is a

Figure 9. Federal vessels cut out the schooner *Aid* at the mouth of Mobile Bay, June 5, 1861.
Courtesy Mobile Municipal Archives.

strong-built and well-found vessel of about 100 tons . . . and belongs to Mobile." Still aground, the *Amstel* was left as bait to catch future salvors, and she
steadily broke apart during the years that followed.[31]

The Union blockade would never be completely effective, but Alabama's
residents began to feel the pinch early nonetheless. Life's little luxuries were
the first things to be missed. Noting the disappearance of New England ice,
Cumming lamented, "We were fast awakening to the distressing fact of our
great dependence on the North for almost everything." The Confederate government was most concerned about military supplies and medicines, of course,
but civilians mourned the dwindling of fine silks and thread, the latest magazines and newspapers, fancy shoes and clothes, not to mention tea, coffee,
sugar, and cigars. A Greensboro lawyer complained, "The Yankees are threatening the coast & to come down the Miss with a great force—When oh when
will this ever end? Meat is getting very scarce."[32]

The war became much more immediate on December 9, when what were
likely Alabama's first shots in anger rumbled over Mobile Bay. A young Con-

federate officer named James M. Williams was stationed at Fort Gaines and described the incident to his wife, Lizzie, in Mobile. "Yesterday one of the enemy's steamers came up on the west of pelican island and fired eight or ten shells in the direction of our pickets," he wrote. The shells landed short, but the garrison at Fort Morgan "fired two or three shots as a challenge for them to come on if they felt like it, and the other blockader fired her guns also, so that for an hour we had quite a lively little cannonading at safe distances." It reminded Williams of two roosters "all crowing without pitching in to fight it out." Things heated up on Christmas Eve, when there was another action, brisker and far more exciting than the first. Skies were clear and seas calm when a small Rebel gunboat named the CSS *Florida* (later rechristened the *Selma*), sallied out to attack the blockaders. Flags fluttering gaily from stubby masts and her funnel vomiting black smoke, the *Florida* gamely approached the bar. Hearing his comrades' excited shouts, Williams "ran up the sand hills and there was the glorious little steamer going out alone to meet the new vessels of the enemy!" A white puff appeared from her deck as she opened fire, and then Williams heard the delayed report. Cicero Price, the Union commander, observed that the little ship was "firing rapidly from two rifled guns and one or two of smoothbore." Most of the projectiles passed harmlessly over the blockader, while a few "burst all around us, without, however, doing any damage to the hull or crew." Yankee sailors watched from the rigging and tops of neighboring vessels, and Rebels crowded Forts Morgan and Gaines's ramparts, cheering their respective sides. "Boom! Boom! goes the Lincolnite," Williams excitedly wrote to his wife. "Bang! Bang! The Florida replied with her sharp rifled guns, the difference in the sound was so great that without looking at the vessels you could tell which had fired." After about forty-five minutes, the Southern vessel prudently retired behind Mobile Point and the protection of Fort Morgan's glowering guns. "The most magnificent scene I ever witnessed!" Williams declared, while the *Mobile Evening News* dubbed the set-to "a nice little affair." No one was hurt on either side, but one Union officer mused, "The activity of the enemy in these waters seems to call for a more active force here." Distant and protected as it was from the primary scenes of action, Alabama's war was clearly going to be a hot one.[33]

# 2

# War in the Valley

Truly our town is full of the enemy.
—Mary Jane Chadick

They were ungainly looking things. Cut-down riverboats with soaring paired stacks amidships, boxy pilothouses, big side-wheels flanking the stern, massive smoothbore cannons hugging the decks, and five inches of unpainted solid oak plank wrapped around everything, earning them the sobriquet "timberclads." The troops more derisively referred to them as "bandboxes." Both names were apt. While not liable to be of much use against artillery, the oak siding was more than enough to stop the small-arms fire they would likely encounter on Southern waterways. These vessels certainly looked intimidating enough to civilians, and in the winter of 1862 a pair of them brought the war directly into north Alabama.[1]

By fall of the war's first year, the euphoria and confidence that had attended secession and early enlistments were tempered by the realities of absent loved ones, camp sickness, and battlefield horror. In the East, the Confederates had been unable to capitalize on summer's triumph at Manassas, and the armies now faced one another across what was destined to be some of the world's most fought-over real estate. Alabama troops were there, and they proved to be brave and capable soldiers. John Pelham, who had been so embarrassed trying to drill tobacco-chewing Calhoun County rustics in front of family and friends, was a phenomenon under fire at Manassas, ignoring the snapping bullets and bursting shells while efficiently and effectively managing his battery. He earned the praise of numerous officers, and in a letter to his father

Figure 10. USS *Tyler*. This formidable timberclad routinely ran the Tennessee River early in the war, frustrating Rebels and cheering Unionists. Courtesy Library of Congress.

he expressed the sentiments of many of his comrades: "We are battling for our rights and homes. Ours is a just war, a holy cause."[2]

In the West, barely 50,000 Southrons faced twice their number across a looping 400-mile front between Cumberland Gap and Columbus, Kentucky. Here the Union enjoyed a decided advantage in its ability to run the rivers. While the Rebels were restricted to land and a rickety rail network to maneuver across long distances, Yankee ironclads, timberclads, steamboats, barges, and flats could transport troops and reinforce them with heavy guns, conduct lightning raids (especially against railroad crossings), facilitate supply, and even serve as floating hospitals and chapels. The Mississippi, Tennessee, and Cumberland Rivers all beckoned as handy invasion routes, poorly protected by hastily erected forts and batteries. The Tennessee and Cumberland pierced the middle South like a pair of cotton hooks, with prime farmland and metropolitan Nashville the immediate prizes. They joined the mighty Ohio River in Kentucky where they were only separated by three miles and should have each been fortified there, allowing for mutual support. But because of dicey early war politics, when it was considered unwise to push Kentucky too hard to secede lest its citizens reject the Confederacy entirely, the rivers had been fortified farther upstream just across the Tennessee state line, where they were 12 miles apart. Fort Henry protected the Tennessee and Fort Donelson the Cumberland. North Alabamians' hopes rested on Fort Henry, and they were none too reassured. The fort was built in a bottom, and with winter's onset and rising waters, the river was as likely to accomplish its destruction as the Federals. To further add to the distressing picture, nearby commanding heights had been left unoccupied by the Rebels. Even the fact that the river flowed north was considered a Federal advantage, since any disabled vessels would quickly drift free of further danger. South of Fort Henry there was no defense at all.[3]

Concerned about their vulnerability, a group of prominent Alabama and Mississippi citizens called on the Confederate high command at Columbus in late November. They met with Gen. Gideon Pillow, a Tennessee lawyer, planter, and Mexican War veteran known for his vanity, bravery, and willingness to bend the truth. Years before, Gen. Winfield Scott had called Pillow an "anomaly, without the least malignity in his nature," but "the only person I have ever known who was wholly indifferent in the choice between truth and falsehood, honesty and dishonesty." Nonetheless, when the civilian delegation asked him if "he considered the defenses of the Tennessee River safe," his answer was sincere. "He said they were as good as could be constructed in the time allowed and with the means afforded," the committee reported, "and most cheerfully accepted the tender of aid which we were sent to make." As it turned out, they couldn't offer much—at best a "regiment of men past middle life" armed with shotguns and rifles, slaves to help dig, and "our wives and daughters to prepare clothing and tents." The unvarnished truth was that north Alabama's security depended on an undermanned river fort that was flooding as fast as the Yankees were approaching.[4]

To no one's surprise, Fort Henry fell to the combined army and naval forces of Gen. Ulysses S. Grant and Flag Officer Andrew H. Foote on February 6. Even as the Federals then swung their focus toward Fort Donelson, the opportunity of a wide-open Tennessee River was not lost upon them. In fact, four days earlier Foote had already issued orders to Lt. Seth Phelps, a saltwater veteran with service from west Africa to Mexico, that once Henry capitulated, he was to conduct a raid "as far up the river as the stage of water will admit." Accordingly, as soon as the Stars and Stripes snapped from the gaff above the conquered bastion, Phelps took the timberclads *Tyler*, *Lexington*, and *Conestoga* and steamed south, or "upbound" in Tennessee River parlance. The *Conestoga* took the lead because she had the only local pilot willing and available to work for the Yankees. Phelps's immediate objective was the Memphis, Clarksville, and Louisville Railroad bridge 25 miles upstream, which the Rebels could use to shuttle troops east. The gunboats reached it after dark, only to find the drawbridge disabled and several Confederate steamboats beyond it fleeing upriver. Lacking neither energy nor ingenuity, Phelps dispatched several mechanically inclined bluejackets to repair and open the drawbridge. He then pushed the *Conestoga* and *Lexington* through, leaving the *Tyler* to destroy the span. Throughout the following day, Rebel sharpshooters fired sporadically into the timberclads' thick sides but did no harm. Unintimidated, Phelps kept on and late that afternoon arrived at Cerro Gordo, Tennessee, where his crews seized a Confederate ironclad under construction and 250,000 feet of prime lumber. Early next morning, the vessels passed Eastport, Mississippi, and then crossed over the Alabama line.[5]

Still unopposed by any serious force, Phelps's timberclads soon reached Florence, 150 miles beyond their starting point. Situated on the north side of the river at the Muscle Shoals, Florence was as far as the gunboats could navigate, but it held both strategic and psychological significance. A short bridge connected the town to the Memphis and Charleston on the south bank, which former Secretary of War Walker, now a brigadier general, had just labeled the "vertebrae of the Confederacy." Florence also possessed flourishing cotton mills, brick warehouses, well-built steamboats, and some capable small manufacturers. But more than anything, it represented the deepest penetration yet by the Federals. Phelps's raid was an astonishingly bold stroke, highlighting the Confederate government's inability to defend its citizens. From Richmond, Rebel war clerk Jones lamented: "Three of the enemy's gun-boats have ascended the Tennessee River to the very head of navigation, while the women and children on its banks could do nothing more than gaze in mute despair. No batteries, no men were there." This wasn't completely true, as there were a few Confederate cavalrymen, but other than taking a few potshots at the Yankees and setting three steamboats on fire, they could do little. Phelps landed some men, who quickly seized "considerable quantities of supplies, marked 'Fort Henry.'" Anxious about what might be next, a "deputation of citizens" called upon the Yankee lieutenant. As Phelps put it in his official report, they wanted two things—first, to reassure their wives and daughters "that they would not be molested," and second, that he would not destroy their relatively new railroad bridge. Phelps was comforting on both points. "As for the first," he declared, "I told them we were neither ruffians nor savages, and that we were there to protect from violence and to enforce the law." As for the second, Phelps stated that because of the shoals his vessels couldn't ascend farther and he saw no need to burn the bridge. Compared to what was to come later in the Tennessee Valley, this was remarkably light-handed treatment.[6]

There was a reason, of course. Lincoln wanted it that way. He believed that the Southern fire-eaters and big planters had brought on the war but that it was not widely supported by the people. If the Southern common folk realized that Federal soldiers and sailors had no intention of ravishing their daughters, robbing them, burning their houses, or freeing the slaves, then they would quickly see the wisdom of abandoning the rebellion and returning to the national fold. War was to be made on the Confederate army only, not innocent civilians. During the early months, this conciliatory policy seemed logical. Everyone knew about the loyalist pockets in places like east Tennessee and north Alabama, and if more Rebel citizens came to see the Yankees as benevolent rather than malevolent, the Confederacy was surely doomed. Whether or not this was realistic was about to be revealed as Union troops began taking territory.[7]

First indications were good. In his report, Phelps emphasized what he considered the most interesting lesson learned from his daring waterborne foray. "We here met with the most gratifying proofs of loyalty everywhere across Tennessee and in the portions of Mississippi and Alabama we visited," he declared. "Most affecting instances greeted us almost hourly." Crowds of men, women, and children numbering in the hundreds had "shouted their welcome," he asserted, "and hailed their national flag with an enthusiasm there was no mistaking; it was genuine and heartfelt." Phelps believed even more citizens felt this way, but as one confided to him, "a reign of terror makes us afraid of our shadows." The *New York Times* couldn't wait to share the heartening news. "The people of Florence are so delighted at finding the Stars and Stripes once more giving protection to them that they were prepared to give a grand ball to the officers of the gunboats, but they could not remain to accept their courtesies."[8]

Positive developments just kept coming. Fort Donelson fell on February 16, and its 12,000 defenders were made prisoners. Nashville tumbled bloodlessly a week thereafter. Of a sudden, the center of the Confederacy's long Kentucky line was broken, and its troops to the east and west were exposed to flank attack. Bested in battle and outmaneuvered, the disgruntled Southrons abandoned Kentucky and middle Tennessee and reestablished themselves along a new line stretching from Chattanooga to Memphis. Determined to protect their critical "vertebrae" and make a stand somewhere, they concentrated at Corinth, Mississippi, through the early spring. The West's first great battle came at Shiloh, Tennessee, just 20 miles north of Corinth, on April 6 and 7. It was an awful collision of arms, with combined casualties of almost 24,000 killed, wounded, and missing, ruthlessly dispelling any lingering hopes that the war would be short or easy. The immediate result was a draw, and the Rebels fell back on Corinth to tend their wounded and regroup. Kate Cumming, eager to help, arrived days later and was appalled at the human wreckage. "O, if the authors of this cruel and unnatural war could but see what I saw there," she wrote, "they would try and put a stop to it!" That wasn't to be, but another battle wasn't likely anytime soon, and in the meantime Alabama's fertile Tennessee Valley lay undefended and inviting.[9]

An astronomer led the Federal invasion. Gen. Ormsby M. Mitchel was a fifty-something Kentuckian with a distinguished and varied career as an attorney, surveyor, mathematician, West Point lecturer, and founder of the Cincinnati Observatory. Despite his age he had a full head of wavy hair, a clean visage, and a steady gaze. His men affectionately called him "Old Stars." They were 8,000 down from middle Tennessee, tough midwestern farmers, lumberjacks, draymen, farriers, teamsters, carpenters, masons, and mechanics with the occasional bespectacled clerk thrown in. During the wee hours of April 11, their advance cavalry reached the Memphis and Charleston just in time to surprise two trains bound for Stevenson, in Alabama's northeastern corner. By daylight the main force was in Huntsville. "The city was taken completely by surprise," Mitchel bragged, "no one having considered the march practicable in the time. We have captured about 200 prisoners, 15 locomotives, a large amount of passenger, box, and platform cars, the telegraphic apparatus and

Figure 11. Kate Cumming worked as a Confederate nurse and was appalled by the war's human wreckage. She witnessed and commented on many aspects of Alabama's war. From Kate Cumming, *Gleanings from Southland* (Birmingham: Roberts and Son, 1895).

offices, and two Southern mails." Huntsville's sleepy citizens were thunderstruck. What few Confederate soldiers and officials who were in town skedaddled. They included Walker and Brig. Gen. John Bell Hood. Jeremiah Clemens, true to form, was the exception. When he saw the blue columns tramping downtown's macadamized streets he switched sides again, professing his renewed love for the Union. "They entered at daybreak," wrote Mary Jane Chadick, a Presbyterian preacher turned soldier's wife and, as it turned out, eloquent diarist. "The southern train was just coming in, having on board 159 Confederate soldiers, some wounded, going to their homes, and others, who had been on furlough, rejoining their regiments." In what must have been an understatement, Chadick recorded "a great deal of excitement and consternation among the citizens." Another local woman shared her direct impressions of the invaders in a letter printed by the *Mobile Register*. "You should see them as they troop past the gate sometimes, on horseback, forty or fifty of them together, with their murderous looking spurs attached to their heels, great long swords encased in brass and dangling with terrific clamor against the horses' sides." She further described rattling pistols and scary-looking knives attached to wide black leather belts. This fearful martial procession with its menacing racket was exacerbated by mysterious barked commands and rough soldiers' talk, all of which left Huntsville's female faces "fever blanched with terror." The correspondent explained that their reaction was to pull their sunbonnets down snug and "stop our ears with our fingers, that we may shut out as much as possible the terrifying and humiliating noise."[10]

Mitchel dispatched other units to the east and west, seizing and occupying Stevenson and Decatur. There was minimal resistance, and to secure his flanks he had several small bridges destroyed. "Thus in a single day," he proudly reported, "we have taken and now hold a hundred miles of the great railway line of the rebel Confederacy." His superiors were both surprised and pleased by his rapid advance, and he was at once promoted to major general. A correspondent traveling with the army shared the excitement: "His movement was almost as sudden and luminous as the meteors which he so often followed through the skies." Not only had Mitchel severed the South's best east–west rail connection, seriously compromising its communications and ability to reinforce one theater with troops from another, but he had also placed a large armed force deeper in Dixie than any other Union commander. Now he could swing west on Corinth or east on Chattanooga as the military situation dictated.[11]

Mitchel's fondest hope was that he would be given a field command with the Army of the Potomac, but Lincoln wasn't about to foolishly tinker with success, and the "unwinking stargazer" was ordered to assume occupation duty in Huntsville. His men bivouacked around the magnificent domed Greek Revival courthouse, their white canvas tents blossoming under the north Alabama sun. Regular searches for weapons and concealed Rebels were initiated and guards posted. Citizens kept a wary eye. "Truly our town is full of the enemy," Chadick wrote. "There is a sentinel at every corner. Everybody keeps the front door locked, and I make it a point to answer the bell myself, not permitting children or servants to open it." This was to be the first large-scale test of the federal government's conciliation policy, and the Union soldiers studied civilian reactions closely. "The men of Huntsville have settled down to a patient endurance of military rule," wrote Col. John Beatty, Mitchel's provost officer. "They say but little, and treat us with all politeness." The women, however, were another matter, "outspoken in their hostility, and marvelously bitter."[12]

Figure 12. Federal troops camped around the courthouse in Huntsville. They would occupy and evacuate the city several times during the war. Courtesy Huntsville-Madison County Public Library.

While Huntsville proper remained in uneasy equilibrium, the countryside became agitated by troubling instances of guerilla warfare. Beguiled by Phelps's glowing account and the *New York Times*, the Federals had badly misjudged the Valley's degree of Unionist sentiment. This wasn't the hill country. The situation deteriorated throughout late April and by early May was ugly and violent all along the river. Mitchel complained of "bitterest feeling" among the Rebels. "Armed citizens fire into trains," he reported, "cut the telegraph wires, attack the guards of bridges, cut off and destroy my couriers, while guerrilla bands of cavalry attack whenever there is the slightest chance of success." In a steady trickle, blue-clad corpses were brought back into town for burial. Chadick wrote of witnessing two or three funeral corteges a day. "When a member of the cavalry dies," she continued, "his horse is led in the procession, as chief mourner, with the blankets and accoutrements of the deceased thrown over him, which looks inexpressibly sad." The conciliation policy obviously wasn't working. This was a different and unexpected kind of warfare, vicious and unstinting, and Mitchel was all too ready to fight fire with fire.

Thoroughly exasperated by the depredations, he raged: "Unorganized bodies of citizens have no right to make war. They are outlaws, robbers, plunderers, and murderers, and will be treated as such."[13]

Two nearly simultaneous incidents in early May graphically demonstrated just how far the Federals were prepared to go to suppress such activity. While riding a train through the picturesque little village of Paint Rock, a few miles south and east of Huntsville, a Union detachment commanded by Colonel Beatty was ambushed. Scattered rifle shots peppered the cars, and half a dozen men were wounded. Infuriated, Beatty halted the train and marched "a file of soldiers" back into Paint Rock. "The telegraph line had been cut, and the wire was lying in the street," he later wrote. Calling the citizens together, Beatty harshly told them "that this bushwhacking must cease." The Federals had tolerated it long enough, he shouted. It was time for an ultimatum. "Hereafter every time the telegraph wire was cut we would burn a house," he promised; "every time a train was fired upon we should hang a man; and we would continue to do this until every house was burned and every man hanged between Bridgeport and Decatur." The Federals were more than happy to engage in an open honorable fight between uniformed opponents, he continued, but "assassin-like" attacks by skulking civilians were cowardly. Beatty vowed that if townspeople didn't hand over the bushwhackers, "we should make them more uncomfortable than they would be in hell." His men then set the town's quaint wooden buildings alight, took three prisoners, and returned to Huntsville.[14]

And then came Athens. What happened there May 1 and 2 sparked an outcry North and South and ultimately led to the end of conciliation and the beginning of total war. Located some 30 miles west of Huntsville and above the river, Athens is the Limestone County seat. During the Civil War it was a small town with a population of under a thousand, nearly half of them slaves. A neat courthouse square anchored the community, with modest businesses and homes around it. A few churches, a school, and nearby columned mansions like that of the Reverend James Donnell completed the picture. Before the war the town had been anything but a secessionist hotbed. Up until February 1861 it enjoyed the novelty and stimulation of an antisecession newspaper, the *Union Banner*, Yancey had been burned in effigy by white laborers during the lead-up to the Montgomery Convention, and after Alabama's withdrawal the American flag flew above the Limestone County courthouse longer than anywhere else in the state. When it was hauled down, Mayor Press Tanner lovingly folded it and kept it safely in his house. But with war and the enlistment of so many young men in the Confederate army, a different sentiment came to the fore, prompting Reverend Donnell to state, "On the whole I think the sympathies of the people here are with the Confederate government."[15]

Unfortunately for both sides, Yankee occupation didn't elicit gestures of warmth and cooperation from Athens' residents. At first, however, there was little sign of the trouble to come. When the officers of the Eighteenth Ohio quartered around the square and their men pitched tents on the local racetrack the evening of April 29, locals tried to ignore them and make the best of the situation. It helped that the soldiers mostly kept to themselves and were frequently absent on routine patrols and expeditions. Surveying the situation, Mayor Tanner pronounced the occupation "Unexceptional! The citizens were congratulating themselves on having such a quiet and orderly set."[16]

It turned on a Liberty dime. Early on the morning of May 1, gunfire west of town announced an advancing Rebel force. First there were pistol shots, then musketry, then the sound of heavier guns. This was worrisome and a sign that it might be a sizable contingent. Jittery Union scouts confirmed their officers' worst fears, reporting several hundred gray-clad cavalrymen, at least two cannon, and, because they had seen "three flags," many infantry.

Sensibly worried, the Yankees beat a hasty but confused and disorderly retreat, leaving their tents, backpacks, and camp equipage in the process. Athens' citizens made no effort to hide their delight at the spectacle. Women jeered and waved exaggerated farewells, and there was general shouting and jumping for joy. To add to the humiliation, a train from Huntsville carrying none other than Old Stars himself ran into the shabby withdrawal and had to laboriously chuff into reverse lest the general become a Rebel trophy. Eager to explain the situation, the Eighteenth's shamefaced officers told wildly exaggerated stories of an overwhelming Rebel phalanx; civilian men cursing them; women spitting on their weapons, chasing them, and "throwing filth and garbage"; and bolder souls sniping at them from inside houses around the square. The Confederate juggernaut turned out to be 200 men of the First Louisiana Cavalry dragging two small mountain howitzers. Athens' citizens welcomed them heartily, after which they all had a fine time plundering the

Yankee camp and distributing the stuffed knapsacks to blacks and children of whatever color.[17]

Safely arrived back at the Huntsville Depot, Mitchel was in a towering rage. He immediately ordered 500 men to ride the train west, "attack the enemy there, and take and hold the town at all hazards." As the designated companies, made up of youngsters from Illinois and Indiana, milled about waiting to board, Mitchel loudly harangued them. He was done tolerating the Rebel ambushes and disrespect, he said. Rising to his theme, he commanded the troops to "leave not a grease spot." Then he heard that two members of the Eighteenth had been killed and swore: "I will build a monument to these men on the site of Athens. I have dealt gently long enough with these people. I will try another course now." The impressionable soldiers no doubt enjoyed the display and took it to heart. They were far from home, had slept on the cold ground, suffered sickness, been shot at, lost friends, and were eager for an end to the whole mess. So it was that they resolutely bundled onto the cars with their muskets, bayonets, cartridge boxes, tin cups, and canteens, believing they understood what the old man expected—namely, as one captain put it, to "clear things out generally."[18]

Their colonel was the right man for the job. Ivan Vasilyevitch Turchaninov, known as John Basil Turchin in the States or, more colorfully, the Russian Thunderbolt, was a forty-year-old immigrant from the Don Cossack Host, a province between the Black and Caspian Seas. Thickset and balding with streaks of gray lightening his dark beard, he was a veteran of the Russian Imperial Army who had helped quash the Hungarian Revolution of 1848. In a newspaper profile shortly after Turchin came to America, the *Chicago Tribune* explained that "having imbibed Democratic notions, and being thoroughly disgusted thereby with the Russian government," he had finagled a furlough to a German spa and, accompanied by his wife, "made his way to free America." When the war came, he joined the Union Army as a colonel of Illinois volunteers and by the spring of 1862 found himself in Huntsville, Alabama. As he and his men grimly rode the rails alongside the glistening Tennessee, the happy residents of Athens were about to learn that his attitude toward civilians in wartime was very different from that encouraged by the conciliation policy.[19]

The Yankees disembarked several miles outside of town, sending scouts ahead. These soon returned to report the Confederates all gone. Deprived of a fight, Turchin ordered his men forward. Early morning on May 2 they flooded the town. Donnell's home was occupied, artillery placed on the grounds, and other troops and guns were positioned at various points in and around the square. Mayor Tanner anxiously watched as "the soldiers were breaking down the board fence in front of my yard, and the artillery men with the long knives they had commenced cutting down my peach trees." Residents began to gather about, and some mildly taunted the Yankees. But they quickly sensed a different tone to this day. Ignoring them, Turchin ordered his men to begin searching houses and stores. By all accounts the men were gruff and disrespectful. Mildred Ann Clayton's home was searched for weapons. She said she had none. One man called her a liar and a "Goddam Bitch." He pointed a pistol at her, and she gave up several guns. But the Yankees weren't done and wrecked the house before leaving. Other female residents experienced similar treatment. Rowena Webster reported that the soldiers' "chief delight" was to "strew molasses and lard all over the carpets, break up furniture and smash the mirrors, and to leave nothing that they could possibly destroy." Stores and businesses were similarly ransacked. One soldier claimed the "sidewalks of the town were almost covered with dry goods," a pharmacy was ankle deep in medicine bottles, and burly bluecoats whaled on iron safes with sledgehammers and axes. Finally, as if any further proof were needed of the soldiers' philistinism, several private libraries were vandalized, the books ripped and strewn on the floor. Turchin sat his horse in the square and saw it all and approved.[20]

But did he order it? There is no evidence that he did. Two Union officers who were not present later said he had told his troops that he would turn his back or shut his eyes for two hours, or something to that effect, allowing them to loot the town. One of his soldiers who was there said pretty much the same: "Colonel Turchin allowed us to take our revenge, which we were not slow in doing, although it was not his orders, still he winked at our proceedings." Many Confederate officials and civilians believed the blame went up the chain of command and that Mitchel had dictated the sacking. Such a command certainly would have matched his level of exasperation at the time. Contemplating her ruined carpets and broken mirrors, Webster stated, "No worse order was ever given in the days of the French Revolution than he issued to old Gen'l Turchin."[21]

To use a quaint Southern expression, it was all over but the shoutin', and there was a lot of that. Anger was universal in the South, and Northern news-papers lined up on both sides of the issue. The *Cincinnati Commercial* declared the sack of Athens "disgraceful," while the *New York Times* praised Mitchel for a policy that handled "rebels as if they *were* rebels." Mitchel's superior, Gen. Don Carlos Buell, was a determined proponent of the conciliation program, however, and in June he traveled to Huntsville in an attempt to restore con-ciliation among Mitchel's troops. Frustrated by months of guerilla warfare and insults, the men preferred Mitchel's fiery rhetoric and aggressive tactics to Buell's kid-glove approach. After Buell ordered the release of a civilian sus-pected of firing into a train, one bluecoat grumbled, "These Southern conspira-tors [are] always innocent [to Buell]." A Wisconsin officer was more blunt, stat-ing that Buell's "conduct makes my blood boil." Predictably, Buell and Mitchel clashed, with the latter ultimately decamping for Washington. That summer Turchin was court-martialed and found guilty. Buell ordered him drummed out of the army. But thanks to the influence and activism of Turchin's wife, the Lincoln administration intervened, overturning the verdict and even pro-moting the Russian Thunderbolt to brigadier general. No clearer sign could have been asked for—conciliation was done, hard war had come.[22]

On the scale of wartime destruction, Athens and its citizens had actually not fared so badly. No homes or barns were burned, and no one was killed. There was one report of a female slave raped outside of town, but Union offi-cers promised to aggressively prosecute the perpetrators. There was no denying that restraints had been thrown off, however, and that Southern sympathiz-ers could now expect vandalism and destruction along with routine searches and seizures. Houses, carriage houses, smokehouses, and barns were targets, as were crops in the field, horses, mules, cattle, hogs, and sheep. Chadick's home and property were frequently intruded upon, and some two weeks after Athens she wrote of a "horse panic." "Nearly all of the carriage horses about town were taken," she noted. "They called to examine Old Henry, but pro-nounced him too clumsy for cavalry." Matters steadily deteriorated, and as Confederate cavalry strikes and partisan activity continued, civilians were in-creasingly abused, especially in the countryside. By March 1863, fourteen-year-old Ellen Virginia Saunders wrote in her journal that the Yankees were "destroying and burning property and compelling the people to pay war tax and insulting ladies by searching them and even running their hands into their pockets." Protests up the Union chain of command were fruitless. Gen. William Tecumseh Sherman, soon to become one of the most infamous hard-war practitioners in American history, stated that the federal government "has in North Alabama any and all rights which they choose to enforce in war—to take their lives, their homes, their lands, their everything—because [civilians] cannot deny that war exists there, and war is simply power unrestrained by constitution and compact."[23]

Slaves were profoundly affected by these changes. Southerners considered them property, of course, and used them to support the rebellion as laborers, teamsters, cooks, and body servants. As such, any disruption to the Peculiar Institution was a disruption to the Rebel cause, and Union soldiers openly encouraged slaves to escape. While some postwar Southern families frequently comforted themselves with heartwarming stories of faithful servants remaining on the plantation and hiding silver or Confederate soldiers, the reality was that most slaves left their plantations and homes at the first opportunity. This was a heavy blow to the status quo and yet another clear sign that this war would change everything, including the South's vaunted social order.

In June 1862, Chadick disapprovingly wrote of Union officers visiting residents' kitchens to flirt with the black cooks and maids. "Many of the negroes have refused to work for their masters and are constantly going to the Federalists," she continued. Two months later she complained again that the Yankees "are playing mischief with the negroes, and the poor ignorant creatures don't know which way to turn, or who are their real friends. The Yankees can be seen at the corners, in the alleys, in confidential chats with them." As to who their real friends were, however, most blacks appeared to have had no doubt, despite instances of some Union soldiers' racist hostility or indifference. Colonel Beatty declared: "We have in our camp a superabundance of negroes. . . . They lie around contentedly, and are delighted when we give them an opportunity to serve us." Based on his experience, Beatty was adamant: "There are not fifty negroes in the South who would not risk their lives for freedom. The man who affirms that they are contented and happy, and do not desire to escape, is either a falsifier or a fool." After the Emancipation Proclamation on New Year's Day 1863, the effect on north Alabama's blacks was, in the words of one Yankee captain, "marvelously wonderful." Thousands of slaves poured into the Union camps and tagged along after columns, creating no small degree of inconvenience for the troops. The contrabands, as they were known, had to be managed somehow, and the Federals employed them as cooks, teamsters, and personal servants. Able-bodied males were formed into military companies, armed and drilled by white officers in front of their horrified erstwhile masters. Chadick could only mutter: "So they are arming blacks. Truly their course must have become desperate." While many Union common soldiers bristled at the idea of having anything to do with the former slaves, others found pleasure and humor in the circumstances. One Yankee described marching a crowd of blacks and a herd of livestock into Huntsville. "We had 500 hogs," he wrote, "550 sheep, 250 cattle, and nearly 1,000 negroes, counting men, women, and children, and a lot of horses and mules, of which there was never any account taken." The scene resembled something out of Exodus: "The hogs waddled along and grunted; the sheep tripped along, panted and bleated; the cattle dragged along and lowed; the mules kicked along and brayed; the negroes followed, the older ones singing and the babies crying; women carried babies on their backs and bundles on their heads; the men carried the larger children and all sorts of cabin 'traps.'" Despite the confusion, disorder, and outright chaos that attended those days, most blacks couldn't have been more thrilled. As one of them rejoiced to a bemused Yankee soldier, "Bress Mars Abraham foh long time sah, we all ready to fall into Abraham's bosom."[24]

Scenes like the foregoing unfolded against the Valley's beautiful natural and agricultural backdrops. Even in the midst of destructive civil war, both soldiers and civilians couldn't help but occasionally notice and favorably comment upon their surroundings. When Mitchel's replacement, Brig. Gen. Lovell H. Rousseau, arrived in the summer of 1862, he inspected the country from Huntsville to Tuscumbia and wrote, "The Tennessee Valley, for 70 miles long and from 5 to 7 miles wide, is one immense corn field." Chadick found relief from the stress of military occupation by visiting Monte Sano Mountain with several female friends. This 1,600-foot-high horseshoe-shaped eminence overlooking Huntsville has long been a favorite retreat for locals and tourists. Chadick rode her faithful Old Henry "in true equestrian style." Union pickets viewed her little party "with a great deal of curiosity" but didn't bother to examine passes. Chadick had a delightful time. "Bushwhacked about on the top of the mountain and spent a couple of hours with Mrs. Toney, who is rusticating up there," she wrote in her diary. Jenkins Lloyd Jones, a Wisconsin private, proved himself a talented wordsmith during his time in the Valley. At one point he toured Russell Cave, a "stupendous piece of God's handiwork," penetrating as far as the light allowed. "A truly impressive scene," he wrote in his journal, "solid rock under one's feet, pure crystal water trickling down its walls, streams fell from above on [illegible] of rock, which by constant trickling were now smooth and symmetrical." But even here, the war was present; evidence of Rebel saltpeter mining included piles of dirt and big vats outside the entrance. Jones was no less susceptible to Huntsville's attractiveness. On a January day in 1864 his unit was wearily marching through winter cold when the community appeared ahead. "The sun shone brightly on the snow-covered roofs of this beautiful town with their tall church spires raising their snow-capped peaks to the heavens as a witness of better and happier days gone by. On either side broad fields with beautiful mansions were spread to view, the whole enclosed by the frost-covered range of low mountains." Their spirits lifted, Jones and his comrades jauntily stepped through town "with colors flying and bands playing, much to the satisfaction of the large crowds of contrabands that flocked at every corner."[25]

Despite the presence of thousands of armed Federal troops and an increasingly harsh occupation, many locals remained hostile, and Confederate cavalry kept up their activity. Barely three months after the sack of Athens, a small band under the command of Madison County native Capt. Frank Gurley ambushed and killed a Yankee general. The incident sparked furious retaliation by Federal troops in the vicinity and widespread Northern outrage. It happened around noon on August 5, as a detachment of Ohio and Minnesota soldiers tramped north from Athens to Winchester, Tennessee. Their commanding officer, Brig. Gen. Robert L. McCook, was well ahead in an ambulance, clad only in his underclothes and nursing an old wound and a nasty case of dysentery. Accompanied by a small escort, McCook wanted to find a suitable campsite. Near the Tennessee state line, the small party was surprised by about ninety hard-riding Rebel cavalrymen. In desperation, McCook's driver turned the ambulance, but its canvas top caught a tree branch, and the vehicle ran up an embankment. Skilled teamster that he was, the driver got it righted and took off with the general. As one Union officer described it: "He was soon overtaken and surrounded although his horses were running at the top of their speed. In reply to the oft-repeated cry of 'Stop!' 'Stop!' the general rose in his bed and exclaimed, 'Don't shoot; the horses are running; we will stop as soon as possible.'" Whether or not the Confederates could hear this amid the noise, confusion, and gunshots is unknown, but one of them, thought to be Gurley, fired into the wagon bed, mortally wounding McCook. The general was taken to a nearby farmhouse, where Gurley, insisting that he hadn't been able to see into the ambulance, apologized for shooting him. The Rebel captain's supporters later claimed that the Yankee general chalked it up to the fortune of war and absolved him of any blame.[26]

As soon as the main body of Union troops arrived, a few shots sufficed to scatter the Rebels. When they discovered their general suffering at death's door, they went on a rampage. That at least was the charge in the Southern press and from beleaguered Valley citizens. The *Charleston Mercury* wrote that when McCook's men found him, they "seized their muskets, and, breaking through all discipline, dashed forth with feelings amounting to frenzy." An Athens woman backed up this account, citing seventeen civilians hung and all the plantations and farms burned within five miles of the ambush. Members of Gurley's outfit later claimed that local civilians hadn't had anything to do with the ambush and hadn't helped them in any way. Unfortunately, given everything that had already transpired in the Valley, the Yankee common soldiers weren't convinced.[27]

As Gurley's lightning strike demonstrated, organized Rebel resistance in north Alabama was almost exclusively conducted by small cavalry detachments. Traveling fast and light, these units were frequently comprised of local recruits who already thoroughly knew the country. They were expert horsemen and good pistol shots, and if they got lost or left behind, they could blend into the civilian population. One of their most effective leaders was Philip D. Roddey, a former tailor, Lawrence County sheriff, and steamboat captain. In the fall of 1862, Roddey raised a cavalry outfit in and around Tuscumbia and led it on raids in northwest Alabama, middle Tennessee, and the northeastern corner of Mississippi. Union wagon trains, railroad bridges, mail shipments, and isolated garrisons were his favorite targets. His commanding officer, Gen. Braxton Bragg, informed a fellow general, "Capt. Roddey has the entire confidence of the commanding general, who wishes to commend him to you as one eminently worthy of trust."[28]

Figure 13. Gen. Philip D. Roddey,
the "Defender of North Alabama."
Courtesy Library of Congress.

The reason for Bragg's remark was that he was launching an invasion of
Kentucky and had assigned Roddey to help maintain a Confederate presence
in north Alabama. He wanted the cavalry captain's new commander there to
know he was leaving him a good man. Bragg's bold move was meant to regain
all that had been lost the previous year and firmly plant the Stars and Bars
on the Ohio River's southern bank. It very nearly worked. Buell, forced to
abandon his Tennessee River line, withdrew all the way to Nashville. Without
so much as a minor skirmish, much less a major battle, Bragg had suddenly
freed the Valley's oppressed Rebel citizens from their tormentors. Chadick was
awakened after midnight on August 31, 1862, "by the sound of heavy tramping
of feet, the sound of voices, uttering the most dreadful curses, the rattling of
wagons in the street." Springing out of bed, she peered through the window
to behold a long jumbled column of men, mules, horses, and wagons as the
Yankees evacuated Huntsville. "Could hardly believe it," Chadick exulted,

"so joyful the thought. All the children were up and in a state of great excitement. Joined them on the back porch to look at lurid glares of fires burning in different directions, fearing they had set fire to some parts of the town." It turned out to be just supplies "and other articles destroyed to prevent them from falling into our hands." Fortunately for the citizens and Rebel troops who quickly moved in to access their spoils, the Yankees didn't do a very thorough job. According to the *Richmond Whig*, the Confederate quartermaster found warehouses stuffed with goods, including "over 500,000 pounds of leather," bolts of wool cloth "enough to make 5,000 coats and pants for our soldiers," and 1,000 bales of cotton. Captain Gurley and his men soon appeared and were cheered by civilians. "A perfect crowd of ladies and gentlemen rushed to the square to greet them," Chadick recorded, "and Capt. Gurley was literally crowned with wreaths of ivy and flowers." Several Federal pickets who hadn't got word of the retreat were arrested, as were those enemy soldiers left in the local hospitals. In an uglier turn, Chadick approvingly noted, the Rebel troopers "shut up some of the Jew stores, who had been purchasing goods from the Feds."[29]

Freed of the Union yoke at last, Huntsville's Confederate women discovered renewed delight in old pleasures. Rebecca Vasser wrote that she was again able to "enjoy the calm night air, and the sweet moonlight that falls around me and is reflected in brighter gleams from my ring." Sarah Lowe offered profound thanks to "the Ruling Power" that although the Federal occupation had been a "long and disagreeable one," it was "not permanent." To be sure, the hated Yankees had gone, but much had irrevocably changed. To begin with, tens of thousands of blacks followed them into Tennessee, disrupting the region's daily life and economy. Catherine Fennell spoke for many whites when she stated that she for one was "glad to get rid of them." Others were angry, including two men who told the retreating Yankees they ought to be ashamed for stealing their slaves. More upsetting to others was the nasty little civil war that had been unleashed between the Rebels and Unionists in north Alabama. Unable to leave, the Valley's Unionists, as well as stronger concentrations in the hill counties immediately south, experienced their own brand of harassment and abuse by the ascendant Rebels. Farms and houses were raided, able-bodied men were pressed into military service, and crops and livestock were destroyed or seized by butternut troops. Those accused of spying for the Union or materially aiding the occupation were subject to arrest and even hanging. One local woman could only shake her head, calling the situation "a miserable condition for a country to be in, when a part of the inhabitants are leagued against the other part."[30]

As for those Confederate loyalists who hoped retreating Yankees augured a return to peace and prosperity, they were to be sadly mistaken. The armies would ebb and flow again. Huntsville would be occupied at least three more times, Florence and the Shoals would change hands dozens of times, clashing cavalry would crisscross the Valley and hill counties, gunboats would steam the river, plantations would be burned and looted, muskets would spit fire and lead, and more people would die. But all that was yet in the future. Five months of Yankee rule had bent but not broken the region's Confederate civilians. Women in particular were proud of their defiance, resourcefulness, and resilience during a period of daunting adversity. Little did they know their trials had only begun.

# 3

## Mobile under Blockade

Our boats were much injured and all the standing
rigging shot away: our hull well peppered.
—Capt. John Newland Maffitt, CSA

Early on the morning of June 5, 1861, a "very dark, sallow man with black hair and eyes, whiskers down each cheek but shaved clean off his chin" eased out of a Liverpool hotel and cautiously wended his way toward the waterfront. He suspected that his every move was monitored by Union spies, and he was right. One was nearby, in fact, and provided the above less-than-flattering description. Their intense interest in this slightly seedy-looking fellow was more than justified. His name was James D. Bulloch, just arrived as the Confederacy's chief foreign agent, charged with contracting and building warships for the Southern navy. Bulloch was in his late thirties and had already had a varied and interesting career. Born into a distinguished Southern family (Theodore Roosevelt was to be a nephew), he had served fifteen years in the US Navy and was the captain of a civilian mail packet when the Civil War began. Like dozens of other ambitious Southerners, he had made his way to Montgomery early and was there appointed foreign agent. His uncanny administrative acumen was widely known and appreciated on both sides of the Mason-Dixon Line, and no one with a troy ounce of judgment dared underestimate him. "He is the most dangerous man the South have here and fully up to his business," the chief Union spymaster in Europe, Henry Sanford, informed his government. "I am disbursing at the rate of $150 a month on this one man which will give you an idea of the importance I attach to his movements."[1]

Within a few blocks of leaving his hotel, Bulloch arrived at 10 Rumford

Place, the elegant three-story brick offices of Fraser, Trenholm and Company, a prominent commercial house. Rather than risk being seen at the handsome Classical Revival main entrance, Bulloch slipped around and came through the back door, but he was observed nonetheless. That he had made his way straight to Fraser, Trenholm was no surprise. The firm was partially owned by a Charleston, South Carolina, family and prided itself on strong Southern loyalties. One of its Liverpool principals, Charles K. Prioleau, also happened to be the Confederacy's de facto British banker, and after he warmly welcomed Bulloch, the two quickly got down to business. "No funds had yet reached them, and they had no advice of remittances on behalf of my mission," Bulloch later recalled. But Prioleau, "perceiving the necessity of prompt action, authorized me to give out such orders as were of pressing importance, and to refer to his firm for the financial arrangements." Within a matter of weeks, the industrious Bulloch had successfully contracted for two vessels, the *Oreto* and the *290*, soon to become famous as the CSS *Florida* and the CSS *Alabama* respectively. Both would wreak fearsome havoc upon the Union's merchant fleet in the months to come, but only the *Florida's* bright coppered hull would actually course Alabama state waters, and it is her story that concerns us here.[2]

Building a warship on English soil intended to harry United States vessels was a decidedly risky proposition, and Bulloch did his best to cloak the endeavor. Besides evading Union scrutiny and interference, he had to remain cognizant of British laws forbidding the construction of vessels for use by belligerent foreign powers. However, if anyone was equal to the challenge, it was Bulloch. When he contracted with the William C. Miller and Sons shipyard for the hull, masts, rigging, boats, and "general sea-outfit," he told them the vessel was to be named the *Oreto* and was for the Italian government. It is doubtful that the shipyard's savvy owners and workers truly believed that, but they didn't care and were simply happy to have interesting work. Considering what Bulloch needed from them, they were clearly the logical choice. Miller had extensive experience as a Royal Navy shipwright and knew about old-style vessels from bowsprit to sternpost, which perfectly suited the job at hand. Bulloch's order called for a wooden vessel because it would have to "carry heavy weights on deck and berth large crews." Miller already had on hand a scale drawing of a Royal Navy gunboat that with minor adjustments would do for the plans, and the *Oreto* began to take shape on the ways. The engines were contracted for separately, the job going to Messrs. Fawcett, Preston and Company, every specification carefully emphasized by Bulloch in person.[3]

By late winter of 1862 the *Oreto* had been launched, and she floated regally in the River Mersey dockside. She was a beautiful thing to behold: 695 tons, 191 feet long, 27 feet in the beam, three raked masts, a bark rig, twin collapsible smokestacks, big gunports, and a two-bladed screw that could be ingeniously lifted by a winch to reduce drag and increase sailing speed. Below decks was a pair of 200-horsepower engines with forward and reverse capacity, along with bilge pumps, cabins, a ward room, a dispensary, a sail room, a magazine, storage rooms, and a galley. By this time, of course, US government agents and officials were well aware of the *Oreto*'s purpose and mounted increasing pressure on the British government to intervene. Bulloch had remained on his game, however, taking care not to supply the vessel with any guns or accoutrements of war that would justify British interference. Before his adversaries could have the ship seized or contrive to delay him further, Bulloch sent the *Oreto* on a supposed sea trial complete with female passengers to fool any spies. At the harbor mouth, the ship slowed and the women descended into small boats for the return to port, then the *Oreto* bolted for open sea. By the standards of the time, she was a greyhound underway. During the run from England to the Bahamas her master recorded a speed under steam of 10 1/2 knots, and under canvas alone "with quartering wind, so that we could carry main top-gallant studding sail, 13 1/2 good." Although she was intended to be a commerce raider, the *Oreto* would soon prove to be a handy blockade runner as well. Bulloch had managed his challenges well and given the Confederacy an extraordinarily seaworthy and swift vessel.[4]

By high summer 1862 the ship was sheltering at Havana under Spanish protection while Union warships shadowed her every move. During the intervening months since her run out from England, she had been commissioned as a Confederate naval vessel; been rechristened the *Florida*; acquired a commander, Lt. John Newland Maffitt; been armed with eight rifled guns but no rammers, sponges, or sights to operate them; and been joined by a crew since afflicted by yellow fever. In the ship's log for September 1, Maffitt wrote that because he could neither recruit a crew in Havana, "as 'twas the season of sickness, when sailors did not congregate in this port," nor obtain the military supplies needed, "I reluctantly came to the conclusion that there was nothing

Figure 14. CSS *Florida*. From J. Thomas Scharf, *History of the Confederate States Navy from Its Organization to the Surrender of Its Last Vessel* (Albany, NY: Joseph McDonough, 1894).

left to me but to force my way into some Confederate port." With Pensacola and New Orleans in Union hands, Mobile was the obvious choice, a straight shot northwest, 545 nautical miles across the glittering Gulf. Suffering from fever now himself, Maffitt ordered the *Florida* to set sail that very night with fewer than twenty men aboard. Skirting the Cuban coast to avoid detection, she then darted out and enjoyed an uneventful three-day crossing. By the afternoon of September 4, Mobile Bay and the comforting ramparts of Forts Morgan and Gaines were in sight. "There was not a cloud in the sky," Maffitt wrote, "or a zephyr breath on the sea, to disturb the serenity of the surroundings; but when the eye sighted the approach of the vengeful foe this poetry of view faded before the harsh and stern reality."[5]

Maffitt had been into Mobile Bay before, of course, but that was with a knowledgeable and competent pilot, which he did not have aboard the *Florida*. From his coastal survey days he likely knew that there were three possible entrances from the gulf. The least attractive was the shallow Pelican Channel to the west, but since the *Florida* drew 12 feet, that was risky, and with the channel markers removed he wasn't sure about the exact entrance there anyway. To the east the 12-foot-deep Swash Channel ran just offshore along the Fort Morgan peninsula. This was a great favorite among light-draft blockade run-

Figure 15. John Newland Maffitt's daring runs into and out of Mobile Bay inspired the South and infuriated the Union high command. Courtesy History Museum of Mobile.

ners as it was easily defended by Confederate field pieces and sharpshooters placed behind the sand dunes. But getting over to it would have required time and complicated maneuver. As Maffitt anxiously observed the Union blockading vessels steaming hard for him, he knew his best option was the main channel, which crossed the bar with 21 feet of water and ran immediately under the guns of Fort Morgan into the bay.[6]

Although his decision to make the run in broad daylight with enemy vessels approaching might have been considered suicidal, Maffitt had one significant consideration in his favor. As he tried to reassure one of his worried officers, "We will hoist the English colors as a '*ruse de guerre*,' and boldly stand for the commanding officer's ship; the remembrance of the delicate *Trent* affair may perhaps cause some deliberation and care before the batteries are let loose upon us; four minutes of hesitation on their part may save us." What Maffitt was referring to was the international uproar created the previous December when the *Trent*, a British vessel, was stopped by a Union warship, and a pair of Confederate envoys aboard were arrested. The British public and government were outraged at this breach, and the two nations came close to war. Ultimately, Lincoln ordered the envoys released, muttering, "One war at a time," but tensions remained high. Thus, when Union officers off Mobile Bay trained their brass spyglasses on the advancing *Florida* they saw a vessel that looked exactly like a British warship flying that nation's red ensign. Was she indeed such, approaching to ask permission to enter the harbor, a not uncommon occurrence, or was she something more sinister? A wrong guess could have drastic consequences.[7]

The decision as to what to do lay with Commander George Henry Preble, a forty-six-year-old native Mainer with extensive naval experience that included sailing into Tokyo Bay with Commodore Matthew Perry in 1853. He was a brave and competent officer, recently promoted for his role in the capture of New Orleans. Preble had only been on blockade duty off Mobile a few days and was still learning the local shoals and channels and sizing up Rebel gun ranges when the *Florida* appeared. His vessel was the USS *Oneida*, a handsome 1,488-ton, 10-gun screw sloop that drew only 8 feet, allowing her to operate relatively close inshore. Unfortunately for Preble, the *Oneida* at best could manage 12 knots, and as the *Florida* came on directly with black smoke tumbling out of her twin stacks, he attempted to get up steam with one of his boilers shut down for repairs. This effectively halved his speed, and as the *Oneida* struggled, the *Florida* made directly for her.[8]

Two other Union warships also took up the chase but were farther astern. If the *Florida* was indeed a Confederate ship, only Preble could stop her. When the vessels were about a hundred yards apart, he hailed "the stranger," but "receiving no answer I fired a shot across his bow. He ranged ahead without stopping, but still thinking him an English man-of-war I fired two more shots across his bow, and then directed a shot *at* him, which unfortunately went over, between his fore and mainmasts." Racked with fever, Maffitt had himself lashed to the rail, while his skeleton crew raced aloft to set as much sail as possible and lower the British flag. No longer in doubt as to the *Florida's* intent, Preble ordered a broadside. At just that moment a heavy swell rolled the *Oneida*, and her shots swished high through her quarry's rigging. "Had their guns been depressed," Maffitt remarked later, "the career of the *Florida* would have ended then and there." Now all three Union ships opened what Maffitt termed, with grim respect, a "rapid and precise" fire. Master seaman that he was, Maffitt was able to adjust course so that two of his pursuers were in a line, allowing only the forward vessel to fire and, at that, only by veering off course to bring her guns to bear. In the meantime, fearing a collision, Preble had turned his own vessel slightly, costing more valuable moments. As the *Florida* raced past her, the *Oneida* unleashed another thundering broadside, which proved more effective than the first. A big 11-inch shell smashed through the *Florida*'s port coal bunkers, hit the forward boiler, "and entering among the men on the berth deck wounded nine men and took off the head of James Duncan." Fortunately, despite making a hole large enough to push a cotton bale through and wrecking things generally, the shell failed to explode. Otherwise the *Florida* would likely have been crippled or sunk. Meanwhile, high in the rigging, a blizzard of humming shrapnel prevented further adjustments to the sails. As several beleaguered Rebel tars hastened to regain the deck, one lost the bottom of his foot and another, a finger. Somehow, in the middle of this chaos, one of them managed to "re-rove" a halyard, and "the Dixie flag" floated defiantly in their enemy's faces. On the *Florida* plowed as rigging, spars, and blocks crashed onto her deck amid the *Oneida*'s persistent pounding. Maffitt clung to the rail, determined to "enter the destined harbor."[9]

After what must have seemed an eternity for the men of both sides, though in reality it was less than half an hour, shoal water and Fort Morgan loomed, and the Union vessels were forced to fall away. Amid wild cheering from the crowded brick ramparts, the *Florida* glided into Mobile Bay and dropped anchor. While two Confederate gunboats steamed for her, their crews exulting, Maffitt untied himself and assessed the damage. "Our boats were much injured," he wrote, "and all the standing rigging (except three shrouds) shot away; our hull well peppered." One man was dead, eleven wounded, and practically everyone was still suffering from some stage of fever. But the *Florida* was safe, and Maffitt was a hero. From Mobile, Adm. Franklin J. Buchanan, the very same who had commanded the CSS *Virginia* (formerly the *Merrimac*) at Hampton Roads before a wound forced him to miss the epic clash with the *Monitor* and now in command of local waters, sent down his hearty congratulations. The *Florida* was immediately quarantined, but that didn't stop civilians from crowding her sides in small boats to shout up their approval. Bursting with pride, Maffitt informed his daughter that his exploit was featured in all the newspapers and that his cabin was "like a flower garden."[10]

There was no such adulation for Preble. Due to hesitation and uncertainty, he had allowed a dangerous enemy vessel to escape Union capture and find safe haven. The *Oneida* had very nearly run aground at the end, which would have been ignominy multiplied. In his report to Rear Admiral David Glasgow Farragut at Pensacola, commanding the West Gulf Blockading Squadron, Preble explained the circumstances and credited the *Florida*'s success to her "superior speed and unparalleled audacity." These were not words calculated to warm his superior's heart, and Preble knew it. He signed the report "with great mortification" and waited for his medicine. The embarrassment quickly went up the chain of command. In his report to the secretary of the navy, Farragut expressed frustration and mystification as to why Preble hadn't opened fire sooner. Southern papers gloated, the foreign press had a field day lampooning Union officials, and as soon as all the reports landed on Lincoln's desk, Preble was out, his dismissal announced from the quarter deck of every vessel in the fleet. The *New York Times* expressed satisfaction, calling it "a just judgement." Unfortunately for the Union war effort, the extraordinary John Newland Maffitt wasn't done humiliating his enemies.[11]

Preble's ouster was a painful reminder, if Federal naval officers needed it, of the dire wages attending hesitation or timidity while on blockade duty. They had to be vigilant at all times, and numerous factors were ranged against their success. Preble was not the only officer who let an enemy vessel slip through his grasp, though none of the other ships stood to pose as serious an offensive threat to Union commercial interests as the *Florida*.

In the wake of the *Florida*'s successful run, Farragut increased the blockade off Mobile to nine vessels, some crisscrossing the sea lanes well out, others prowling the various channels at the bay mouth. Every man jack on station knew the *Florida* was undergoing repair and refitting, and under no circumstances whatsoever must she be allowed to escape back into the gulf. But even with nine ships on duty, determined Rebel captains could still dash in and out, and they did so with infuriating frequency. Schooners, brigs, small steamers, and larger custom-built fast steamers continually made the effort, ingeniously exploiting foul weather, sheltered bayous and coves, and Union inattention or mechanical trouble. The most successful blockade-running vessel was the British-built *Denbigh*, jokingly dubbed "the mail packet" by Union sailors for the regularity of her trips. She sat long and low in the water and drew only 7 feet, allowing her to steam all the way up to the city wharves with ease. Powered by big engines and feathering side-wheels that could deliver 14 knots or better, she did much to keep up civilian morale. During the war, there were 220 attempts to run the Mobile blockade by the *Denbigh* and other vessels, 208 of them successful. This was more than enough to justify the risk and the expense. Little wonder that today nearly every Old Mobile family worth its salt can point to a daring blockade runner somewhere in the family tree.[12]

The typical run ferried cotton to Cuba and returned with military supplies for the Confederate government and sundry civilian goods for general sale. The government supplied the cotton and agreed to let the ship owner have half of it if he would deliver the entire cargo and give the government "at least one-half of the carrying capacity of the steamer in the return voyage." Besides the captains, who enjoyed profit margins of a mouthwatering 500 percent, Mobile's citizens were the most immediate beneficiaries of this brisk business. One English visitor noted that they "seem to drive a thriving trade with Havannah by running the blockade—their swift, well-handled steamers going in and out just when they please." Only a month before the *Florida*'s dramatic run, the *Mobile Register* reported that "a fine schooner was to be seen just about sunset yesterday evening, lying off Matthew's [cotton] Press, concerning which all we are able to state is that she ran in yesterday morning in the face of the blockade, and that her cargo consists chiefly of powder, lead, caps, salt, coffee, cavalry sabers and soap." Weeks later, a small ad in the paper trumpeted, "Just Run the Blockade! 100,000 cigars!" Smart Mobile housewives and comely belles learned how to navigate the wharves and cut private bargains with old-salt captains, handing them private shopping lists for needles, buttons, thread, bobbins, fine gloves, calico, muslin, or hard candies for the children. Augusta Jane Evans scored a beautiful gold pen to replace the crude steel nibs she had been forced to use. Liquor was a perennial favorite for many civilians, and virtually every blockade runner had some quantity of wine, rum, gin, or champagne aboard. The hard-pressed Rebel government was more interested in the military cargo and desperately needed every bit that got through. There was never enough, but what did make it helped keep the war going longer than otherwise.[13]

As for the Union sailors and their officers offshore, every blockade runner that got by them was fresh cause for anger, frustration, and humiliation, but those captured made them believe their effort was making some difference. Even so, service afloat in the open Gulf of Mexico was no pleasure cruise. Some ships were known for their uncomfortable qualities, none more so than the *Winona*, a notorious "roller." One of her officer's grumbled, "the sea was like a tight rope to her, and she was forever trying to keep her balance. A sea-gull flying over her mast-head or a tarpon swimming under her bottom seemed quite enough to set her in motion." No matter the vessel, summer heat was searing above decks and positively murderous below, where temperatures could reach a smothering 130 degrees. When there was a flat calm, the sea's surface acted like a giant mirror, slowly baking the ships and afflicting the men with throbbing headaches. Sails hung limp, damp laundry festooned the lower rigging, decks were uncomfortably hot to toughened bare feet, and tar melted between the boards. At night clouds of mosquitoes appeared, keeping the men awake. During winter, howling northers whipped the Gulf into a fury, and stinging cold rain made duty on deck or aloft a trial. It was at such moments, when God-fearing sailor men preferred to be huddled below decks warming their hands over heated cannon balls nestled in little sand boxes, that blockade runners most often chose to make their attempts. Because the blockading vessels anchored at night, Farragut explained the difficulty of stopping a runner when she suddenly loomed out of mist and rain. "You are lying still, & the vessel is upon you before you see her going 12 or 14 knots & before you can get your men to aim a Gun she is past you." To improve the chances of spotting the runners at night, Farragut ordered heavily armed Union sailors to patrol the bay's choppy mouth in small picket boats, showing a signal light if they spied an enemy vessel. Then the chase was on, assuming the big ships on station had adequate coal supplies, fully functional engines, and enough steam up. At any given time, a third of the Federal ships were down for engine maintenance or off to Pensacola for coal or repairs. Those that remained did the best their crews could manage, and when they did catch their prey there was general rejoicing in the fleet.[14]

Despite the omnipresent blockaders, Mobile developed a reputation as a pleasure capital during the war—the "Paris of the Confederacy." Far removed from the scenes of immediate dire threat in Virginia, Tennessee, or along the Mississippi River, the city enjoyed a robust social scene with frequent parties and balls. While Rebel officers danced the Virginia reel with beautiful belles in gas-lit ballrooms on floors designed to spring at their steps, the common soldiers explored every nook and cranny of the town seeking pleasure, sometimes free-spirited and harmless, other times nasty and illicit. When one group of Kentucky soldiers were caught trying to get into the Battle House Hotel dining room, they explained to the officer who apprehended them that they were looking for stragglers. "You are looking for straggling oysters," he huffed. "I know what you are up to." The theater was popular with one and all, and each performance met with "rounds of heartfelt applause." In the winter of 1863, an Englishman named Fitzgerald Ross visited Mobile and enjoyed "a capital breakfast at a French restaurant" as well as a wedding party "where all the beauty of Mobile was assembled." On a trip down the bay to look at the forts with some Confederate brass and civilians, Ross was entertained by band music and dancing. Among those who joined in the fun was Admiral Buchanan himself, who "created a great deal of confusion and merriment, at which he was in high glee." Another Englishman, Lt. Col. Henry Fletcher of the Scots Fusilier Guards, was especially intrigued by the city's balmy climate— "oranges were growing in the open air"—and by the *Florida*, still at anchor down the bay as Christmas and New Year's Day passed. He found her repaired and the crew "anxiously awaiting an opportunity of again passing through the blockading squadron, and entering on her mission of destruction of the Federal merchantmen."[15]

Once again fit and well, Maffitt was impatient, too, but he wryly noted that Buchanan "seems to fancy the retention of the *Florida*, considering her not badly employed in keeping a large fleet to watch her." Old navy man that he was, Buchanan doubtless took pride in that, as well as having the trim *Florida* to look at and visit when he wanted relief from inspecting poorly armored gunboats, chastising men out of uniform, and wrangling with recalcitrant civilian contractors. Certainly there was much serious work for him to do. The city's defenses were inadequate and the naval squadron yet a poor and primitive creation. Nonetheless, Buchanan was laboring to improve matters. His vessels included two new wooden gunboats, the *Morgan* and the *Gaines*, each about 200 feet long, drawing 7 feet, armed with 10 guns, and manned by over 100 officers and men. They were handsome ships, locally built in part through the monetary contributions from earnest citizens. Initially much hope was placed in their breaking the blockade. This illusion was shattered when dur-

Plate 1. Colton's Alabama Map of 1859. There were fifty-two counties in Alabama at the time, about a million residents slave and free, and an embryonic railroad network. Courtesy Alabama Department of Archives and History.

Plate 2. Flag of Selma's Magnolia Cadets. One local woman called the 1861 presentation ceremony "a beautiful sight!" Alabamians' early enthusiasm for war would soon fade. Courtesy Alabama Department of Archives and History.

Plate 3. Emma Sansom monument, Gadsden, Alabama. Courtesy Library of Congress.

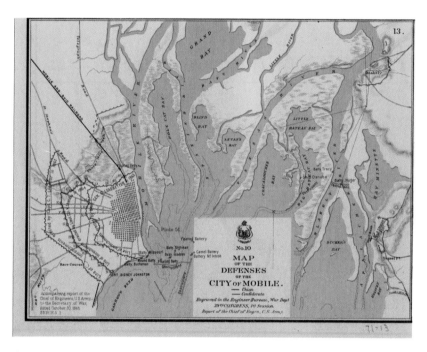

Plate 4. Upper Mobile Bay defenses as drawn by Federal engineers. The names of the Blakely (as they spelled it) and Apalachee Rivers were switched in error. The defenses at Spanish Fort are at lower right, and those at Blakeley upper right. From *The Official Military Atlas of the Civil War.* Courtesy of the Mobile Municipal Archives.

THE UNITED STATES SLOOP OF WAR "RICHMOND" ON BLOCKADE DUTY, OFF MOBILE.—[See Page 106.]

Plate 5. The USS *Richmond* on blockade duty off Mobile Bay. The Alabama coastline is just visible on the horizon. Blockade runners often chose heavy weather to make their attempts. Courtesy Mobile Municipal Archives.

SEARCHING FOR REBELS IN A CAVE IN ALABAMA.—SKETCHED BY MR. HORNER, 7TH ... OHIO VOLUNTEERS.—[SEE PAGE 683.]

Plate 6. Federal troops and a black guide search for Rebels in a cave. Partisan activity plagued both sides in north Alabama throughout the war. Courtesy Mobile Municipal Archives.

Plate 7. The Battle of Mobile Bay as painted by Julian Oliver Davidson, ca. 1886. This is the best panoramic presentation of the battle, depicting the moment of the *Tecumseh*'s sinking. The Confederate warships *Tennessee*, *Morgan*, and *Gaines* are at lower left, engaging the Federal fleet. Courtesy Library of Congress.

THE FIGHT BEFORE MOBILE—STORMING OF FORT BLAKELY, April 9, 1865.

Plate 8. The Battle of Blakeley, April 9, 1865. Sixteen thousand Federals, including several black regiments, participated in Alabama's largest Civil War infantry assault. The thunderous gunfire was clearly audible for miles. Courtesy Mobile Municipal Archives.

ing an early action off Fort Morgan the gunboats quickly retired after firing only a few rounds. If what one of the *Morgan*'s officers said of his boat was true, that was the only sensible move. "Her steam pipes were entirely above the water line," he observed, "and her boilers and magazines partly above it, so we have the comfortable appearance of being blown up or scalded by any chance shot that may not take off our heads." The men didn't inspire much confidence either. Recruited from among the steamboats, barges, ships, shacks, and taverns riverside, they were a dissolute mix of idlers, brawlers, drunkards, and coal heavers, plus the occasional idealistic youth. One officer groused, "To call the *Morgan*'s crew sailors would be disgracing the name. Out of a hundred and fifty not one is even *American*, much less a Southerner." Buchanan agreed, calling them "vagabonds."[16]

What Buchanan needed was an ironclad fleet that could smash and scatter Farragut's wooden ships. He had the beginnings of one, but again, the vessels weren't especially intimidating. They included the *Baltic*, the *Huntsville*, and the *Tuscaloosa*. The *Baltic* was placed into service first and served as his flagship. She was a converted Alabama River tug with high side-wheels, a tall smokestack forward, and inadequate cotton bale and iron cladding. She drew only 6 feet and mounted half a dozen guns, but was woefully underpowered with a top speed, if that's the right word, of 5 knots. It took her twenty-four hours to steam from the city down to the lower bay, and it was so hot inside her casemate that the crew was forced to sleep on a flat moored alongside. She wasn't likely to be much use in a fight, one of her officers dismissing her as "rotten as punk" and little better than a "mud scow." The *Huntsville* and *Tuscaloosa* were small ironclads mounting only four guns each, built at Selma and floated downriver for completion. What iron plating they did acquire came from the Shelby Ironworks in central Alabama and the engines from the Columbus Naval Iron Works in Georgia. But these vessels were even slower than the *Baltic*. Unable to breast the Mobile River's steady current, they were converted into bulky floating batteries that could be towed around the upper bay.[17]

Better was to come, however—two gigantic craft begun in 1863 and finished about a year later. These were the *Tennessee* and the *Nashville*, built at Selma and Montgomery respectively, and sent downstream to Mobile where each saw much service. The *Tennessee* was to be one of the Confederacy's best ironclads, a casemated 1,000-ton leviathan, 209 feet long, 50 feet in the beam, screw propelled, protected by 2 feet of oak and pine overlaid by 5 inches of iron, mounting six rifled guns—the fore and aft pivot, meaning they could swivel to fire in three different directions—sporting a fearsome beak at her prow to ram enemy ships, and drawing 13 feet. Her draft was to be a significant challenge in getting the vessel over the shallow bars between Mobile and the lower bay, but almost everyone who saw the *Tennessee* was awed. Kate Cumming toured her while she lay in the Mobile River and wrote: "It is a ram, and has many a dark-looking corner where the men are to be stowed away in case of a battle. All looked very mysterious. I certainly felt I should not like to be one of the crew." The *Nashville* was even bigger, with a length of 270 feet and huge boxed, plated paddlewheels arching over everything. She was never to be fully armored, but one of her men called her "a tremendous monster," and her profile at the city wharves was heartening proof that Confederate naval authorities were not idle.[18]

Fortunately for Mobile, Buchanan's efforts were complemented and reinforced by those of the local Confederate army commander, Maj. Gen. Dabney H. Maury, who arrived in the spring of 1863. Sporting a trim goatee, Maury was a native Virginian, a West Point graduate, and a Mexican War veteran. He was an energetic officer and surprisingly open-minded toward newfangled ideas, but he was short and liked to wear ridiculously large thigh-high cavalry boots. Ever alert to the absurd, the troops promptly nicknamed him "puss in boots." By fall, Maury and Buchanan enjoyed the services of a new and remarkably capable chief engineer, Lt. Col. Victor von Scheliha, a former Prussian army officer and meticulous planner. Operating beautifully in tandem, these three men—diminutive general, hawk-nosed admiral, and efficient European engineer—designed and constructed a well-thought-out, coordinated defensive system for the lower and upper bay as well as the city proper. Work proceeded on the various elements throughout the war and was truthfully never finished, but enough progress was made to qualify Mobile as one of the most heavily fortified places in the Confederacy. After the Battle of Mobile Bay, Farragut estimated that an army of 30,000 men would be needed to take and hold the city.[19]

Besides Buchanan's steadily improving naval squadron, local defense work included strengthening Forts Morgan and Gaines; building Fort Powell between Dauphin Island and the mainland, which protected the entrance into

Figure 16. General Dabney H. Maury
enjoyed his assignment as the
Confederate Army commander at
Mobile. He worked hard to protect the
city, but his short stature made him
a laughingstock. Courtesy Alabama
Department of Archives and History.

Mobile Bay through the Mississippi Sound; seeding waterways with torpedoes, or mines in modern parlance, gunpowder-filled wooden kegs anchored
to the bottom; driving iron-tipped wooden pilings in serried rows spaced by
rubble-filled hulks; erecting batteries at the five river mouths; and digging
what would ultimately be three lines of earthworks defended by big guns
around the city. What with their 25-foot-wide parapets and 18-foot-wide tra-
verses, Ross thought the earthworks "perfect models of strength and judicious
arrangement." Despite white Mobilians' professed enthusiasm for the cause,
they balked at helping with all this digging, hauling, and lifting, even when
promised wages and meals. Confederate troops did what they could but were
continually being shuffled off to other departments or tasked with quotidian
military duties like patrols, drills, and artillery practice. Thus the Confederate government resorted to impressed slave labor, sending agents around
Alabama to procure able-bodied black men for the work at Mobile. Masters
were promised a dollar a day per slave as compensation but had to provide
valuable tools like picks and shovels, which would invariably be lost or broken through the hard usage to come. Impressment was universally unpopular

and politically risky, but the workers were desperately needed. The government also used captured black Union soldiers, many of whom had been taken by Forrest in Tennessee, northern Alabama, and Mississippi. These men's lot was miserable. Clad in their soiled blue coats with the buttons cut away, they were the object of vile invective and harsh treatment. One of them later complained, "If we lagged or faltered or misunderstood an order we were whipped and abused, some of our own men being detailed to whip the others." On any given day, hundreds of black men toiled on the city's earthworks and batteries. Visitors marveled, one remarking there were so many that "they look like ants on the side of an ant hill." At the end of their day, exhausted and filthy, the slaves were marched back to brick warehouses riverside, fed corn meal and mule meat, and locked in for the night. Bad as all this was, however, at least one Federal officer believed these men were better off than their white comrades in hellholes like Andersonville Prison in Georgia. "They are not bereft of hope," he declared, "as are the Union soldiers dying by inches." In such a context, unappetizing food and stuffy warehouses were preferable to grubs and shoe leather for breakfast and flimsy shebangs constructed of pine boughs and tattered coats to keep out rain and cold.[20]

Spies and deserters kept Union commanders well informed on the defense work in and around Mobile, and their reports were worrying. The city and bay were gradually becoming impregnable. Farragut's repeated requests to attack the forts early had been pushed aside amid more urgent priorities elsewhere, like the Vicksburg and Red River campaigns, and all too soon the opportunity of an easy victory vanished. By 1863 Mobile was a tough nut, and cracking it was going to cost a lot of lives. A British merchant traveling through about this time ticked off its defensive strengths: "the forts at the entrance of the bay; shore batteries all the way up; then lines of obstructions sunk, one within the other, across the channel below the city, these commanded in turn by water-batteries and iron-clad rams waiting inside to pounce upon any assailant" and, lest it be forgotten, a railroad network that could funnel in "an army of 100,000 men . . . in a very few days." Neither Maury nor Buchanan believed Richmond could muster that large a host to defend Mobile, but both were relatively sure they could hold their own with as few as 10,000, a much more achievable figure in an emergency.[21]

Mobile's military authorities had resigned themselves to a defensive posture,

IMPRESSMENT RECEIPT.

Slaves and other Property impressed under the Act of the General Assembly of Alabama, of 31st October, 1862, from *J. G. Johnson* _____ by *J. Moseley & J. B. Harrison* _____ Impressment Agent for *Dallas* _____ county.

| Slaves, Tools, Wagons, &c. | No. of each. | Provisions and Forage. | No. of Pounds. | Value of Provisions and forage. | |
|---|---|---|---|---|---|
| | | | | DOLLARS. | CENTS. |
| Slaves ....... | 3 | Meal ..... | 54 | 1 | 50 |
| Club Axes... | | Flour..... | | | |
| Broad Axes... | | Bacon .... | 12 | 6 | 00 |
| Spades ...... | | Beef...... | | | |
| Picks........ | | Corn...... | | | |
| Cross Cut Saw | | Fodder ... | | | |
| Chisels ...... | | Hay ...... | | | |
| Augers ...... | | | | | |
| Wagons ..... | | | | | |
| Mules ....... | | | | | |
| Setts Harness. | | | | | |
| Oxen........ | | | | | |
| Log Chains... | | | | | |

These receipts should be signed in duplicate; one given to the owner, and the other filed in the Executive Department of Alabama.

REMARKS.

If any of the Slaves are impressed as mechanics, the number and trade should be stated under this head.

Impressment Agent of *Dallas* county, certify that *we* have this day impressed and received from *J. G. Johnson* in said county, the slaves and other property herein specified, and that the valuation of the provisions and forage as herein stated is correct. Signed by me in duplicate.

DATE: *Dec. 10   1863*

*John Moseley*
Impressment Agent,
*Dallas* ..........County.

Figure 17. Impressment form as filled out by a Dallas County agent, December 10, 1863. Alabama farmers and isolated plantation women resented constant Confederate government demands on their scarce resources. Author's collection.

but in the spring of 1862, three civilians called on General Maury with an improbable offensive scheme. They were a thirty-eight-year-old lawyer and sugar broker named Horace Hunley; James McClintock, an engineer; and Baxter Watson, a gifted tinkerer. Before New Orleans fell they had been experimenting with submersible craft on Lake Pontchartrain, and they wanted to know if Maury would support them as they transferred their endeavor to Alabama's port city. Maury, open-minded as ever, liked what he heard and offered the inventors free use of the Park and Lyons Machine Shop riverside. There they rapidly set to work, ably assisted by interested helpers like William A. Alexander, a British-born mechanical engineer, and 1st Lt. George E. Dixon, a twenty-two-year-old infantryman and a veteran of Shiloh, where his life was saved when a gold coin in his pocket deflected an enemy bullet. Together with the machine shop's mechanics and blacksmiths they built a submarine boat, the *American Diver*, but it was lost in choppy seas at the bay's mouth, fortunately with no loss of life. After this, Buchanan was skeptical, but Maury remained enthusiastic, and the Crescent City trio redoubled their efforts.[22]

Postwar mythology has made much of the resulting vessel's slapdash character—it was said to be a repurposed boiler cut in half and the pieces extended and fastened by crude longitudinal iron straps—but when it was raised off the Atlantic seabed in 2000, the *Hunley*'s elegant lines surprised conservators, readily explaining its Mobile nickname, the *Fish Boat*.

Indeed, from above it looks just like a porpoise, beautifully fashioned to glide through water. After the war, Alexander carefully detailed the design, and it was he who told the boiler story. While he was wrong about that and some details, he was right about others, especially the boat's general operational features. The *Fish Boat* (it was only after its transfer to Charleston that it became known as the *Hunley*) was 40 feet long, 4 feet high, and crewed by eight men. It was made of forty-two wrought iron plates meeting flush and affixed to interior butt straps. The outside rivet heads were hammered flush to reduce drag, and the propeller was protected by an iron ring. Two short conning towers with glass portholes and a series of dead lights along the hull provided limited visibility and light. The pilot stood in the forward tower while the men sat on a long low bench and turned a shaft to drive the propeller. The engineering was sophisticated and included differential gears and an off-center drive shaft. The former had the effect of smoothing and multiplying the men's effort, while the latter required that they bend over the shaft to turn it, rather than sit up right. This balanced the craft by putting the center of gravity where it belonged and eliminated the need for bulky counterweights. At best, strong men could give the *Fish Boat* 4 knots, but that was almost as good as the *Baltic* and just enough to make it operational. Bow and stern ballast tanks could be flooded with sea cocks, allowing the vessel to submerge, and a pair of dive planes controlled the angle of descent. Detachable cast iron weights along the keel allowed for a quick ascent. A candle provided interior light and had the additional advantage of indicating when the air was going bad. The armament was a towed torpedo. It was only later that the boat acquired the long bow spar with a charge attached.[23]

Conscious of prying eyes, Hunley's team assembled the vessel in the center aisle of the Seaman's Bethel on Church Street downtown, the pews removed to facilitate the work. Despite official precaution, the submarine was an open secret. Children played around it during construction, and spies kept Union authorities apprised of its progress during every stage. By July of 1863 it was time to cast security aside and test the boat. A clutch of Rebel army and naval officers, including Buchanan and Maury, as well as curiosity seekers, interested citizens, and the omnipresent gaggle of small boys, crowded the Mobile River bank as the vessel was pulled out of the sanctuary, loaded into a wagon, and hauled to the Theatre Street wharf. While everyone watched, the crew, each man chosen for his small, wiry frame and endurance, slithered through the narrow hatches and cast off shore. The target was a coal flat anchored mid-river, and at a signal from the pilot the hatches slammed shut and the *Fish Boat* disappeared beneath the surface, a long tether snaking behind with a torpedo attached. The choice of the river rather than Mobile Bay for the test was a wise one, since its waters were deeper and more protected from dangerous chop that could easily slosh over an open hatch on the surface. Aboard the submarine the men cranked furiously away as the pilot opened the sea cocks, depressed the dive planes, and then leveled off at about 20 feet. Visibility was only 1 to 2 feet at that depth, but the pilot had taken a careful sighting before the vessel submerged, and the men drove it ahead. Within minutes a loud explosion rocked the *Fish Boat* and violently jostled the crew. On shore the crowd erupted into cheers and applause, which turned into roars when the vessel popped to the surface well beyond the smoking remains of the coal flat. Buchanan was now convinced that the *Fish Boat* could do real service, but not off Mobile Bay where bars and shoals would prevent it from getting under an enemy keel. He thus wrote to his counterpart in Charleston, then undergoing a heavy siege, and offered him the submarine. It was gladly accepted, and the *Fish Boat* left Mobile concealed under heavy tarpaulins aboard a railroad flatcar. Three crews would subsequently perish aboard the vessel in Carolina waters, among them Hunley and Dixon, but the submarine ultimately sank the USS *Housatonic*, revolutionizing naval warfare.[24]

Unfortunately for Mobile, and Alabama, the *Fish Boat* wasn't going to break the blockade in the gulf. The cat-and-mouse game between the runners and Farragut's captains continued, and numbers of the runners still managed to get through. But in no way did their ships bring in enough to feed or clothe a people, and not every woman could exploit a maritime connection. Hardship and privation became increasingly common, particularly among the lower classes. In September of 1863 things were so desperate that a group of poor white women staged a riot in Mobile. According to the *New York Times*, which reported the story regretfully and with compassion, they met "in large numbers on the Spring Hill road, with banners on which were printed such devices as 'Bread or Blood,' on one side, and 'Bread or Peace' on the other, and armed with knives and hatchets . . . marched down Dauphine-street, breaking open the stores." In an ugly and foul mood, the rioters especially targeted Jewish merchants. Maury ordered troops to stop the angry women, but the soldiers "refused to obey the order, saying that they would, if they took any action, rather assist those starving wives, mothers, sisters and daughters of men who had been forced to fight the battles of the rebellion." Ultimately the mayor appeared with a provost guard and pleaded for calm, pledging increased relief efforts. This had the desired effect, and the mob dispersed, according to the *Times*, "promise-crammed."[25]

Upstate, Confederate women prided themselves on making do through ingenuity and innovation. At Cahaba, Anna M. Gayle, who was a young girl during the war years, recalled how they managed. "Sugar was scarce and hard to get," she wrote, "for while sorghum was grown in abundance, it would not make sugar, and only a few were able to get seed of the ribbon cane." People cobbled together crude mills with wooden cylinders to extract the juice and threw the crushed cane to the hogs. Watermelon sugar was used to make candy, and parched peas ground and mixed into a paste with their own oil made a good chocolate substitute. "Each household became a factory within itself," Gayle proudly noted. "On every plantation scores of negro women were kept busy spinning and weaving. Spinning wheels, reels, and warping frames stood around everywhere." Good dyes were obtained from the surrounding woods— gray from the wild myrtle, brown from sumac berries and walnut hulls, garnet from pine root, "a dark, rich magenta" from pokeberry, and "a lovely blue" from the wild indigo. Shoes were fashioned from deer skin at the local tannery, and muscadine wine rewarded a hard day's labor. In Eufaula, Parthenia Hague described how she and her neighbors made hats and bonnets. "There was variety enough of material to makes hats for both men and women, palmetto taking the lead for hats for Sunday wear. The straw of oats or wheat and corn husks were braided and made into hats. Hats which were almost everlasting, we used to think, were made of pine straw." Nearby, Victoria Clayton reported that like the women along the Alabama River, Barbour County's females kept the spinning wheels and looms going and sometimes traded foodstuffs with poorer women in exchange for help making clothes. Hague found medicine substitutes in the surrounding woods. Blackberry roots made a "soothing and efficacious cordial for dysentery and similar ailments." Extract from dogwood bark was used for chills, and its berries made passable quinine to reduce fever, while wild cherry bark tamed coughs.[26]

Confederate civilians prided themselves on their ability to bear up under pressure. But confidence and good cheer were best assured by battlefield victory or some other kind of martial success. Down on Mobile Bay, Maffitt was prepared to deliver it. He was going to have another run at the blockade. In a long letter dated October 25, 1862, Navy Secretary Mallory had expressed confidence in his abilities. "The Department does not deem it necessary to give detailed instructions for your guidance," Mallory wrote, "relying as it does upon your judgement and discretion for the conduct of your cruise, and believing that your success will depend entirely upon your freedom of action." Maffitt's mandate was simple, the secretary explained, "to do the enemy's commerce the greatest injury in the shortest time." Buchanan agreed. Much as he loved having the *Florida* under his authority, he knew he had to let her go. On January 6, 1863, he instructed Maffitt to paint the vessel's hull "lead color when she runs through the blockading squadron." He had it on good authority from other runners that "a vessel of that color cannot be seen well at night." For the rest, Buchanan instructed, Maffitt should have his ship ready for action on the run out, "hammock nettings taken down, men at quarters, etc."[27]

As for the *Florida* herself, she was at last shipshape. Patched, re-rigged, fully provisioned, crewed by 116 men, and her guns operational, she was, bragged the surgeon's steward, "a tiger preparing to spring." During the first two weeks of January, Maffitt steered her about the lower bay, waiting for the right moment. The Yankee blockaders were ready, too, or at least they thought they were. A dozen ships covered the bay's mouth, alternately lying at anchor directly in the main channel, coming as close to Fort Morgan as they dared, and steaming back and forth just over the horizon. The senior officer on station was Commander Robert B. Hitchcock, a forty-year veteran determined not to let his quarry escape. His two fastest ships, the *R. R. Cuyler* and the *Oneida*, were tasked with overhauling the *Florida* once she sallied out of the bay. Since Preble's dismissal, the *Oneida* had a new captain, Samuel F. Hazard, like Hitchcock a forty-year veteran. Despite his long record, Hazard was no Maffitt, in love with the rolling deep. "A more sea-sick man I never saw," one of his officers recalled. "He ate, to my knowledge, nothing but tobacco and hard tack." It was the *Oneida*'s unhappy fate to once again be the blockade's weakest link at a critical juncture.[28]

At last, on January 14, the weather turned dirty, and Maffitt wanted to go, but with visibility less than 20 yards his pilot declared it too dark. Impatiently, Maffitt kept the deck, waiting and watching. It rained and blew hard all the next day and by 2:00 a.m. on January 16 cleared overhead with a "light mist" covering the water. It was time. Steam up, hands aloft clutching loosened sail ready to drop it on command, the *Florida* made her move. "You might have thought her a phantom ship, manned by spectres," one of her men proudly recalled. Burning coke that left no telltale smoke, the trim vessel trembled slightly, like a thoroughbred released from the starting gate. The enemy was close but seemingly yet ignorant of her presence. "Sail right ahead, sir!" whispered one of the Rebel tars. "Port your helm!" Maffitt softly responded. Eyes peeled, the excited crew spotted one, two, then three, and more sail stacks and looming hulls around them. At this perilous moment the *Florida*'s coke supply ran out and the engineer was forced to switch to coal. As the first shovelfuls hit the furnace, billows of black smoke and a shower of red sparks shot from *Florida*'s funnels. A Union gunboat instantly signaled, "Vessel running out of this pass." Astounded, the *Oneida*'s signal officer helplessly witnessed the *Florida* rocket through the fleet. All attempt at stealth gone, Maffitt barked, "Let fall and sheet home your topsails!" The canvas tumbled down in ghostly white curtains and instantly bellied out, driving the cruiser even faster across the swells. All around signal lights flashed as the blockaders attempted to respond, but the *Florida* was too fast, "off like a deer," one of the crew remarked. Incredibly, the *Oneida* did not immediately pursue, the hapless Captain Hazard claiming he hadn't seen the Rebel or the signals. As Fort Morgan's farewell salutes echoed, Hitchcock paced his cabin "catching convulsively at his hair," positively apoplectic. "What do you mean? What do you mean?" he wailed when Hazard and his signal officer reported aboard the flagship to explain their inaction.[29]

Daylight found the *Florida* well out into the Gulf with two Union ships in pursuit. But there was no catching her. Gale force winds and furiously working engines propelled her to an astonishing 14 knots and faster. Heeled hard over, smashing through the swells and shipping green water, the *Florida* plowed on, her crew drenched and chilled but exhilarated. Their cruise was underway, and before it was finished, *Florida* would capture and destroy thirty-seven vessels, costing US mercantile interests millions of dollars. Together with the *Alabama*, her adventures would cheer weary Southern hearts and infuriate the Northern public. The *Charleston Mercury* was jubilant over the escape and wrote that Maffitt was "as brave as Nelson, as shrewd as a fox, and as thorough a seaman as ever trod a deck." The *Alabama*'s Semmes concurred, and called the episode "most daring and gallant." Hitchcock expected to fare no better than Preble, but an investigation exonerated him. There was no such luck for Hazard, whose health broke under the strain, and he retired from the service. Contemplating it all after the war, Adm. David D. Porter called the navy's failure to capture the *Florida* on her runs into and out of Mobile Bay "the greatest example of blundering committed throughout the war." It was certainly expensive blundering in financial terms.[30]

And so, as the Civil War approached its midpoint, Alabama's contributions to the Southern cause continued to accumulate. Far afield the state's soldiers demonstrated determination and valor, while at home ordinary citizens labored to support their loved ones and keep body and soul together. Montgomery's people had helped birth the Confederate government, Huntsville's had showed how to endure Federal occupation, and Mobile's had sheltered, refitted, and then said Godspeed to a dangerous commerce raider. But there were other Alabamians who did not take joy in these things—Unionists, draft dodgers, Rebel deserters, and slaves, all of whom waited for more hopeful developments to come.

# 4

## Streight's Raid, 1863

My highest regardes to Miss Emma Sansom.
                              —Gen. Nathan Bedford Forrest

He came home by ferry, train, steamboat, and wagon. But this was no joyful arrival of a living, breathing hero. It was, rather, the mournful return of his mortal remains, encased in a cast iron coffin with a glass face plate. John Pelham, so young, handsome, and brave, had been hit by an exploding artillery shell during a clash at Kelly's Ford, Virginia, on March 17, 1863. Theretofore, his remarkable valor and tactical genius had inspired thousands of beleaguered Southrons, who eagerly followed his exploits on distant battlefields from Sharpsburg to Fredericksburg. At the latter fight he had famously checked an entire Federal corps, 16,000 men, with only two guns, and earned the open-mouthed admiration of officers and men on both sides, including George Armstrong Custer, perhaps the supreme egotist of the war, who sent him a congratulatory note. The violent and stark end to his youthful martial exuberance was a deeply sobering reminder of war's futility and waste.[1]

Because of the difference in railroad gauges, Pelham's body crossed the Chattahoochee River into Alabama aboard a rickety ferry and was then placed upon the Montgomery and West Point Railroad for the 80-mile trip to the capital city. As had occurred at stations and sidings large and small all the way from Richmond, a silent crowd was on hand when the engine chuffed to a halt. Former Governor Moore was there, though whether he had any thoughts about the consequences of a war he had helped precipitate is unknown. As the people looked on, Pelham's body was reverently taken off the train and escorted by troops to the capitol building where it lay in state heaped with flowers and attended by a mute sentinel. From Montgomery, the body traveled to Selma via steamboat, then by train on the Alabama and Tennessee River Railroad to Blue Mountain, where it arrived late on the night of March 28. There it was placed into a hearse drawn by four white horses and taken to the steps of the family home, 7 miles away. As Pelham's sister-in-law described the scene, "The Father and Sister were crushed and in sorrow kept their rooms, but that Spartan Mother met her beloved son on the threshold as she would have done had he been living and led the way into the parlor and directed where he must be laid where the light would fall on his face when Sunday came." Three days later he was buried in nearby Jacksonville, where serious children filled his grave with lilac blossoms. John Pelham's war was over, but not so that of his northern Alabama friends and neighbors. They were about to bear first-hand witness to a Union raid that would cost lives, property, and not a little anxiety. But when it was all over, the South would have yet another youthful hero, this one an indomitable country girl in homespun dress and sunbonnet.[2]

By the spring of '63, the Union war effort hardly presented an encouraging picture. In the east, Robert E. Lee continued to win big battles despite fearsome casualties. On the Mississippi River, Grant was bogged down before a seemingly impregnable Vicksburg in what was clearly going to be a complicated, costly, and lengthy campaign. And in middle Tennessee, Gen. William S. Rosecrans's Army of the Cumberland licked its wounds opposite Bragg's Army of the Tennessee after a bloody stalemate at Murfreesboro. While many of Rosecrans's veterans were no doubt content to rest and avoid another fight, at least one of their officers chafed at the inactivity.

Abel D. Streight, thirty-three, was an Indiana infantry colonel noted for his impatience and abolitionist sympathies. A native New Yorker, he had moved to Indianapolis before the war, where he owned a lumberyard and a printing company. Physically impressive if a bit overweight, and sporting a dour beard but no moustache, he took pride in his reputation as a successful businessman and committed Republican. In the fall of 1861, despite his lack of military experience, Streight was commissioned a colonel in command of the Fifty-First Volunteer Infantry Regiment and took his staunch beliefs into action. His men were held in reserve at Shiloh and Perryville but saw action at Corinth

Figure 18. Col. Abel. D. Streight was a good tactician and a brave man, but his daring raid was doomed by persnickety mules, repeated bad luck, and a ferocious opponent. Courtesy Library of Congress.

and Murfreesboro. After the latter clash, Streight fretted in his canvas tent. He desperately wanted to strike another blow and, not incidentally, to advance his prospects. Time spent in camp was time wasted by his lights.[3]

While pondering the frustrating strategic situation, Streight hit upon a bold idea. He would propose a raid into enemy territory to break the stalemate. He wrote on March 5 to his immediate superior, Gen. James A. Garfield, "I hope you will continue to favor me with your influence to induce the General [Rosecrans] to give me a suitable command for the purpose of penetrating the interior of the South. I am more and more satisfied as I study the matter more carefully that I could do them more harm and our cause more good in a three month campaign than I am, situated as I have been during the last year, in a whole lifetime." Rosecrans liked the idea and authorized the raid on April 8. The plan called for Streight, in command of a mounted provisional brigade, to advance into north Alabama at Tuscumbia, his movement screened by a supporting force, and then strike south and east with the goal of cutting the railroad between Chattanooga and Atlanta at Rome, Georgia. This was Bragg's supply line, and its disruption could have a profoundly positive effect for the Federals.[4]

Streight already had some familiarity with this route, having served in north Alabama during the recent occupation. Like a number of other Union officers, he had been impressed by the Unionist sentiment he encountered there and even wrote a report on the subject. "Suffice to say," he declared, "that I have never witnessed such an outpouring of devoted and determined patriotism among any other people; and I am now of the opinion that, if there could be a sufficient force in that portion of the country to protect these people, there could be at least two full regiments raised of as good and true men as ever defended the American flag." Streight was well aware of the risks his daring new move entailed, but he fully expected to draw support and strength from north Alabama's Unionist population. This was to be a woeful miscalculation, one of many in the star-crossed adventure.[5]

Streight picked his men, 1,700 total, from four midwestern infantry regiments and two cavalry companies made up of loyalist north Alabamians. This represented yet another miscalculation, since the foray was supposed to be a mounted one, and many of the men had no meaningful experience with horses. Then, Rosecrans, worried about his cavalry, which had been continually bested by the likes of Forrest and Roddey, wouldn't give over any horses to Streight's command. Instead, the Indiana infantry colonel's troops were assigned mules, thought to be superior for the task at hand anyway given the rugged nature of the country to be traversed. In his 1973 novel *Flags in the Dust*, William Faulkner penned a famous hymn to the intractable character of the mule, declaring, "it is a known fact that he will labor ten years willingly and patiently for you, for the privilege of kicking you once." Such was to be the experience of the youthful bluecoats of Abel D. Streight's command. When they boarded their steamers at Nashville to begin the southward thrust, they discovered their new situation at once. "We found the lower deck crowded with mules," Sgt. Henry Breidenthal of the Third Ohio wrote, "the odor of which was not agreeable to our 'oil-factories.'" To everyone's consternation, there weren't enough mules to mount the entire command, and those supplied were decidedly inferior, many sick with distemper, others unshod, and most unbroken. Getting these beasts ready for mounted service proved better entertainment than a three-ring circus. "The animals, though lean and scraggy, so soon as saddled, went off on what the men called a 'sheep gallop,'" another soldier recalled. "Running about a hundred yards, some planted their fore feet firmly in the loose soil, and kicking up their hind feet, sent their riders flying into the air as if shot from a bow." And then there was the braying, constant and loud, day and night. The upshot was that a blind, half-deaf man could have easily traced this raucous host over hill and dale from 3 miles away. Little wonder that bemused observers quickly dubbed the force "the Jackass Cavalry."[6]

The Union plan called for Streight to link with his screening force, 8,000 cavalrymen commanded by Gen. Grenville M. Dodge, near Tuscumbia. From there Dodge would drive east into the Valley, keeping the Rebels to his front, while Streight cut south and east, hopefully unopposed by significant force. The two commands met on April 22 and marched east with Dodge in the lead. They were lightly contested by some of Roddey's cavalrymen, who steadily fell back before the inexorable blue tide. Dodge's thrust was devastating for the Valley's residents. One of his men wrote: "Today we witness war's desolating scourge on the plantations. The devouring elements of fire are doing their work." At least one historian has contended that Dodge's Raid has been too much de-emphasized by later Southern chroniclers. While the story of Streight's running battle and ultimate surrender is certainly colorful, Dodge's efforts were more effective and significant to the Union war effort. In his report, Dodge tallied the destruction: "1,500,000 bushels of corn, besides large quantities of oats, rye, and fodder, and 500,000 pounds of bacon." Over a thousand horses and mules were confiscated, along with hundreds of sheep, cattle, and hogs, hundreds of cotton bales, and over a thousand slaves. Tan yards, flour mills, and the military school at LaGrange were torched, as well as flatboats and ferries in the creeks and on the Tennessee. One of Dodge's cavalrymen, a Kansas Jayhawker with no sympathy for the South, put it into perspective: "We found the country beyond Tuscumbia about the best and richest I ever saw and left it nothing but a wilderness with nothing scarcely but the chimneys left to show where once had been the habitations of men."[7]

Finally, late on the evening of April 26 in a driving rainstorm, Streight turned his raiders south for Russellville. Despite the weather and the mules, he and his men were in good spirits. He had written his wife, "If I succeed it will aid our cause more than everything that has heretofore been done by our entire army." Early prospects looked good. Opposition was light, and Dodge's feint had distracted the Rebels according to plan. But then, contem-

Figure 19. Confederate cavalryman. This is the only known wartime photograph of a mounted Alabama soldier. His musket has its bayonet attached, and his right hand appears bandaged. Courtesy Alabama Department of Archives and History.

plating the success of his movements, Dodge decided his work was done and headed back toward Corinth. At first puzzled by this turn, the Confederates soon realized what was happening and lit out after Streight. They were outnumbered, but in the words of one of them, they were "fine high strung young men who loved adventure." Well-armed with double barreled shotguns and pistols, astride good horses, and accompanied by several artillery pieces, they gobbled up miles of real estate in an effort to catch their plodding quarry.[8]

They were also very well led. Colonel Roddey was earning a reputation as the "Defender of North Alabama," and native Tennessean Brig. Gen. Nathan Bedford Forrest was a fearsome force of nature on any battlefield. Born in Chapel Hill, Tennessee, in 1821, he had grown up poor with almost no formal education. Rough and unlettered, he worked as a slave trader, amassing enough wealth to become a planter and Memphis city alderman. In 1861 he joined the Confederate cavalry as a private, then raised and equipped his own command. He proved a genius in combat, fearless and focused with an admirably simple guiding strategy: "Get there first with the most men; put the skeer on 'em, and keep up the skeer." In overall command of the hard-riding Ala-

Figure 20. Gen. Nathan Bedford Forrest, the "Wizard of the Saddle." Courtesy Alabama Department of Archives and History.

bamians and Tennesseans, Forrest dispatched Roddey with several regiments to shadow Dodge, while he charged ahead with the rest. Soon enough Roddey was able to return and report that Dodge's retreat was ongoing and Streight was the main threat. Together, they caught up with the mule brigade quickly, prompting one butternut to quip: "Colonel Streight was too slow of motion for the business he had in hand. . . . He must have considered that he was on a May-day frolic; he seemed to be trying to coddle the negroes."[9]

The first clash came April 30 at Day's Gap on Sand Mountain, south and east of Moulton. Unaware that they were being pursued, Streight's men were strung out for over a mile leading up to the mountain. Their line of march was a churned-up mess, littered with discarded equipment, trash, and, in the words of one bluecoat, "exhausted horses and mules, many of them dead and dying." On the morning of the thirtieth, while the mules loudly brayed for their breakfast and the Union rear guard stopped to cook up a little something for themselves, the Confederates opened fire. Two miles up ahead, Streight heard "the boom of artillery" and knew he had a fight on his hands. He hurried his men through the gap and deployed them on a ridge just beyond, their left anchored by boggy ground and their right by a steep ravine. The horses and mules were placed down in the ravine for protection, every fourth or fifth man designated to hold the reins. The rest were to fight dismounted, the usual practice with western cavalry during the war.[10]

Eager to get at the foe, Forrest's men hurried forward, but after routing the rear guard lost time when they stopped to scarf down the abandoned Yankee breakfasts, still hot in the frying pans. There was a running skirmish all the way up the mountain, and Forrest's brother, William, leading a detachment of scouts known as the Forty Thieves, was severely wounded in the thigh. Then the Rebels spotted the main Union line, and Forrest rapidly deployed for an assault. As Sergeant Breidenthal of the Third Ohio put it, "they came thundering on," while the artillery on both sides banged away. Day's Gap was a small affair compared to the massive battles like Shiloh and Murfreesboro, where many of these veterans had seen action, but it was a sharp scrape nonetheless with Streight's 1,700 men facing down about a thousand gray coats. And as every solider knew too well, one could be killed just as dead in a little battle as a big one. Streight had chosen his ground well and proved cool and smart under fire. Forrest's men attacked piecemeal and were repulsed by a capable and determined defense. Then Streight ordered a counterattack against one of the Rebel batteries. Breidenthal and his comrades fixed bayonets and "skipped off on a run, gun and hat in one hand, yelling like so many Mohawks, taking their battery of two pieces and one limber, and some horses, without firing a gun, the rebels taking to their heels and horses and 'lighted out.'" In the awed words of one Johnny Reb, Forrest was "ferocious and wild as a lion" at the loss of the guns and wanted to attack again. But his men were disorganized, and while he raged, Streight made good an orderly withdrawal. The fight at Day's Gap hadn't lasted long. Streight had successfully preserved his command and continued his drive for Georgia. His loss amounted to about seventy-five killed, wounded, and captured. Bloodied by the stout defense, Forrest lost twice as many or more, though there was never an official tally. It was clear to both commanders now that they had their work cut out for them. Streight's men were already fatigued and saddle sore, the mules were as intractable as ever, and though they were in supposed Unionist country, farms were widely scattered and the civilians eager to stay out of the way. Forrest and his men regrouped and renewed their pursuit, sobered by the realization that this "Jackass Cavalry" consisted of "brave and formidable" men who were "practiced and patient fighters." They had caught up to their enemy well enough, but stopping him would not be easy.[11]

Fortunately for Forrest, Streight's mandate was to get to the railroad and wreck it as soon as possible, not engage Rebel troops. Otherwise, given the Indiana colonel's numerical advantage and tactical competence, Forrest might have been in real trouble. And so the chase continued toward Crooked Creek, 10 miles south of Day's Gap, a tributary of the Black Warrior River. Hog Mountain, a 1,200-foot eminence, rose just beyond. This was home ground for Streight's Alabama units, and they provided invaluable help with the route and in choosing superior defensive positions. At dusk on the thirtieth, the strong Yankee rear guard, which included Sergeant Breidenthal, reached the creek "under full mule-way." But as soon as the hot, thirsty animals splashed into the water they stopped to drink their fill, and there was no moving them. The Rebels took advantage and attacked. Once again, 2 miles ahead at the front of the column, Streight heard the racket and, as he later reported, "was compelled to prepare for battle." He placed his men along the mountaintop, his guns covering the valley below, and the mules and horses below the crest to his rear.[12]

Despite the gathering darkness, Forrest threw his men forward, shouting, "Whenever you see anything blue, shoot at it and do all you can to keep up the scare!" The result was a surreal nocturnal slugfest. "This was the first night battle I had witnessed," one Confederate trooper later wrote. "The pine trees were very tall, the darkness of their shade was intense, the mountain where the enemy was posted was steep, and as we charged again and again under Forrest's own lead, it was a grand spectacle. It seemed that the fires which blazed from their muskets were almost long enough to reach our faces." Once again the Yankees repulsed their pursuers—Forrest had at least one horse shot out from under him—and Streight pulled away again, leaving behind several dozen wounded in care of a surgeon named William Spencer and a handful of male nurses. When the Rebel cavalrymen tromped into the rude field hospital, they methodically went about emptying the pockets of the helpless bluecoats. Spencer was outraged. "I find myself surrounded by a mongrel set of armed men," he fumed, "rude and illiterate, who taunt and jeer me for my devotion to my country and its honor, while their companions rob our wounded and strip our dead." The Yankee doctor was told Forrest wanted to meet with him, and he was taken over to the general, whom he found directing matters from a carriage. Forrest made a more favorable impression than his gruff, ragtag troopers, thanking Spencer for his selfless devotion to the wounded and promising what little aid he could offer as well as freedom from further abuse. "The general is a pleasant, good-looking man," an obviously charmed Spencer wrote, "a little above the medium size, with dark eyes and a profusion of dark hair." Forrest complimented the fighting abilities of the Yankees, telling the surgeon, "Well Sir your Hoosier soldiers fight well Sir, *damned well Sir* and Colonel Streight has a fighting devil in him, bigger than two yokes of oxen." This was high praise indeed coming from the legendary Wizard of the Saddle, but Spencer's more immediate concern was treating "our brave wounded." As the Confederates rode on after his erstwhile comrades, he returned to his grim task, a prisoner.[13]

At eight o'clock on the morning of May 1, Streight's weary men rode into Blountsville, 43 miles from Day's Gap. The town was preparing to hold a May Day Festival, and the arrival of bedraggled Federal soldiers, noisy mules, and a motley crowd of contrabands took everyone by surprise. In an attempt to improve his chances, Streight burned his creaky supply wagons and redistributed the loads among the cantankerous mules. He also reluctantly decided to leave the contrabands behind. These desperate, hopeful people had joined the column along the way, expecting freedom. Abandoning them to their fate had to have been a bitter pill for a committed abolitionist like Streight. Milling about Blountsville's dusty streets, the bluecoats finally dismounted to get a little rest and according to Breidenthal "took a good meal of ham and coffee, and gave our gallant chargers a good feed of corn." Their respite was short-lived, however, as "the rebs were again harassing our rear." Sleep deprived and saddle sore, the Federals moved on again, deeper into Dixie.[14]

The chase continued toward Gadsden, both commanders playing their advantages as best they could. Streight kept moving ahead, while his rear guard set up small ambuscades to keep the Rebels cautious. Forrest rotated his men in and out of the immediate pursuit, allowing them short periods to tend their mounts and rest. It wasn't much, but it was more than the Federals were getting, most of whom had now gone over twenty-four hours without sleep. Both forces were steadily depleted along the way. Mounts continually gave out, stragglers couldn't keep up, and the numbers of killed and wounded mounted with each clash. Unfortunately for Streight, the significant Unionist support he had expected failed to materialize. His men seized horses and mules from civilians, paying in greenbacks if the owners were loyalists. "He recruited his horses almost every mile," one of Forrest's men remarked. "It was a common thing to find standing in the highways the wagons and carriages of citizens from which he had removed horses, leaving his exhausted mules in the place for them." Nobody in hardscrabble country whether Unionist or Rebel wanted to part with a valuable animal, and Streight's seizures didn't win him any friends. Many civilians harbored Rebel sympathies. East of Blountsville, two sisters seduced a trio of horse-hunting Yankees with soothing words and morphine-laced mint juleps. The barefooted farm girls astonished the Rebels by marching into their camp the next morning with several horses and the sheepish Yankees as prisoners. Forrest was delighted and sent the girls on their way with high praise.[15]

On May 2, Streight deployed a strong skirmish line to hold his rear and crossed the Black Warrior River. The ford was rocky and swift, and two mules burdened with wooden boxes of hardtack, a bland cracker that was standard soldier fare, lost their footing and were drowned. The skirmishers kept the Rebels at bay and then followed the main force. Once they were no longer under fire, Forrest's men plunged into the stream. Several graycoats retrieved the waterlogged boxes and broke them open. One of the men waved a handful of the crackers in the air, yelling, "Boys, it's wet and full of mule-hairs, but it's a damn sight better than anything the old man's a-givin' us now!" Forrest rested his men again beyond the stream and took the opportunity to walk among them and praise their performance. He acknowledged the ardors of the chase and then asked for volunteers to push it to the end. This winnowed his force to six hundred men. More were certainly willing but were either too exhausted or their mounts broken. Amid whoops of encouragement and confidence, the select gray phalanx spurred east after the Yankees.[16]

Yet another large stream lay between the two forces and Gadsden. This was Black Creek, a tributary of the Coosa. Alabama's thousands of creeks vary greatly in size and current, some burbling rivulets a child can easily step across, others sluggish, deep, and able to drown a poor swimmer. Black Creek is one of the latter, and in the spring of 1863 there were only two bridges across it, one of them rickety and abandoned. Streight's men thundered over the good bridge and then set it afire. A strong rear guard was posted on the east side. If the bridge burned through and the rear guard held, Streight stood to gain valuable time.[17]

Forrest arrived to find the bridge aflame. His men rode up to the stream but the rear guard was on alert, and there was no getting across without significant casualties. Both sides started firing. Not far away was a plain farmhouse occupied by a widow named Sansom and her two teenaged daughters. Like many families in the area, the only male in the household was in the Confederate army. In the Sansoms' case it was a son named Rufus, but at least he was nearby in Gadsden on sick leave. When the firing began, Mrs. Sansom and her sixteen-year-old, Emma, were near the bridge. They had gone to make sure their split fence rails wouldn't be damaged. Unfortunately, they discovered the Yankees had piled them on the bridge for the fire. When the shooting started, they sensibly hurried back home. And that was where Forrest rode up to them, and an Alabama legend was born. "Can you tell me where I can get across the creek?" he excitedly asked. Years later, Emma, married and living in Texas, related what happened next to Forrest biographer John Allan Wyeth. "I told him there was an unsafe bridge two miles farther down the stream, but that I knew of a trail about two hundred yards above the bridge on our farm, where our cows used to cross in low water, and I believed he could get his men over there, and that if he would have my saddle put on a horse I would show him the way." Forrest snapped that there was no time to saddle a horse and to "get up here behind me." Lithe country girl that she was, Emma hopped onto the horse and grasped the famous general about the waist. "Just as we started off mother came up about out of breath and gasped out: 'Emma, what do you mean?'" Forrest had a weakness for the ladies, and he reassured the mother that Emma was only going to show him a ford. "Don't be uneasy; I will bring her back safe."[18]

Leaving Mrs. Sansom anxiously wringing her hands in the farm yard, Emma and the general rode off. When they got near the ford, Emma suggested they dismount and creep up to the location. As they got closer, Forrest realized that he was sneaking up on the enemy with a young girl ahead of him. This would not do. "He stepped quickly between me and the Yankees," Sansom told Wyeth, "saying, 'I am glad to have you for a pilot, but I am not going to make breastworks of you.'" While the nearby forces banged away at each other, Emma pointed out the ford. Satisfied, Forrest "asked me my name, and asked me for a lock of my hair." There was to be much postwar mythmaking about Emma and the general. One account claimed that Yankee bullets actually clipped her dress, causing her to quip, "They have only wounded my crinoline." Yet another says that when she and Forrest mounted to ride away, she waved her sunbonnet defiantly in the air, causing the Yankees to cease fire and cheer her courage. At least one Union officer, no doubt humiliated by the circumstances of the raid's demise, claimed that the Emma story was a complete fabrication. In a book published immediately after the war (by Streight's Railroad City Publishing House), he wrote that it was Rufus Sansom, whom Streight had captured and paroled, who showed Forrest the ford, "notwithstanding his solemn oath not to aid or comfort in any manner whatever the enemies of the United States." Other than wounded pride, there is nothing to reinforce this version, and most historians agree that it was Emma. Whatever the particulars of the episode, there is little doubt that she was a brave young woman who did the Confederacy some service at her peril. Before he followed after Streight, Forrest left a semiliterate note for his youthful heroine. "My highest regardes to Miss Emma Sansom," it read, "for her gallant conduct while my forse was skirmishing with the Federals across Black Creek near Gadisden Alabama."[19]

Thinking they had gained a little time by burning the bridge over Black Creek, Streight's men poured into Gadsden and immediately starting seizing horses and mules. They also took the opportunity to visit a little punishment on the town. Breidenthal wrote that they destroyed "four thousand dollars worth of good flour, five hundred stand of arms, and the ferry-boat." Then they rode on for Rome. Forrest's men followed and continued to marvel at Streight's seemingly leisurely pace. "Why should he be sauntering at Gadsden during those precious hours?" one of them asked. "It seemed as if he had made up his mind to fail." But from Streight's perspective, his command was barely making it. "Many of our animals and men were entirely worn out and unable to keep up with the column," he later wrote, "consequently they fell behind the rear guard and were captured."[20]

Eager to alert Rome's citizens that a Yankee force was coming their way, Forrest dispatched a courier at Gadsden. But even as he did so, a local ferryboat operator, forty-four-year-old John Wisdom, decided to do the same.

Wisdom was from Rome originally and still had family there. Knowing his horse and buggy couldn't make the trip in enough time, he borrowed a pony and galloped out of town on his self-appointed mission. He rode hard, exchanging mounts with sympathetic farmers and residents along the way. In the darkness north of Cave Springs his mount stumbled, "throwing me full length into the road ahead of him." Dazed and dusty, Wisdom sat up, regained his wits, remounted, and continued. "I arrived at Rome a few minutes before twelve o'clock that night," he wrote, "making the ride 67 miles in eight and a half hours, including the stops for changing horses and the time I was delayed when the horse fell down with me." Suitably alarmed, the Romans hastily erected rude defenses at the roads and bridges that led into town. There weren't many regular troops in town, but combined with convalescing wounded and brave citizens, there were enough to man the barricades and present an intimidating presence. It was almost, but not quite, the final touch in the cascade of bad luck that doomed Streight's Raid.[21]

The end game played out between Gadsden and the Georgia line. Still closely followed by the Rebels, Streight deployed his men into yet another defensive stand, this one along a low ridge near Blount's Plantation. The terrain consisted of a field alongside the road backed by small pines and scrub, providing plenty of cover for the defenders. Forrest's men crashed into this line like a wave and were repulsed. After several more failed charges, the Rebels took up a position on a ridge opposite. During the firing, Col. Gilbert Hathaway, the beloved commander of the Seventy-Third Indiana, was hit in the chest and killed by a bullet shot from 600 yards away. Civil War rifle muskets were well known for their long-range accuracy, but even by those standards such a deadly reach was a marvel. Morale can be a delicate thing, especially when men are tired and under sustained stress. Hathaway's death hit everyone hard and effectively extinguished what little spirit the Yankees retained. "His loss to me was irreparable," Streight mourned. "His men almost worshipped him, and when he fell it cast a deep gloom of despondency over his regiment which was hard to overcome." Streight's gloom wasn't eased when he asked a captured Tennessean how many men Forrest had. The man was probably uneducated, but he had a shrewd appreciation for the situation and was a convincing actor to boot. He hemmed and hawed, before ticking off the names of the various brigade commanders and stating that there were others whose names he couldn't recall. Streight had always believed he was outnumbered, and the Tennessean's remarks solidified it in his already disturbed and agitated mind. All he could do was flog his command onward, at the same time dispatching an advance element of two hundred men to secure the entrances to Rome and, if not defended, take it.[22]

It was not to be. Streight's advance discovered the barricades and got the word back to their commander, who had reached Cedar Bluff on May 3, just 21 miles from his goal. "The boys were so overcome with drowsiness that they would go to sleep on their animals," Breidenthal remembered, "for we had not slept more than six hours in the last seventy-two, and had fought three general engagements, and rode one hundred and fifty miles." Yet again, Streight ordered his men into a line of battle to deal with Forrest, and they spread out along an open ridge. But as soon as the troops lay down on their arms, sleep overtook them, and they were "dead to the world." Meanwhile, Forrest's men, refreshed after ten hours of rest, rode into view, shattering the quiet, warm Alabama morning with the spine-tingling Rebel yell and scattered gunshots. Streight knew that his situation was untenable. His animals and men were played out, his ammunition diminished and much of what remained wet from the numerous streams forded, Rome was too strong to attack, and to top it all off, he believed Forrest outnumbered him three to one. It was time to parley.[23]

Sensing he had won at last, Forrest sent a courier forward to ask for a meeting with his Yankee counterpart "in order to stop the further and useless effusion of blood." A nearby Rebel cavalryman heard Forrest confidently declare, "If he ever talks to me then I've got him." The "old man," this particular graycoat chuckled, "had large experience and skill in such emergencies." Streight hastily gathered his officers and discussed the possibility of surrender. "I yielded to the unanimous voice of my regimental commanders, and at once entered into negotiations with Forrest to obtain the best possible terms I could for my command."[24]

The two officers met in the no-man's-land between their troops. After a brief greeting, Streight said that he would not surrender unless Forrest showed him how large a force he had. Forrest was no fool and instead talked on while his officers rode about busily issuing orders to nonexistent regiments and two cannons were repeatedly circled around a nearby hill, creating the illusion of many more. All the while Forrest watched his adversary's reactions to the sham display. "I seen him all the time we was talking," Forrest later said, "looking over my shoulder and counting the guns. Presently he said, 'Name of God! How many guns have you got? That's fifteen I've counted already!' Turning my head that way, I said, 'I reckon that's all that has kept up.'" Fully convinced that he faced overwhelming force, Streight surrendered. The little valley where his dream finally collapsed was snugly situated between the Coosa and Chattooga Rivers, in an area known, ironically enough, as "Straight-Neck Precinct."[25]

"At nine a.m. we were marched out into a field and there stacked arms," remembered Breidenthal. "Streight had about fourteen hundred and fifty men," one Confederate figured, "and we had about four hundred and seventy-five in line. We were drawn up on both sides of them, and every man of them carried a loaded rifle and some likewise loaded pistols. If they had concluded to renew the struggle, it is difficult to understand how any of us could have escaped alive." But Forrest successfully preserved his ruse, barking continual orders to "imaginary regiments and imaginary batteries to stop and feed their animals and men." It probably helped that Streight's men were simply too dog-tired and relieved to be done with their crazy adventure to care anymore. When Streight finally realized the disparity, he angrily demanded the surrender be revoked and that he be allowed to renew the fight. Forrest reportedly laughed and patted his seething adversary on the shoulder, saying, "Ah, Colonel, all is fair in love and war, you know." A woman living nearby described what happened after the Federals capitulated. "Their arms were stacked a half mile from our house, and the hungry men poured in," she wrote. "Every negro on the place was put to work with pot, oven, and skillet cooking for the exhausted soldiers. I continued till midnight serving one table after another."[26]

Streight's humiliating surrender, like the *Florida*'s daring escape in January, cheered Alabamians and Southerners desperate for good news. But as 1863 unspooled, those exciting events were to prove rare highlights in what was to be a veritable *annus horibilis* for the Confederacy. Herding their Yankee prisoners into Rome shortly after the surrender, one young Rebel trooper wrote of the terrible news that greeted them. "Our victory was embittered by a message that Stonewall Jackson had been wounded in a battle in Virginia. . . . I can never forget the sorrow and foreboding it produced." The battle was Chancellorsville, one of Lee's most brilliant victories, but Jackson's loss, as it turned out by friendly fire, was devastating for the South. Elsewhere, disaster piled on disaster with each passing month. After a long siege, Vicksburg capitulated on July 4, taking 30,000 Rebel troops out of the fight, and Lee's storied Army of Northern Virginia began its retreat from Gettysburg the very same day. In September, Bragg defeated the Federals at Chickamauga, in northern Georgia, and drove them back into Chattanooga. But Confederate losses were staggering, and in November Grant and Sherman broke the Rebel siege and threw Bragg out of Tennessee, opening Atlanta to invasion.[27]

Wracked with fever and a bad kidney infection, William Lowndes Yancey, one of the principal authors of the whole bloody business consuming the nation, dejectedly contemplated the fruits of his labors from his Mount Meigs plantation, near Montgomery. His wartime career had been less than stellar. After helping propel the South and Alabama into war, his fiery temperament unsuited him for effective public service at home, and President Davis sent him abroad to secure foreign recognition. It didn't take long to discover how difficult that would be. "We are satisfied that the public mind here is entirely opposed to the Government of the Confederate States on the question of slavery," he wrote from London on May 21, 1861, "and that the sincerity and universality of this feeling embarrass the Government in dealing with the question of our recognition." Discouraged at his failure to win over Britain or France, Yancey returned home in 1862 and served in the Confederate Congress as an Alabama senator. He was a caustic critic of Davis, his earlier ringing pronouncement of the man and the hour having met now long buried in bitterness and acrimony. Around the middle of June 1863, Yancey fell seriously ill and steadily declined over the coming weeks. The twin defeats at Vicksburg and Gettysburg put him into a deep depression. He blamed the defeat at Vicksburg on Davis's "prejudice and littleness" and worried over one of his sons wounded there. Realizing that the Confederacy was almost certainly doomed, William Lowndes Yancey breathed his last on July 27.[28]

Newspapers North and South noted the milestone. The *Montgomery Weekly Advertiser* declared his loss "to the politics of the country" equal to that of Stonewall Jackson's to the army "in the field." The *Richmond Dispatch* called his death "an event that occasions much public regret." The Northern press was understandably less respectful. The *New York Herald* labeled him "a restless, plotting revolutionist, a noisy fire-eater, an eloquent blatherskite, always in hot water, and never satisfied with anything. With his decease a great bag of wind has collapsed, and nothing more." *Harper's* dismissed him as "the most virulent but not one of the most able of the traitors who have conspired for the ruin of their country." And the *New York Times* lambasted his "traitorous heart." Two days after his death, Yancey's remains were borne to Montgomery's City Cemetery (Oakwood Cemetery today) and reverently lowered into the soft Alabama loam. "We can and will survive this blow, as we have others that have preceded it," the *Weekly Advertiser* wrote on August 5. But the blows were coming appallingly fast now. And the end was nowhere in sight.[29]

# 5

# Rousseau's Raid, 1864

The bugles sounded "Forward."
—Capt. Thomas C. Williams, USA

Winter 1864. Cold gripped the land and the Union vise was set, ready to tighten. Frigid northers barreled over the sere fields and leafless woods, plunging temperatures from the already ice-choked Ohio River to the southern Atlantic and Gulf coasts. In northern Virginia, the respective armies hunkered down in cozy log huts divided by the Rapidan River on the north and the Blue Ridge to the east. In the western theater, the Father of Waters flowed "unvexed to the sea," and Union forces held everything north of the Memphis and Charleston Railroad between the Arkansas state line and Chattanooga. In northeastern Alabama, not far from Bridgeport, Yankee artilleryman Jenkins Jones registered the weather in his diary. "The new year came in very cold with a little snow," he wrote, "the first of the season. Ground frozen several inches in depth." Jones and his comrades coped by chunking fence rails onto blazing fires, sending showers of sparks skyward, and cushioning their bedding with piles of dry leaves. They were hardy young men, inured to harsher temperatures at home, but they took solace when the cold fronts passed and the air slowly warmed. After the New Year's Day freeze, they endured periods of heavy rain, mist, and overcast skies but then delighted in "a soft sunny day." Smiling skies buoyed their faith and optimism.[1]

Rebel Alabamians were less cheered. Augusta Jane Evans's new novel, *Macaria; or, Altars of Sacrifice* rolled off presses North and South (the latter edition with wallpaper-covered endboards and rough wrapping paper pages), as an exhortation to persevere, but public officials, military men, and ordinary citizens from the Tennessee River south to Mobile Bay felt vulnerable, and they worried about what might happen next. Even as white flakes dusted Jones's tent and Huntsville's rooftops, four politicians penned a letter to Confederate secretary of war James A. Seddon "relative to the present condition of North Alabama." Noting that the Federals were in force everywhere north of the Tennessee, the correspondents continued, "A glance at the map of the country will satisfy that if the raiding parties of the enemy be permitted to cross the river there is no natural barrier to prevent him from sweeping as low down the country as the Alabama River, penetrating that region of the State in which are located the mining and manufacturing establishments." They begged that to protect against "such calamities as would result from the incursions of the enemy," General Roddey be reinforced by five companies of Alabamians then under General Forrest. They further warned that should the enemy get across the river "without meeting serious opposition," Unionists "in the mountain regions" would be emboldened. Likewise, on the coast, despite months of tireless preparations, Confederate officers believed Mobile Bay faced imminent attack and that their various forts and small naval squadron were as yet too weak. Dissatisfied with the city defenses, Scheliha started construction on a third line of entrenchments, and Admiral Buchanan candidly informed Evans that he "had not more than half" the number of men he needed for his gunboats.[2]

Their fears were well-founded. Studying the overall strategic situation after Vicksburg, General Grant wanted to immediately strike Mobile. "Having that as a base of operations," he later explained in his memoirs, "troops could have been thrown into the interior to operate against General Bragg's army. This would necessarily have compelled Bragg to detach in order to meet this fire in his rear. If he had not done this the troops from Mobile could have inflicted inestimable damage upon much of the country from which his army and Lee's were yet receiving their supplies." Grant was overruled that time, but by February another opportunity of at least putting some extra fear into south Alabamians presented itself. General Sherman was to launch a land attack across Mississippi from Vicksburg all the way to Meridian, which would cripple three critical railroads. From there he could either strike farther east for Demopolis, Selma, and Montgomery, head down the Mobile and Ohio's tracks for the Port City, or fall back on the Mississippi River. In order to divert Rebel troops during Sherman's advance, Farragut was to make a strong demonstration against Mobile Bay. It was never meant to be more than a feint, but if it convinced the Rebels that Mobile was Sherman's ultimate goal, they would swiftly funnel men there and away from the rampaging redhead. In a letter to Navy Secretary Gideon Welles on February 7, Farragut agreed to "amuse myself in that way for the next month."[3]

Fort Powell was to be the focus of Farragut's attentions. It wasn't much to look at, a sand and earthen installation perched in the middle of the Mississippi Sound 3 miles north of Dauphin Island. It had been constructed atop an oyster bank, enlarged by sand- and oyster-filled cribs to half an acre, and it guarded Grant's Pass, a shallow channel into Mobile Bay. The pass had been dredged to about 7 feet and offered a safe route for blockade runners and coastal traders. The fort was protected by 8-foot-high parapets that were 25 feet thick, six large guns, and a few torpedoes seeded in the pass. Its commander was Lt. Col. James M. Williams, the very same who had provided his wife, Lizzie, with the breathless description of a gunboat duel early in the war. Williams was a twenty-seven-year-old midwesterner who had moved to Mobile in November 1860 as bookkeeper for the well-known silver merchant and jeweler James Conning. Despite his Northern birth, he enlisted in the Twenty-First Alabama Infantry, was stationed at various places around south Alabama, saw action at Shiloh, and then found himself again on the coast. As early as January 24, 1864, he guessed trouble was on the way. "I am fixing myself up here for a siege," he informed Lizzie.[4]

Trouble came in the form of six mortar schooners and a few shallow-draft gunboats. Farragut's big warships couldn't navigate the shallow Mississippi Sound, and even the lighter vessels could only approach within 2 miles of the fort. Steamers towed the schooners into various positions or pulled them off mudbanks and sandbars when frequent north winds pushed water out of the sound. The mortar schooners had seen considerable prior service on the Mississippi River, and one Union naval officer lamented their "most dilapidated condition." Still, they were formidable craft, capable of delivering strong blows. The typical mortar schooner was about 100 feet long with a pair of raked masts and a giant round turntable positioned on deck amidships. Atop this sat an awesome eight-and-a-half-ton, 15-inch mortar gun. Yankee jack tars, with their usual talent for felicitous metaphor, dubbed these stubby guns "chowder pots." With a 20-pound black powder charge, a mortar could throw a 200-plus-pound projectile over 4,000 yards along a high, arcing trajectory. Upon firing, flame shot many feet from the muzzle, and the recoil was terrific. In order to cushion the effect, the schooners were heavily braced below decks by big square timbers, and in some cases planks were stacked from keelson to deck for further support. Once discharged, the projectile's entire career could be easily followed with the naked eye for half a minute. One observer compared the racket to "a train of cars passing over a wooden bridge." On impact the shell penetrated the earth up to 4 feet and blew out a 7-foot crater.[5]

The bombardment began on February 16 at 9:00 a.m. Most of the Federal shots fell short, sending up geysers of spray, but a few hurtled into the fort, slinging sand and debris. Rebel troops fired their guns when they could and scrambled into secure bomb proofs between shots. One of the shells smashed into the officers' quarters, and Williams was wounded. The *Mobile Register* sensationally reported that the "shell grazed the front of his arm and body, entirely tearing away the sleeve and breast of his coat." Anxious to reassure his wife that it really wasn't so bad, Williams wrote her a few days later. "The account of my accident was very much exaggerated in the newspapers," he explained, but then went on to describe anything but a trifling experience. A shell fragment had knocked him down, he admitted, and his coat and vest were torn, "but not so much." He was terribly sore for days and reported his side "still of a bright yellow color." He had vomited a great deal that night but remained in command. More than three hundred enemy shells were fired the day he penned his letter but had done "little or no damage" to the fort. Williams closed his note to Lizzie gamely, "I like the fun finely so far." Her feelings, home with their young son, can only be imagined.[6]

Not surprisingly, many Mobile residents were in a panic. General Maury ordered all nonessential personnel out of town, and for days, trains and wagons creaked and swayed north with their jittery burdens. Family silver was hastily hidden or buried and trusted servants strictly admonished to guard empty households. Augusta Jane Evans rode the rails into Georgia, but others elected to stay. From Montgomery, Governor Thomas H. Watts urged all militia and every able-bodied man to spring to the defense of the state. "Our foes have commenced the attack on the water defense of Mobile," he announced, "and their army said to be thirty thousand strong, has marched across the

State of Mississippi, and on the Western border of Alabama, confronted by Gen. [Leonidas C.] Polk, threatens to invade the state." Lives and property were in jeopardy, he declared, "unless this army of our hated foe is repulsed." Every measure had to be taken: "Alabama *must*, Alabama *shall be* defended." Throughout the department, Confederate troops were shuffled hither and yon to meet the developing crisis, but the best troops were far away in Virginia, facing Grant. Meanwhile, Sherman reached Meridian and went about wrecking things in his usually efficient manner. Believing Mobile to be the ultimate Federal objective, Polk sent Maury as many troops as he could spare. Eventually almost 10,000 butternuts manned the city's defenses, anxiously awaiting Sherman and listening to the rumble of the big guns down the bay.[7]

Contrary winds made a sustained assault against Fort Powell challenging, but on February 29 Farragut gave it a third go. Among the Union vessels was the *John P. Jackson*, a 750-ton steamer with six guns. The *Jackson* opened fire that morning and discharged twenty-four rounds from her 6-inch Sawyer gun before the twenty-fifth shattered the breech with a terrible concussion, splintering the deck and slightly injuring seven men. The dramatic episode occasioned an illustration in *Frank Leslie's Illustrated Newspaper*. "Evidently there is some oversight in the Ordnance Department that requires remedy," the paper wryly editorialized. Despite this mishap, the *Jackson* remained in the fight, and the artillery duel between fort and vessels continued most of the day. A Confederate officer aboard the *Baltic*, anchored a bit beyond the fort in case she was needed to evacuate the garrison, was an enthusiastic witness. "I saw some beautiful line shots made," he wrote. Unfortunately, none of the enemy vessels was sunk, though a few were hit. Later inspections also determined that the torpedoes, frequently bumped by enemy vessels, had failed to explode. Oysters, barnacles, and teredo worms clustered on the striker mechanisms were to blame. For his part, Farragut was exasperated at wasting powder and shot to so little seeming effect and, believing that he had spotted the CSS *Tennessee* in the lower bay, called off the action. The feint had been a success, lightening Sherman's opposition and causing considerable heartburn among Rebel commanders.[8]

Despite the pounding, Powell had held. The Rebel flag still fluttered from its sandy ramparts, and the defenders, ears ringing and heads aching, took pride in their stand. One graycoat remarked with satisfaction, "Not a single

Figure 21. A gun explodes aboard the USS *Jackson*, February 29, 1864. Despite the shock and damage, the vessel continued shelling Fort Powell. A Federal mortar schooner is visible in the background. Courtesy Mobile Municipal Archives.

gun had been dismounted, not a single traverse had been seriously damaged, nor had the parapet and the bombproof lost any of their strength, all damage done by the exploding shells being at once repaired by throwing sandbags in the open craters." Casualties were remarkably light—one dead and five wounded, including Williams. Further good news came when the Confederates finally realized it was all only a feint. Instead of heading for Mobile as feared, Sherman returned by the route he came, and the threat diminished. Determined to return to town before the all clear, Augusta Jane Evans boarded a train at Columbus, Georgia, with a special pass. The weather was frightfully cold, "twice we were obliged to stop and thaw the pipes of the engine which froze stiff before we reached Opelika," and at Greenville a provost ordered all the ladies off the train. Evans's pass worked its magic, however, until she reached Pollard, where an officious functionary made her party detrain. The young writer bunked with friends, laughing and telling stories in a big fire-warmed hall, before being allowed to continue on her way. Soon enough, Evans was again ensconced amid the comforts of her Mobile home, Georgia Cottage. She was further delighted to receive a "small box of champagne" courtesy of a blockade runner and puttered happily about her flower garden when the weather began to moderate. Mobile, for the time being at least, was safe.[9]

On March 9, Grant was made a lieutenant general and placed in command of all Union armies east and west. At last he could put his strategic ideas into motion without fear of veto. Grant realized that capturing territory and cities mattered little if Confederate armies remained intact to fight another day. Therefore, he determined to go hard after those armies no matter the cost. For the first time in three years, Federal troops coordinated their movements in both theaters. In the east, Grant attacked Lee, who was forced to defend Richmond, and in the west, Sherman assaulted Joseph E. Johnston (who had replaced Bragg) and the Army of the Tennessee, positioned north of Atlanta. Throughout the spring and summer the armies slugged it out east and west, the Federals slowly but inexorably advancing as their foes retreated after each engagement. The South's only hope was that war-weary Northerners would throw Lincoln out of office in the coming election and let the Rebels go in peace.[10]

Sitting behind his desk in Nashville, Maj. Gen. Lovell Harrison Rousseau was following Sherman's progress and hit upon the idea of a swift cavalry raid deep into Alabama. Such a thrust carried several advantages, including pulling Forrest out of middle Tennessee, where he was playing hell with Union communications, and wrecking the critical Rebel industrial hub at Selma. Rousseau sent his suggestion to Sherman on June 29. His timing couldn't have been better. Sherman had just been repulsed at Kennesaw Mountain and well knew that any more such bloody checks would likely doom Lincoln's reelection chances. Rousseau's proposal was attractive to the Ohioan, but Sherman had different ideas about the objective. Rather than Selma, the Montgomery and West Point Railroad was to be the target. This line daily served to transport reinforcements and supplies into Atlanta and Rebel wounded and civilians out of harm's way. Sherman sent lengthy and specific instructions to Rousseau on June 30. "The expedition should start from Decatur," he wrote, "move slowly to Blountsville and Ashville, and if the way is clear, to cross the Coosa at Ten Islands or the railroad bridge, destroying it after their passage,

Figure 22. Gen. Lovell H. Rousseau raided east Alabama with almost no opposition in the summer of 1864. Southern women were pleasantly surprised by his good manners, but he was less charming toward Rebel prisoners and wealthy planters. Courtesy Library of Congress.

then move rapidly for Talladega or Oxford, and then for the nearest ford or bridge over the Tallapoosa." Once past that river, Sherman continued, Rousseau "should move with rapidity on the railroad between Tuskegee and Opelika, breaking up the road and twisting the bars of iron." After doing as much damage as possible, he should rejoin the main army at Marietta. Sherman emphasized that "the party should avoid all fighting possible," a prospect much improved by the fact that Forrest and Roddey were tangled up with a separate Federal force in northern Mississippi.[11]

While disappointed not to have a crack at Selma, Rousseau was eager to get started. His endeavor was to be no Jackass foray but rather an efficient raid conducted by skilled horsemen with the latest accoutrements and weapons. Rousseau was an impressive and accomplished officer by any measure. A native Kentuckian, forty-six years of age and slightly balding with a heavy moustache and sideburns, he had worked as a lawyer and state senator before the war. He raised several companies for the Union and was a veteran of the big western battles, where he had proven himself a natural leader of men. "When he showed himself on the battlefield," one observer remarked, "with his hat raised on the point of his sword, encouraging or urging them into the fight, his influence over them was unbounded." Southerners had taken note of him as well. Mary Jane Chadick met with him in Huntsville in 1862 and thought him a "handsome, fine looking man." Less charitably, one newspaper opined that he was a "fair third rate lawyer," who could "drink as much *good* whisky as the next best man."[12]

Throughout early July, Rousseau assembled his command at Decatur. All told it came to 2,700 stalwart midwesterners—Indianans, Iowans, Ohioans, and Michiganders, as well as some Kentuckians and loyal Tennesseans. Many of the men were armed with the new Spencer carbine, a formidable force multiplier if ever there was one. While on the march, each trooper carried this weapon hooked to ring on a leather shoulder strap. It hung just behind the right leg, where it was secured to the saddle by a leather cup. Short and easy to handle, the Spencer featured a tubular, spring-loaded metal magazine filled with seven rim-fire cartridges. Extra rounds were carried in a leather cartridge box or simply stuffed in pockets. When ready to reload, a trooper withdrew the empty magazine from the butt of the weapon, dropped in fresh rounds, and reinserted the magazine with a twist. Each new round was fed into the chamber with a trigger lever that dropped the breech block and ejected the spent cartridge before rolling back into position and channeling the new round. When the trigger was squeezed, the Spencer discharged with a sharp crack, distinct from the deep thunder of an ordinary Civil War musket. A practiced marksman could easily lay down fifteen to twenty rounds per minute, an overwhelming rate of fire against the usual two to four shots typical of older-style weapons.[13]

Besides a carbine, each man also carried a Colt revolver, holstered butt first on his right side; a scabbarded 35-inch-long, 2-pound cavalry saber at his left side; and a tarred canvas haversack over the shoulder filled with several days' rations—hardtack, bacon, sugar, salt, coffee—and personal effects. Hanging from his saddle or stuffed into saddle bags were a tin cup, canteen, utensils, skillet, two sets of extra horseshoes complete with the nails, and some clothes. An Iowa private informed the home folks, "We are only allowed to take 2 shirts, 2 pair drawers, 2 pair socks and a rubber blanket." Each man rode his horse easily on a leather McClellan saddle tightly cinched over an indigo-blue blanket with yellow border. Two light cannons were brought along, and extra baggage, ammunition, rations, and tools like axes, crowbars, and picks to tear up the railroad followed on pack mules and in a few wagons. The intent was to travel as fast and light as possible, avoiding unwieldy encumbrances.[14]

At last, on the evening of July 9, men and animals were as ready as they were likely ever to be. "The boys are now drawing their rations and everything is in a regular bustle," one soldier wrote his mother. "I understand we have to leave tomorrow morning at six o'clock. The boys are all anxious for a fight and ready to go." Dawn brought all the familiar sights, sounds, and activity of a cavalry troop about to depart. Mules brayed and horses shifted, stamped, and whinnied while men scurried about checking girth straps, saddles, bridles, and stirrups. Teamsters inspected loads, axles, and wheels, and cracked their whips. Officers busied themselves with maps, lists, and last-minute dispatches. Meanwhile, Rousseau hurriedly wired Sherman: "I am off today after all sorts of petty annoyances composing delays. I hope to accomplish fully what you desire, and shall do my best." His first day's goal was 16 miles. Rousseau was blessed with experienced cavalrymen on good horses, but even so he didn't get fully underway until afternoon. "The bugles sounded 'forward,' and the command moved out," his adjutant, Capt. Thomas C. Williams, recorded as the men finally trotted off four abreast. "Hazardous it might be," Williams mused, "but there was a smack of daring and dash about it, which was captivating, and gave to officers and men an inspiriting feeling different from that of an ordinary march." While the officers sat on their horses and watched, raced along the line, or took their positions with their units, the long blue column clopped, rattled, creaked, and clanked through the midsummer haze. The January fears expressed by those four Alabama solons looked to be coming frighteningly true.[15]

The first day's march was uneventful. Rebel guerillas took a few potshots at the column but missed, and by 9:00 p.m. it reached Somerville, 15 miles from Decatur. The following day, buglers awoke the camp before light, and the men mounted up again. After another uneventful march, the column reached the top of Sand Mountain and bedded down for a second night. Williams attached significance to the fact that this geographical feature represented the dividing line between "the waters flowing into the Tennessee river from those flowing into the Gulf of Mexico." Crossing the mountain, they were in the Deep South, and there was no turning back.[16]

Traversing the same portion of Alabama that Streight's ill-starred command had traveled over a year previously, Rousseau's men grumbled about its hard-scrabble qualities. Roads were narrow and hemmed by bogs and impenetrable jack-oak thickets, fields overgrown or poor, farms few and far between, and the people appallingly ignorant. When a couple of troopers stopped to ask a white woman for something to drink, she gave them some water and corn pone. "And who mout you'ns be?" she asked. When they told her they were Yankees she remarked, "I know you'ns ain't no Yankees, for you'ns haint got no horns." Good-humoredly, the troopers answered that theirs hadn't sprouted yet, but that the horned Yankees "are in the rear and will be up directly." She was genuinely frightened by their jibe.[17]

Relieved at being on the march at last and free of opposition, Rousseau indulged in a little cruel joking of his own. A couple of his scouts picked up a Rebel soldier on furlough and presented him to the general. "I presume you are a spy," the general growled, "you intended to get behind a tree and count every man I have in my command as they passed, and then report to your rebel commander. We'll just hang you and save further trouble. Major, where's that rope?" Shocked and horrified, the soldier begged to be spared, saying he was a regular on leave, nothing more. Rousseau told him he could go if he ran like hell and didn't look back upon penalty of being shot. Needing no further encouragement, the man bolted for the woods, while Rousseau, scarcely able to contain his laughter, yelled, "Faster! Faster! Faster!" A Yankee private recalled that the Rebel "seemed to dodge the trees, but overlooked the smaller growth of brush, which he swept down with the force of a cyclone. The scene was ludicrous to a laughable degree and yet pathetic; a man running for his life, or at least thinking he is, should not be laughed at." Doubtless many other troopers shared this view, knowing that they themselves might face similar circumstances one day.[18]

On July 13 the column reached Ashville, routing a few Rebel scouts. Most of the civilians had already fled, and the troopers helped themselves to corn, bacon, and fodder for their mounts. Rousseau ordered all the horses checked and then reshod if necessary. Meanwhile, some ex-newspapermen in the command broke into the offices of the local paper and decided to restart the presses. And so a special edition of the *Ashville Vidette* was distributed among the troopers featuring an article titled "Distinguished Arrival." Chuckling alongside their mounts or sitting on fences, benches, or commandeered chairs, soldiers read about their history-making enterprise. "Maj. Gen. L. H. Rousseau, of U.S. Army, paid our town the honor of a visit this morning," the tongue-in-cheek piece began, "accompanied by many of his friends and admirers. The General looks well and hearty. It is not known at present how long he will sojourn in our midst." The answer, of course, was not long. Copies of the paper were left behind to tweak the citizens when they returned. "In the afternoon the march was continued over a rough, barren country," wrote Williams, "and in the evening the expedition reached the Coosa river at Green[s]port." River crossings could be tricky and dangerous even without opposition, and the Coosa at this point is 300 yards wide, and deep. Rousseau was now getting intelligence that Rebels were on the other side and knew he had to be careful about his next move.[19]

While awaiting retrieval of a ferryboat from the opposite bank, the command learned of its first death, a young Iowa captain in the rear guard. William Curl had been riding with another officer when bushwhackers knocked them down in a hail of gunfire. Curl was killed instantly and his companion badly wounded. The bushwhackers got away. The incident had the useful effect of sobering the troops at a critical moment. Determined not to be similarly surprised on the crossing, Rousseau used the ferry to send over a small detachment to set up an ambush and protect the landing spot. He then decided to divide his command, crossing some of the men at Greensport, while others went downstream to Ten Islands where, though wide, the stream was fordable.[20]

Fortunately for the Yankees, their opponent was not Nathan Bedford Forrest but rather Gen. James Holt Clanton. Convinced that Blue Mountain and ultimately Selma were the raiders' intended targets, Clanton had been slow to get in front of his foe. He owned the typical Civil War officer's résumé— Mexican War veteran, lawyer, state legislator—and was said to be "Gallant to rashness," an all too common attribute among Confederate officers. His command consisted of barely two hundred young and inexperienced men. Clanton knew he was badly outnumbered, but that didn't stop him from dividing his small force as well and throwing half of it against the Yankees at Greensport and the other half at Ten Islands. When these butternuts arrived at the Greensport locale they began skirmishing with the Yankees, confirming Rousseau's wisdom in securing a landing spot early. Fully in keeping with his reputation, Clanton and some soldiers from the Sixth Alabama dismounted and blindly charged right into the Yankee ambush. A sharp volley from the Spencers brought them up short, killing and wounding over a dozen and punching a few holes in the rash General Clanton's clothes. The Rebel threat, such as it was, had been eliminated in that quarter.[21]

The situation at Ten Islands was more dangerous. To begin with, fording the river there presented serious difficulties. The stream was interspersed with several small woodsy islands, and the bottom was extremely rocky. On this day the water was high and tumbling and even a sure-footed mount could be swept away. A detachment of the Fifth Iowa was about two-thirds across, their horses deep in the froth, when the Rebels opened fire. Several horses were hit and threw their hapless riders into the water. Desperate to tamp down the opposition, Yankees in the middle of the ford and on the west bank unslung their carbines and began firing into the woods. The Rebels replied briskly, and their aim was good enough to knock a stick out of Rousseau's hand. A regular skirmish was underway with all the advantages seemingly on the east side. A costly charge over the ford proved unnecessary when the Yankees who had already crossed upstream flanked the small Rebel force and put it to flight. "The ford being clear," Williams wrote, "the column commenced crossing." In lines worthy of a poet, the young captain painted the scene. "The passage of the river was a beautiful sight," he recalled. "The long array of horsemen winding between the green islands and taking a serpentine course across the ford—their arms flashing back the rays of the burning sun, and guidons gaily fluttering along the column, formed a bright picture, recalling the days of romance, and contrasting strongly with the stern hardships of every-day life on the duty march."[22]

Rousseau's men spilled into Talladega the morning of the July 15. Almost sixty years later, Hugh Barclay, who had been a boy of twelve at the time, recalled the raid in an article for *Confederate Veteran* magazine. "My father had died the year before," he wrote, "and my two brothers and three brothers-in-law were all at the front, on the firing line." There were no Confederate soldiers in town, and when word came that the Yankees were approaching, Barclay loaded his unmarried sisters and the family valuables—"some old silverware, jewelry, and prized old family portraits and paintings"—into a wagon and made "a quick get-away to the hills." By afternoon Barclay and his sisters were safe, but they could see "dense clouds of black smoke rising in the direction of home" and worried about what was happening. But upon their return, their mother informed them that the Yankees had "refrained from any vandalism." And like Mary Jane Chadick before her, Mrs. Barclay had been favorably impressed by Rousseau, calling him "a Kentucky gentleman" who ordered his men to leave women, children, and private property alone. Public property didn't fare so well, and the raiders destroyed some warehouses, the depot, and a few boxcars.[23]

South of Talladega the column entered better country. "Our road lay through the most beautiful and fertile portion of Alabama I have yet seen," an Indiana private wrote. Troopers marveled at "many splendid, commodious and tastefully decorated dwellings studding the road on either side." They also encountered more slaves, including women who peppered the men with questions such as "Where *all* youns come from?" and "How des *all* youns manage to get out of the weather, when it rains?" The men enjoyed the attention, and an Ohio colonel quipped, "We found the niggers everywhere to be our friends." Some followed along, but the column moved too fast to accumulate contrabands, which suited Rousseau fine. His job wasn't to ferry slaves out of Dixie but to destroy the railroad. Well outside Talladega, Rousseau and his staff stopped at a plantation for refreshment. Because their uniforms were covered in dust, the owner thought them Confederates. He invited them onto the porch, but protested when they said they had to take his mules, saying he had already given Roddey several a week earlier. Ever the funster, Rousseau replied, "Well, in this war you should be at least neutral—that is, you should be as liberal to us as to Rodd[e]y." When the planter asked if they weren't Confederates, Rousseau answered, "No, I am General Rousseau, and all these men you see are Yanks." The planter exclaimed, "Great God! Is it possible! Are these Yanks! Who ever supposed they would come away down here in Alabama?"[24]

The command crossed the Tallapoosa River on July 16 and by sunset the next day reached the Montgomery and West Point Railroad at Loachapoka. The point they had ridden over 200 miles for wasn't much to look at—a few paintless houses and a depot. "No force was there and all was quiet," Williams later remembered. "We had penetrated into the rear of the rebel army, and were now on their most important line of communications." The men got to work at once. "The railroad was built on the old plan with wooden stringers," another officer recalled, "six by eight inches and probably fifteen feet long, mortised into the ties and held in place by wooden wedges; and on these stringers, iron straps one inch by two and a half inches were spiked." Divided into small squads, the men wielded axes, crowbars, and picks, popping out the wedges, and levering the stringers and iron straps into the center of the roadbed. Then another team hauled the primitive rails to the bonfires. "The long lines of fires up and down the track were sending up volumes of dense smoke," Williams wrote, "and lighting up the heavens with a lurid glare, whilst the flames from the burning buildings shot far upward and reached out as if eager for further destruction." Once again, private homes were spared, and even guarded by troopers with wet blankets in case errant sparks landed on their rooftops or porches.[25]

Stoking bonfires up and down the country advertised the Yankees' presence far more effectively than spies, couriers, or rumor. When people realized war was in their midst, consternation and panic became the rule. In Auburn, just 6 miles from Loachapoka, Isabelle Shacklette described church bells "ringing, wagons . . . thundering through town, carriages, buggies, barouches, conveyances of all kinds containing women and children . . . rushing through the streets, excited people talking and crying on the corners, and the greatest confusion and noise possible, for the streets are very rocky and stoney." The ranking Confederate officer in town, Capt. Thomas H. Francis of the Fourth Tennessee Infantry, did his best to assemble a defensive force. There was no local garrison, but he cobbled together about twenty convalescents, some militia, and a few citizen volunteers, arming them with shotguns and mounting them on borrowed horses and mules. In the opposite direction, some 50 miles away, the citizens of Montgomery were in an uproar as well. Even Sherman knew about it, sitting in his works outside Atlanta. Aides brought the general a confiscated Georgia newspaper describing the residents of Alabama's capital city "in great apprehensions about a Yankee raid, and . . . rushing arms for the defense of the city." Nodding satisfactorily, Sherman remarked, "That means Rousseau." A public meeting was held at the Alabama capital, and Gen. Jones Withers, a West Point graduate in charge of the state reserves, called for volunteers. Late on the evening of July 17, a motley force of some 1,500 Confederates—convalescents, University of Alabama cadets, citizen volunteers, and a detachment up from Mobile—boarded the cars and chuffed eastward, reaching Chehaw Station early on July 18.[26]

Gunfire erupted at each end of Rousseau's strung-out force. Outside Auburn, Col. William Douglas Hamilton's Ninth Ohio was interrupted in their railroad wrecking by Captain Francis's tiny command, hidden in some scrubby woods. "As yet we could see nothing of the town on account of the growth of brush," Hamilton wrote, "but when close to it, I stopped the work, mounted all the men, formed in lines as best I could, and ordered all the buglers along the line to sound the 'Charge.' The rush through the thickets could be better heard than seen." Overwhelmed, the Rebels broke and "scattered in every direction." Shacklette saw the Yankees ride into downtown Auburn from her hotel room. They "dashed in shouting and firing at everyone in the streets and into the hospital," she wrote, "the wounded and sick running in every direction . . . and one who was just entering our gate was shot down before my eyes." Hamilton quickly established order and did his best to preserve private property. His men broke open the government warehouses and helped themselves, leaving the remainder for local civilians. Women and children, white and black, swarmed the scene. One dowager ordered her black slave to fetch some choice hams but instead he grabbed them and fled, shouting, "Haint got time, Missus, haint got time."[27]

At Chehaw Station, the Rebel force from Montgomery hopped off the train and fanned out into the woods. By any rational calculus, these men should have been no match for Rousseau's well-armed veterans. They were a patchwork assemblage, many with little or no military training, and most had never seen the officers about to lead them into a fight. Besides all of that, they were poorly armed, mostly old weapons loaded with buck and ball, formidable at close range but ineffective beyond 100 yards. They were in earnest, however, and quickly opened up on the Union marauders. More Yankee troops poured into the fight, and Rebels too, including a Tuskegee unit clad in snappy brown linen uniforms. The volume of fire increased steadily. "Both sides held their position for some time," Williams wrote. The Rebels were "in considerable force," he continued, and "obstinate." This was the very thing Sherman had warned Rousseau about, and as the Kentuckian sat on his horse listening to the mounting roar of battle, he kept muttering: "I shouldn't have got into this affair. I'm very much afraid this isn't judicious." After about an hour the Yankees managed to flank the Rebel line, and their superior firepower quickly told. Nonetheless, it was clear to all that pushing the destruction toward Montgomery might not end well. The clash at Chehaw Station cost Rousseau several dead, wounded, and a handful of captives. Discretion being paramount, he disengaged and moved his men back up the line.[28]

The troopers continued tearing up rail to the east and entered Opelika. According to one Yankee corporal, this was "a pretty country town apparently of some importance." To the men's delight, they found warehouses stuffed with thousands of pounds of bacon, many gallons of whiskey, and thirty boxes of chewing tobacco. "This was a happy find," the corporal recalled, "as rations were getting scarce. The bacon was fine, and it was not long until the men were having some nice broils." Once again, the Yankees opened the warehouses to the public, and people grabbed up "everything in sight." Rousseau and his staff sat down to a hearty meal in a private home. Black cooks and servants eagerly heaped the table with food, and each got paid $50 in greenbacks for their trouble. Before leaving town, the Yankees fired the depot, storehouses, a tool shop, some loaded boxcars, and several hundred cotton bales. Done with the railroad, Rousseau turned his command north, paralleling the Chattahoochee until he could turn east for the return into Georgia north of that stream. At Lafayette, troopers interrupted a church service mid-sermon and arrested some Rebels on furlough. In a departure from orders they "ransacked a number of private houses, and took all the valuables they could find." Officers couldn't watch over every man all the time, and criminally inclined Yankees routinely straggled in order to commit their depredations without fear of reprimand.[29]

On July 21, the column crossed into Georgia and shortly thereafter met up with Sherman outside of Atlanta, having encountered no further opposition. The Ohioan was glad to see Rousseau stride into his tent. "That's well done, Rousseau, well done," Sherman remarked on hearing of the raid's success, "but I didn't expect to see you back." Incredulous, Rousseau asked why not. "I expected you to tear up the road," his superior answered, "but I thought they would gobble you." Rousseau mockingly huffed, "You are a pretty fellow to send me off on such a trip." Sherman reminded Rousseau that it was his idea, but all was well that ended well.[30]

The *New York Herald* praised "General Rousseau's Great Raid." Pleased both with the success and the fact that there had been minimal civilian victimization involved, the *New York Times* opined that the Kentucky general "has demonstrated by this expedition that bold movements into the enemy's lines can be made, and important results achieved against the enemy, without the necessity of violating the usages of civilized warfare." Lincoln's reelection hopes brightened perceptibly. For its part, the Southern press was chagrined. "We doubt whether any other raiding party since the commencement of hostilities, comprising no more men, has penetrated as far into the country, done as much damage, and succeed[ed] in escaping with so little loss," lamented the *Montgomery Weekly Advertiser*. Indeed, the raid had been an extraordinary endeavor, beautifully planned and executed. Over 2,000 men had ridden hundreds of miles deep into enemy territory, losing barely fifty of their number killed, wounded, or captured. Thirty miles of critical railroad between Opelika and Montgomery had been knocked out for two weeks, depriving besieged Atlantans of vital support. Additionally, over $20 million in property had gone up in smoke, including depots, warehouses, factories, and boxcars. Hundreds of mules and horses were taken and hundreds of slaves given a taste of Jubilo. Two brisk actions had been fought, at Ten Islands and Chehaw Station, where discipline and firepower prevailed over poorly armed and organized but dedicated foes. In a July 23 message to his men before they were reassigned, Rousseau expressed his appreciation for their service. He particularly noted their "energy and gallantry" and their "fortitude, courage, and patriotism." He had been proud to command them and would "ever hold them in grateful remembrance."[31]

There was no praise for those raiders wounded and left behind or captured. By the summer of 1864 the customary practice of exchanging prisoners was halted in favor of holding them for the duration. Grant had long been frustrated that captured enemy soldiers, when exchanged, were soon back in action against his troops, perpetuating the war seemingly ad infinitum. In August of '64, as part of his new authority, Grant requested Secretary of State William Seward revise the old policy. "We ought not to make a single exchange nor release a prisoner on any pretext whatever until the war closes," he explained. "We have got to fight until the military power of the South is exhausted, and if we release or exchange prisoners captured it simply becomes a war of extermination." The secretary agreed, and captured soldiers now faced months in squalid prisons rather than a quick release. Grant realized the hardships these men would have to endure, but firmly believed that it was cruel to their comrades still in the field to continually have to fight the same men. It was a hard war, and eliminating the exchanges was yet another example of that unpleasant fact.[32]

The South was ill-prepared to hold large numbers of Yankee captives. Andersonville Prison in Georgia is of course the most notorious example of suffering and privation in Rebel prison pens, but Alabama had several smaller-scale versions of its own scattered around the state. Some of these, such as those at Selma and Montgomery, were little better than glorified holding pens, but one was quite substantial and during the course of the war held over 5,000 men. It sat where the Cahaba River joins the Alabama west of Selma. Here was the dwindling town of Cahaba, one-time state capital. By the Civil War the population had fallen to only a few hundred white residents, but they enjoyed an enduring reputation for wealth and culture and contributed liberally to the war effort. Most of their sons joined the Confederate army, and many were lost on distant battlefields. The prison was called Castle Morgan, for Confederate cavalryman John Hunt Morgan of Huntsville, and was established in June 1863 in an abandoned old warehouse that sat atop the remains of an Indian mound. The building was 193 feet by 116 feet, encompassing 15,000 square feet, and had brick walls 14 feet high. It was only partially roofed. After it was chosen to serve as a prison, Confederate authorities constructed a heavy, 12-foot-high plank fence around it with a fire walk along the outside for the guards. Tiered wooden bunks were hammered together inside the building, but no straw or bedding was provided. The prison's greatest asset, vital to keeping Castle Morgan's mortality rate at an astonishingly low 5 percent, was a freshwater stream running through the building, fed by a nearby artesian well. Residential buildings crowded the prison to the west.[33]

Among the Union soldiers who found themselves at Castle Morgan was Jesse Hawes, an Illinois cavalryman who arrived in the winter of 1864. Life was difficult, but because the exchange program was still in effect, the men were not as crowded as they would soon become. When Hawes was there, roughly 2,000 prisoners milled about, a number that would eventually grow. The men slept in bunks, or "roosts" as Hawes called them, "packed like sardines in a box." Five men shared one blanket. While grateful to have a reliable water supply, there was a drawback. It was, Hawes averred, "warm, of

Figure 23. Castle Morgan at Cahaba. Up to 5,000 Federals were held there, and several hundred died. From Jesse Hawes, *Cahaba: A Story of Captive Boys in Blue* (New York: Burr Printing House, 1888).

a sweetish taste, and impregnated with a sulpher gas, strongly suggestive of eggs 'too ripe.'" There were two commanders at the prison, one compassionate and well-regarded by his charges, the other reviled for his casual cruelty. The guards, of whom there were just over a hundred, were not the best troops and were mostly unsympathetic. But Hawes's greatest trial came when the Alabama rose above flood stage on March 1, 1865. By midnight, he wrote, "there was no dry spot to be found at any point." In an effort to keep out of the cold water, several man clambered into an upper roost, but "their weight crushed it to the earth, or, rather, water." Most simply waded about, "teeth chattering as in an ague," waiting for the water to subside. Kate Cumming happened to pass by the prison aboard the steamer *Southern Republic*, and made light of the situation. She could see several feet of water in the town and people coasting about in small boats, while the prisoners seemed "rather pleased than otherwise with their chances for aquatic sports."[34]

Melvin Grigsby, a Wisconsin infantryman, spent several months at Castle Morgan before being transferred to Andersonville. He complained about the lack of bedding, but found the food "wholesome and sufficient." Not long after his arrival, Grigsby noticed that "many of the prisoners were reading books, and pamphlets, histories, novels, and books on philosophy, science, and religion." When he asked where these came from, he was told that a "young lady who lived near the prison" sent them through a guard. Grigsby had only to make his request to the guard to receive a book. He promptly asked for "one of Scott's novels," devoured it, and asked for another title. The young lady's name was Belle Gardner, and Grigsby soon fell into correspondence with her, sending little thank yous, receiving gracious acknowledgment. Not surprisingly, young, lonely, and far from home, Grigsby developed romantic feelings for his unseen benefactress. When he learned that her house was close by, he cut a hole in the plank fence, sent her a note to appear in the window at a certain time, and eagerly peered out in anticipation. When she did not show, he started making arrangements through a guard to try to actually meet her outside. Alas for poor Grigsby, his efforts were quashed when he was transferred, "and the conditions and materials for an exquisite romance in real life were rudely broken and scattered."[35]

Castle Morgan's inmates suffered the hardships and maladies typical of Civil War prisoners, including overcrowding, cruelty, lice, rats, dysentery, hunger, pneumonia, fatigue, and fever. The prison's exact death toll has never been accurately determined, but records indicate at least 142 and perhaps as many as 224. Additionally, over two dozen guards died of disease there. One Yankee sergeant claimed he saw ten fellow prisoners die in one night. "The rebs would come in with the stretchers and four or five of our boys would help them carry our dead comrades out and bury them." Not content to simply sit and suffer or fantasize about invisible girlfriends, some men plotted escape. Hawes and two friends managed to slither along the drainage ditch, climbing over the fence where it was flimsiest. Unfortunately, a slave saw them and told his master, who ran them down with dogs. In the spring of 1864, at least a dozen men diligently tunneled under the fence to the riverbank, broke out at night and swam across. They then stole horses and rode almost 60 miles before they were apprehended and forced to wear ball and chain for weeks afterward.[36]

Castle Morgan's prisoners finally began to be released during the first months of 1865, and by April they were all gone. In tragic punctuation, many of these men died on their long way home when the steamboat *Sultana* burned and sank in the Mississippi River on May 20. Hawes and Grigsby were more fortunate and lived to write books about their experiences at Cahaba. Grigsby actually returned to the site in the 1880s but found little that he could recognize. The old warehouse had been dismantled for its bricks, weeds grew everywhere, and many of the residents had disappeared. A black ferryman told him, "De City of Cahaba mos' all been moved to Selma." The former state capital and prosperous seat of antebellum planters was well and truly a ghost town, and Castle Morgan existed only in the haunted memories of aging men who when young had worn the blue.[37]

# 6

## The Battle of Mobile Bay

Damn the torpedoes!
—Adm. David Glasgow Farragut

Big guns. If Mobile was to be adequately defended, it had to have them, afloat and ashore. And Selma provided. By the spring of 1864, the Dallas County seat had become a booming war production and distribution center. On April 5, a Connecticut native who had lived there for five years and recently escaped North shared his assessment with the *New York Times*. "The importance of Selma to the Confederacy can hardly be overestimated," he declared. "As a shipping point for iron, coal, ammunition and commissariat stores it is one of the most important in the South. As a manufacturing depot for ammunition, shot, shell, cannon, powder, canteens, and clothing, it is of vast importance." Morning, noon, and night along the high bluffs and on the flats immediately riverside, upwards of 10,000 men, women, and children, black and white, labored away in brick foundries, repurposed warehouses, cotton sheds, and scantling board shelters casting cannon and shot, building gun carriages and wagons, stitching leather cartridge boxes, sewing uniforms, and making gunpowder. "The city was a perfect jam of people," one witness wrote, and nearly all of them were working for the government.[1]

The cannons meant for coastal use didn't come from the arsenal, which had been transferred from Mount Vernon after the fall of New Orleans, but rather the naval foundry, a four-acre complex of brick and frame buildings that included a sawmill; several offices; pattern, molding, and machine shops; a gun foundry; a rolling mill; puddling and melting furnaces; and a sophisticated blacksmith shop. Some 3,000 people worked there under the direction of Commander Catesby ap Roger Jones (a Welsh name in which "ap" means "son of"; Catesby was the son of Roger Jones). Jones was a capable and resourceful officer. Forty-two years old, balding, and distinguished by a gray beard, he was an old navy hand, Mexican War veteran, and recently renowned for commanding the *Virginia* in its duel with the *Monitor* at Hampton Roads, Virginia. He knew artillery, and he knew ironclads. Making powerful guns that could cripple the frightening new warships was his mandate.[2]

Jones's weapon of choice was the Brooke gun, the formidable invention of Capt. John Mercer Brooke, a friend and colleague who had converted the *Merrimac* into an ironclad. Over fifty of these cannons would ultimately be sent to Mobile, where they were mounted on Fort Morgan's ramparts, in the city's earthworks, and aboard the *Tennessee, Selma, Nashville, Morgan,* and *Gaines.* Brooke guns were cast iron, with single or double wrought iron bands at the breach for reinforcement. One Selma foundry worker praised them as "massive, tough, and indestructible." They were designated by the bore size with 6.4-, 7-, and 8-inch rifles, as well as 8- and 10-inch smooth bores. A typical 7-inch Brooke rifle was 12 feet long and weighed more than 15,000 pounds. It was capable of throwing a shot over four miles, or in terms sobering to Farragut's wave-tossed blue jackets, clear across the mouth of Mobile Bay. Casting these behemoths was no easy task. Sweating workers stoked brick furnaces with resinous pine, melting tons of pig iron. When ready, the molten metal was carefully channeled into upright sand molds. The entire process, from the initial pour to cooling, boring out, rifling, and attaching the sights and elevating screw could take weeks. When completed, the guns were barged downriver to Mobile, sometimes accompanied by a steamboat tooting "Dixie" on the calliope. Jones was envious of his fellow naval officers facing imminent enemy action, but in a Christmas Eve letter to Buchanan he shared a little excitement of his own. "An explosion took place whilst attempting to cast the bottom section of a gun pit," he related. The foundry caught fire as a result, but the blaze was quickly extinguished and only a few molds were damaged. Jones himself had a narrow escape, reporting "my hat, coat, and pants were burned." Nonetheless, he found a little dark humor in the incident: "Quite a loss in these times, with our depreciated currency and fixed salaries. As a large casting is never made without my being present, I consider my life in greater danger here than if I were in command of the *Tennessee*." He was only half joking, though he knew Buchanan was in for "hot work" soon enough.[3]

By late May, a big fight at Mobile Bay became increasingly likely. Gen. Nathaniel P. Banks's Red River expedition had ended in humiliation and disaster, but its failure finally freed up troops and vessels for Farragut. Furthermore, Sherman, now hammering away in north Georgia, wanted Mobile attacked to divert Rebel troops from his front, just as he had for his February Meridian raid. But if the Port City fell, he would also have a fine Gulf base with advantageous rail connections. It didn't take long for the Union field commander in the region, a native Kentuckian named Gen. Edward Richard Sprigg Canby, to determine that taking Mobile proper wasn't practical given its defenses and the limited resources available for a land assault, but there were easily enough troops to support Farragut's naval operations at the forts.

For his own part, Farragut was itching to launch an attack. The last two years he had been holding the blockade and watching the runners come and go. He had chafed at the constant delays and strategic blundering and, as 1864 advanced, worried more and more about what the powerful CSS *Tennessee* would do if she got loose among his wooden ships. By late May, the Rebel ironclad had at last arrived in the lower bay, after having been lifted over the shallow Dog River bar by a system of buoyant wooden boxes known as camels. Farragut regularly studied her sloping, dull gray casemate through his telescope and knew he needed ironclads to match her. Like many Yankees, he was suffering a serious case of "ram fever," reinforced by his memories of the incredible destruction wrought by the CSS *Arkansas* at Vicksburg. On May 9, he wrote to Navy Secretary Welles, "I am in hourly expectation of being attacked by an almost equal number of vessels, ironclads against wood vessels, and a most unequal contest it will be, as the *Tennessee* is represented as impervious to all their experiments at Mobile, so that our only hope is to run her down." By "their experiments," he meant Rebel test firing against the *Tennessee*'s iron plates. Several spies and deserters had reported the results, decidedly dismal from the Federal perspective. Welles promised ironclads, but they were slow in coming.[4]

At sixty-two years of age, Farragut was uncomfortable with this newfangled style of naval warfare. He was an old blue-water man enamored of ships,

ADMIRAL D. G. FARRAGUT

Figure 24. Adm. David Glasgow Farragut was a brilliant strategist and absolutely fearless in action. He observed the Battle of Mobile Bay lashed to the rigging of his flagship. Courtesy Mobile Municipal Archives.

sails, and rigging and possessed an innate martial spirit that storied admirals like Hawke and Nelson owned. When news of the *Alabama*'s sinking by the *Kearsarge* reached him off Mobile Bay that summer, he exulted to his son, "I would sooner have fought that fight than any ever fought on the ocean." For all that, he was a native Southerner, born in 1801 in an east Tennessee log cabin, and when six years old had moved with his family to New Orleans. At the tender age of nine, he became a midshipman in the US Navy, serving under the watchful tutelage of Capt. David Porter, and saw bloody action against the British during the War of 1812. He commanded a sloop during the Mexican War, tested artillery in Norfolk afterward, and was "waiting orders" when the Civil War began. Some of Farragut's superiors wondered about his loyalties. Besides his own Tennessee birth and Gulf Coast childhood, his wife was a Virginian, and during the secession crisis he had said, "God forbid I should have to raise my hand against the South." But when the moment came, he announced his intention of "sticking to the flag." His familiarity with the Gulf Coast made him a natural in that theater, where soon enough he distinguished himself in action. Farragut understood tactics and strategy, knew when to be cautious and when to act decisively, and was more interested in winning the war than fighting the interminable political battles beloved by so many of his fellow officers. Above all, he was practical, and now, faced with the *Tennessee*, he knew he had to overmatch her with iron rather than wood.[5]

Farragut's obsession with the *Tennessee* was rational. His combat experience theretofore had taught him that wooden ships could successfully run past brick fortifications, albeit with some damage and loss of life. Because the Mobile ship channel ran close under Fort Morgan's guns, he knew to expect heavy fire there, but was confident of at least getting into the bay. The Confederates, of course, had been laboring for years to strengthen the lower bay defenses into a coordinated and mutually supporting system of forts, torpedoes, obstructions, and vessels. Since March 1, 1864, these defenses had been under the command of Brig. Gen. Richard Lucian Page, a cousin of none other than Robert E. Lee. Despite the family connection, there was no favoritism in the assignment. Page was eminently qualified for his new responsibility. To begin with, he was a physically imposing specimen—one man said he "looked to be about seven feet high"—and wore a neatly trimmed gray beard. He was a strict but fair disciplinarian possessed of an iron will, which, combined with his height, prompted the troops to call him "Ramrod" and "Bombast Page." Like Farragut, he was a navy veteran, but after secession he chose the Confederacy. Early in the war, he served with the Savannah squadron and commanded South Carolina coastal defenses. Because of his familiarity with ships and big guns, he was Davis's first choice to superintend the Alabama coast during its anticipated hour of greatest trial. He arrived on post on March 12, and the men liked him at once. "We are very well pleased with our new general," one officer wrote, "although he hasn't found out the difference between a fort and a ship yet." Mild jesting aside, Page knew the difference between them very well. Both would be needed, along with plenty of stout hearts to man them, if he was to defeat the Federals.[6]

Page's military assets were formidable but not without weaknesses. Fort Morgan sheltered over five hundred men, mostly Alabamians and Tennesseans, and mounted over thirty heavy cannons, most of them *en barbette*, that is, exposed atop the ramparts. Additionally a seven-gun water battery sat at the very tip of Mobile Point, where it promised to effectively blast passing enemy vessels. But despite all of this, Fort Morgan had been built in the era of smaller, smooth-bore artillery, and its elaborate and beautiful arcaded masonry work was unlikely to fare well against Farragut's pulverizing ordnance. The possibility of a sustained bombardment was worrisome. Across the bay's mouth, Fort Gaines bristled with twenty-seven guns and held over eight hundred men, but it was too far from the ship channel to pose a serious threat. In the Mississippi Sound, Fort Powell was the smallest and weakest of the three bay forts, with only six guns and a few dozen men. Pilings and torpedoes obstructed the shallows and the main channel, but a lane had been left open in the latter for blockade runners, with the limits of the torpedo field marked by black buoys. Page begged and cajoled the Torpedo Bureau, in charge of placing the mines out in the water, to continue seeding the bay, but as the February attack on Fort Powell demonstrated, these devices' effectiveness was suspect. Lastly, there was Buchanan's naval squadron, of which only the *Tennessee*, *Morgan*, *Gaines*, and *Selma*, mounting in all twenty-two guns and manned by 470 sailors, were fit for action in the lower bay. Page was only too aware of his defenses' shortcomings, but he could at least take some consolation in the realization that Farragut wasn't. Neither man believed the coming contest would be easy or bloodless.[7]

Farragut's fleet increased to more than twenty vessels during July—big steam sloops like the *Hartford*, *Brooklyn*, *Monongahela*, and *Richmond*; lighter draft gunboats like the *Metacomet*, *Octorara*, and *Galena*; and by August 4 when the *Tecumseh* finally arrived in tow, four ironclads. Of the ironclads, the *Winnebago* and *Chickasaw* were twin-turreted river monitors, not suitable for blue-water work, while the *Manhattan* and her sister ship the *Tecumseh* were single-turreted monsters that Farragut hoped would pound the *Tennessee* into submission. The *Manhattan* and *Tecumseh* were truly awesome vessels, each sporting a steam-rotated turret 20 feet in diameter and 9 feet high. Housed inside were a pair of hulking 15-inch bottle-shaped Dahlgren cannons on slide carriages, each capable of hurling a 440-pound projectile. Any hope Buchanan might have nourished about sallying out quickly faded. Forced into a defensive posture, he kept his little flotilla securely behind Mobile Point, awaiting developments. This suited Farragut fine. "If he won't visit me, I will have to visit him," he quipped.[8]

Aboard his beloved flagship *Hartford*, Farragut had the ship's carpenter make wooden models of the various vessels, and when he wasn't scanning the

CONFEDERATE STATES STEAMER GAINES.

From picture loaned by Mr. George S. Waterman, formerly midshipman C. S. Navy.

Figure 25. CSS *Gaines* raked Federal ships as they entered Mobile Bay, but she was no match for them once they got inside. From *Official Records of the Union and Confederate Navies in the War of the Rebellion*, vol. 21 (Washington, DC: Government Printing Office, 1906).

horizon through a telescope or feverishly scribbling dispatches, he was ensconced in his commodious cabin war-gaming with the little models, laying them out in different arrangements on a large chart, studying possible outcomes. Farragut eventually settled on a logical and wise battle plan that placed his big screw sloops directly in the ship channel facing Fort Morgan, each with a smaller gunboat lashed to her port side to help provide motive power in case the bigger vessel was crippled. Not only did this scheme help the big ships, but it also protected the lighter gunboats from direct enemy fire, getting them into the bay and effectively multiplying the available force once there. The four monitors were to lead the way, with the *Tecumseh* and *Manhattan* first and second in line. Their job was to suppress the fort's fire and engage Buchanan at the earliest opportunity. Knowing about the torpedo field, Farragut also issued strict instructions that his captains keep well away from the menacing black buoys that marked its limits. Perhaps most importantly, he was determined to go in with the flood tide and a light southwest wind. This was vintage Farragut—the tide would carry him in no matter what happened to his ships, and the wind would blow the battle smoke into the faces of his foes. Lastly, almost 2,000 bluecoats under the command of Gen. Gordon Granger were to land on Dauphin Island and besiege Fort Gaines. There weren't enough troops to attack Fort Morgan at the same time, but that was to be next. With the plan settled in his mind, Farragut issued general orders on July 12. "Strip your vessels and prepare for the conflict," he commanded his captains. "Trice up or remove the whiskers. Put up the splinter nets on the starboard side, and barricade the wheel and steersmen with sails and hammocks. Lay chains or sand bags on the deck over the machinery, to resist a plunging fire. Hang the sheet chains over the side, or make any other arrangements for security that your ingenuity may suggest." All through the long hot afternoons and into the muggy evenings Yankee tars busily did their captains' bidding. Decks were cleared of superfluous items that could be turned into deadly projectiles if hit, wooden bulwarks reinforced with sandbags, and the upper masts and spars taken down and stowed away. This last measure was considered necessary since in the existing calm conditions the ships would steam rather than sail into the bay, and spars falling from high above decks promised only further damage and casualties. Below decks, ammunition was prepared, the surgeons laid out their grim tools, and men penned earnest letters to loved ones. Aboard

the *Monongahela*, twenty-year-old Ensign Purnell Frederick Harrington gloried in his admiral's orders, calling them "well written" and a marvelous display of courage and "grandeur." Aboard the *Chickasaw*, Capt. George Hamilton Perkins wrote to his mother, informing her that he was surrounded by "a
lot of mechanics, who are working as fast as they can to get the ship in order.
There is so much noise, and there is so much to be done, that I can hardly
*think*." He reported a temperature below decks of 150° when underway and
closed nobly with the instruction that "if I get killed it will be an honorable
death, and the thought should partly take away your sorrow."⁹

From their forts and little flotilla, the Confederates anxiously watched the
enemy preparations. They knew an attack was imminent. At Fort Morgan,
crews remained at their guns all night, watching the twinkling signal lights offshore, ears attuned to the surf's gentle lap for any disturbance. Aboard the *Tennessee*, Fleet Surgeon D. B. Conrad noted the growing number of Federal warships and soberly mused that the big sloops "appeared like 'prizefighters,' ready
for the 'ring.'" Sitting behind Fort Powell's sandy ramparts, Lt. Col. James
Williams retained his cockiness in an August 1 letter to Lizzie. He counted
twenty-six enemy vessels with more arriving all the time, joked "the more the
merrier," and bragged that he was going to have a "fine time." Perhaps realizing that his wife could use a little more reassurance and a lot less bravado,
Williams promised to "take good care of myself, and make you proud too."¹⁰

On the morning of August 4, Farragut sat in his cabin and contemplated
the coming action. His responsibilities were enormous, and failure was likely
to have significant national consequences. The Northern public was sick of
the war and its horrific human costs, and another bloody defeat might doom
Lincoln's reelection chances. On a personal level, it would be an ignominious end to Farragut's otherwise distinguished naval career, subjecting him to
enduring shame and press opprobrium. In no way did he underestimate his
enemy. Mobile Bay was well and competently defended by officers he had
known and respected in the old navy, but he was confident in his ships and
men and determined to do his duty. Placing a piece of foolscap atop his desk,
he wrote to his wife, Virginia. "I am going into Mobile Bay in the morning,"
he informed her, "if 'God is my leader' as I hope He is, and in Him I place
my trust; if He thinks it is the proper place for me to die, I am ready to submit to His will, in that as in all other things." He told her that the army had

already landed on Dauphin Island "in full view of us" and closed with the assurance that he had "never for one moment" forgotten his "love, duty, or fidelity to you, his devoted and best of wives."[11]

The Union fleet began forming up that evening and into the following morning. At 3:45 a.m. off-duty blue jackets were rousted by bellowing boatswains, "All hands! Up all hammocks!" Men hit the deck, pulled on their blue woolen trousers, frocks, and caps, adjusted their black silk handkerchiefs, wolfed down cold sandwiches, and swallowed their ration of coffee. It was time. As is typical on the Gulf Coast during August, the weather was insufferably hot and humid. Laboring in the sticky gloom, sailors lashed the smaller gunboats securely to the screw sloops' port sides. The ironclads took up their designated positions, and the first tinges of dawn broke through an overcast sky. Light fog clung to the sea surface, and a steady southwest breeze blew. Farragut had reluctantly acceded to his captains' wishes that his flagship not take the highly exposed lead, so the *Hartford*, captained by Percival Drayton, was second in line of battle behind the *Brooklyn*, commanded by James Alden. By five thirty all was at last in readiness, and Farragut signaled the fleet, "Get under way!"[12]

Perched atop Fort Morgan's parapets, officer of the day Lt. Julian Whiting couldn't believe his eyes. With the Federal fleet for a backdrop, a sleek blockade runner, the *Red Gauntlet*, ghosted along the Swash Channel and scooted into the bay, dropping anchor near the *Tennessee*. Her cargo included desperately needed lead bars, harness leather, salted beef, and coffee. She was to be the last blockade runner to enter Mobile Bay. But the real show was in front of him, where strengthening light and lifting fog revealed the Federal line of battle in stately procession, the Stars and Stripes fluttering from every mast. Whiting sent a message to General Page that the long expected attack had finally begun. Page quickly joined his subordinate on the walls and agreed that this was no drill. Since the fleet was yet a few miles out, Page gave the men time to eat a little breakfast and compose themselves before all hell broke loose.[13]

All around the bay, Rebel soldiers and sailors were mesmerized by the unfolding spectacle. From Fort Gaines, Capt. Charles C. Biberon was convinced that "some demonstration of importance was about to transpire." He watched "with intense interest" as the Yankee ships crossed the bar and headed straight into the bay. Turning his theodolite toward Fort Morgan, Biberon could plainly see the men at their guns. Aboard the *Tennessee*, now drawn athwart the channel with the *Selma*, *Morgan*, and *Gaines*, Lt. A. D. Wharton marveled, "It was a grand sight to see when [the vessels] were all in line, the monitors leading singly and the wooden vessels lashed together, two and two." The young lieutenant had "ample time to witness the pageant, for such it was for half an hour, before it became a bloody, fiery reality of war."[14]

At 6:47 a.m., a white puff looking just like a cotton ball appeared at the *Tecumseh*'s turret. This was the first shot in the Battle of Mobile Bay. It fell short and a second followed, which burst over Fort Morgan. Now at the Water Battery, Whiting wanted to reply, but Page thought the range too great and ordered him to hold his fire. By 7:05, the wooden ships were almost 3,000 yards out, still far, but Page thought it time to release the pent-up tension. He nodded to Whiting and said, "Open the fight, sir." Only too glad to obey, the young officer "instantly" complied, and a 7-inch Brooke gun erupted to the men's "soul-stirring-cheer." At once, thick tongues of fire and billows of white sulfurous smoke enveloped the fort as all the other guns followed. "The roar . . . was terrific," Whiting later recalled, "so much so that orders had to be screamed to the gunners who were within three feet. The hulls of the wooden ships could not be seen on account of the dense smoke." Inside the fort, Lt. Joseph Wilkinson recorded in his diary that the men "stood nobly to their guns" and greeted each discharge with "yells of triumph."[15]

Aboard the *Lackawanna*, a big screw sloop in the middle of the van, Assistant Surgeon William F. Hutchison, not yet busy at his trade, watched in awe as a cannon ball approached "looking exactly as if some gigantic hand had thrown in play a ball toward you." Halfway through its trajectory the report followed, and then the projectile flew overhead "with a shriek like a thousand devils." Harrington, commanding several guns aboard the *Monongahela*, declared that "shot, shell, and grape flew as thick as apples fall from a tree in a hurricane." As the Federal ships' guns came to bear, their broadsides answered, shaking the "very earth."[16]

Civilians who lived and worked the waters of lower Mobile Bay had long grown used to Federal ships on the horizon and even sporadic artillery fire. They usually paid little heed. But this was clearly different. North and a few miles east of Mobile Point, a nine-year-old boy and his father were tonging oysters when the attack began. As the first shots reverberated across the calm bay waters, the father dropped his long, wooden-handled tongs and exclaimed:

"They're shootin' boy! We'd better git!" Meanwhile, in the city of Mobile, residents could just discern the distant rumble of artillery. Breakfasting in their Government Street home, two young women, Frances Mosby and Lou Mendenhall, heard frantic bell ringing that became "a pandemonium of sound." Alarmed, they sprang from the table, hastily donned bonnets, and took a horsecar for the riverfront. All along their way were excited neighbors. "We girls locked arms and joined the crowd on the sidewalk," Mosby later wrote. "The confusion was indescribable, but we soon learned the cause. At sunrise that morning Admiral Farragut had formed his line of battle to attack the Forts." Reaction was mixed. John Forsyth, the influential editor of the *Register*, urged calm and predicted that the bay "will be strewed with the wreckage of many a Yankee man-of-war." Others agreed, confident that the forts would hold; failing that, they insisted that the upper bay's defenses and shallower water would protect the city. Others panicked and hurried home to load up buggies and wagons to leave the city.[17]

Modern observers are amazed at how much smoke even small-caliber black-powder weapons generate. Not for nothing did the old-timers refer to Civil War–era revolvers as "smoke poles" or "smoke wagons." During the Battle of Mobile Bay, the Federals had a wind advantage, but with big guns continually belching, heavy smoke rolled and spread across the water, obscuring panoramic combat views. In an effort to get a better prospect and direct the action, Farragut began inching up the ratlines at the *Hartford*'s main mast, finally coming to rest just below the main top. The main top was a wooden platform well above the deck, where the first section of the mast ended and a second, slightly smaller pole continued upward. Another set of ratlines ran from the platform on up to the next section and was secured to the mast by lines known as the futtock shrouds that angled down from the platform's edges. Now high enough to see what was happening, Farragut wrapped one arm around the futtock shrouds and lifted a glass to his eye with the other.[18]

Despite the noise and confusion, an officer standing on deck noticed the admiral's precarious perch, and instantly alerted Drayton. Fearing a cut line or blow to the vessel might pitch the admiral into the bay, Drayton ordered Quartermaster John H. Knowles aloft to secure a line to him. Knowles later recalled, "I went up with a piece of lead-line and made it fast to one of the forward shrouds, and then took it around the Admiral to the after shroud, making it fast there." Impatient at the distraction, Farragut said, "Never mind, I am all right," but wisely let young Knowles complete his task. Now safely secured, Farragut could direct the battle by relaying commands to the pilot, stationed in the main top just above his head; a lieutenant positioned immediately below him who could relay orders to the deck, and Lt. Commander James Jouett, standing atop the starboard paddle box of the *Metacomet*, lashed alongside the *Hartford*.[19]

Situated in the stuffy iron pilothouse atop the *Tecumseh's* thundering turret, Commander Tunis A. M. Craven enjoyed no such advantages. From his narrow viewing port, he felt he was too close to the fort, and then he saw the *Tennessee* ahead. Farragut had ordered all his vessels to stay clear of the torpedo field, but Craven was determined to engage the *Tennessee*. Despite a warning from his pilot he ordered a course adjustment, and the sluggish *Tecumseh* veered across the front of the van and into the torpedo field. This was a direct contradiction of Farragut's orders. Surprised by the sudden change, Alden slowed the *Brooklyn* and signaled the *Hartford*, "The monitors are right ahead; we cannot go in without passing them." Farragut replied, "Tell the monitors to go ahead and then take your station."[20]

And then it happened. The *Tecumseh* bumped into a functional torpedo. There was a dull explosion and a fountain of spray alongside the ironclad. A blue jacket on the *Manhattan*, 200 yards astern, recorded what happened next: "Her stern lifted high in the air with the propeller still revolving, and the ship pitched out of sight like an arrow twanged from a bow." A Rebel sailor aboard the *Gaines* was equally stunned as he watched the hapless ironclad's propeller "wildly clawing the air." In the *Tecumseh's* pilothouse, Craven and the pilot both knew instantly what had happened and grabbed the iron ladder leading out at the same time. Stepping back, the pilot said, "Go ahead, Captain!" Craven demurred, "No, sir! After you, pilot; I leave my ship last!" But as the pilot later said, "There was nothing after me." The *Tennessee's* surgeon recalled that there was "dead silence" aboard the Rebel flagship when the Yankee ironclad suddenly vanished. The men solemnly peered out of the gunports and spoke "to each other only in low whispers." For the common sailors, blue and gray, the instantaneous destruction of so many lives by an unseen weapon was a fearful thing, cruel and convincing evidence that the war was the real enemy, indiscriminate and relentless. Any of them might be next. Only twenty-one blue jackets of the *Tecumseh's* 114 managed to escape. The majority of those were rescued by boats dispatched from the fleet, while four swam ashore and were captured. The remainder found a watery grave at the bottom of Mobile Bay, where they yet lie.[21]

It is a truism that no battle plan long survives once the shooting starts. Farragut now faced a potential catastrophe. Union sailors aboard the *Chickasaw* "turned pale" and "rushed from their guns," and consternation spread throughout the fleet. On the *Brooklyn*, Alden began frantically backing his screws, signaling the obvious: "Our best monitor is sunk." The Union van was thrown into disarray, and with the lead ship slewing and backing, the ships began to accordion up right in front of Morgan's big guns. The Rebels recovered from their surprise faster than the Federals and redoubled their fire. The effect on the Union vessels was horrific. Situated almost 100 feet above the *Hartford's* deck, Lt. John Kinney was appalled by the havoc as shells tore through the ship's vulnerable wooden sides. "The sight on deck was sickening beyond the power of words to portray," he wrote. "Shot after shot came through the side, mowing down the men, deluging the decks with blood, and scattering mangled fragments of humanity so thickly that it was difficult to stand on the deck, so slippery was it."[22]

From his position in the futtock shrouds, Farragut could see that his vessel was in danger of colliding with the lead ship and knew he had to act. "What's the matter with the *Brooklyn*?" he asked the pilot in the main top. "She must have plenty of water there." The pilot declared that she did. Pausing a moment, Farragut turned his eyes heavenward and prayed: "O God, who created man and gave him reason, direct me what to do. Shall I go on?" He claimed later that a voice told him "Go on!" And so he did, taking the lead, which meant steering the *Hartford* right across the torpedo field where the *Tecumseh* had just come to grief. Aboard the *Brooklyn*, a rattled Alden again signaled the obvious: "*Torpedoes Ahead!*" And then came Farragut's immortal command: "Damn the torpedoes! Full speed ahead, Drayton! Hard a starboard! Ring four bells!" Practically within spitting distance, the *Hartford* surged past her stalled sister vessel, the crew cheering Farragut and deriding Alden, while the rest of the fleet followed. Below decks, terrified Yankee tars could hear the bump and thud of torpedoes against their hulls, but fortunately for them, no others exploded. Farragut had made an extremely risky decision. If more torpedoes had worked that day, the Battle of Mobile Bay might have had a different outcome or at least have been an even costlier Union victory.[23]

Having gotten past the fort, over the torpedo field, and into lower Mobile Bay, the Federals now had to contend with the Rebel flotilla. Aboard the *Tennessee*, an officer at the forward pivot gun let off a shot at the *Hartford* 200 yards distant, expecting it to sink her instantly. Unfortunately, the gun was a little too elevated, and the shot tore open a hole above the waterline. The flagship steamed on, and Buchanan decided he would do better trying to ram his enemy. But the *Tennessee* was far too clumsy and slow to effectively butt any of the big sloops. Meanwhile, the *Selma*, *Morgan*, and *Gaines* banged away. The *Selma*'s captain admired the effect of this fusillade, and insisted, "At no time in this action did our shot and shell pour in with greater accuracy." Aboard the *Manhattan*, an engineer described the sensation as Rebel shells rained against the turret. "The scream of the shot would arrive about the same time [as] the projectile . . . and the air would be filled with that peculiarly shrill singing sound of violently broken glass, or perhaps more like the noise made by flinging a nail violently through the air." Despite the frightening sound effects, the *Manhattan*'s sailors were perfectly safe behind their iron armor.[24]

Not so those Union tars aboard the wooden ships, where the little Rebel flotilla inflicted frightening casualties and damage. One shell knocked down fifteen men at the *Metacomet*'s forward gun, and another started a small fire that was quickly extinguished. The *Oneida*, last screw sloop in line, took punishing fire from the *Tennessee*. When a shell fragment shredded the captain's forearm, he gamely bound it up but was soon compelled below to the surgeon's saw. Up and down the van, the air was positively alive with bursting shells and growling fragments. Smokestacks and boilers were hit and men scalded; rigging was cut and masts shivered; bulwarks were smashed, sending showers of splinters across the decks; and screams rent the air. Lt. George Brown of the *Itasca*, the *Ossipee*'s smaller partner vessel, was hit in the leg by a spent wood fragment knocked off the bigger vessel. Bruised but not seriously hurt, he danced in pain. An officer aboard the *Ossipee* asked if a splinter had hit him. "Well, you might call it a splinter on your big ship," he replied, "but over here it ranks as a log of wood."[25]

Once they got into the bay, the Federal ships could at last turn their full attention to the flotilla, and it didn't fare at all well. The *Brooklyn* and the *Richmond* delivered a one-two punch to the *Gaines*, holing her and flooding her magazine. Unable to repair the damage, her crew ran for Mobile Point and beached her, out of the fight. Jouett was eager to get into action, so Farragut released the *Metacomet*, which pursued the *Morgan* and *Selma*. The *Morgan* managed to escape into shoal water and, later that night, up to the city, while the *Selma* fled west and north. It was an unequal contest to say the least. The *Metacomet* was the faster and better-armed vessel, and she soon forced the *Selma*'s surrender. Humiliated by his defeat, the *Selma*'s sixty-five-year-old captain emotionally offered his sword to Jouett, whom he had mentored before the war. Jouett admonished his old friend not to make a fool of himself: "I have had a bottle on ice for you the last half hour!" Alone, the *Tennessee* fought her way down the Union line before anchoring once more under the protection of Fort Morgan. His vessel's steam still up, Buchanan moodily counted the enemy ships brazenly maneuvering in his bay.[26]

It was now nearly 9:00 a.m. The Union fleet anchored in the middle ground, the deepest portion of Mobile Bay, and crews began clearing the decks and assessing damage. Finally down from the rigging, Farragut grimly looked at the wreckage, human and otherwise, littering his beloved flagship. "You may pass through a long career and see many an action," he wearily told a young officer, "without seeing as much bloodshed as you have this day witnessed." But the Battle of Mobile Bay wasn't over. Fuming aboard the *Tennessee*, Buchanan growled to his captain, James D. Johnston, "Follow them up, Johnston; we can't let 'em off that way!" Alerted to the Rebel ram's unexpected movement, Farragut nodded approvingly, "Why, that is fair play, admiral to admiral, I am satisfied."[27]

While the *Tennessee* lumbered toward the *Hartford* at 4 knots, Farragut dispatched a small steamer ordering his vessels to engage the ram. When the admiral's emissary delivered the order to Perkins of the *Chickasaw*, he thought the young captain "would turn a somersault overboard with joy." The ensuing scenes were nothing short of incredible. Farragut aimed his flagship straight for the *Tennessee*, and the two vessels bore on a collision course like two enraged bull elephants. It was time to decide the issue—iron or wood. But before they reached each other, the *Monongahela* smashed the ram amidships.

Figure 26. Adm. Franklin Buchanan didn't
have much to smile about in the summer
of 1864. He fought desperately to keep
Farragut out of Mobile Bay and lost.
Courtesy History Museum of Mobile.

Aboard the *Tennessee*, Captain Johnston was standing in the pilothouse and saw the collision coming. "Steady yourselves . . . Stand by," he shouted to his men on deck below. The blow rocked the ram, knocking everyone down, but she quickly righted, prompting Johnston to cry: "We are all right! They can never run us under now." The *Lackawanna* was next, hitting the *Tennessee*'s port quarter and badly crushing her own prow. As the vessels scraped past each other they exchanged fire only feet apart. Yankees and Rebels could now see each other clearly, and the fight became intimate and personal. One blue jacket flung a spittoon at one of the ram's gunports, and a Rebel webfoot jabbed an opponent through another with a bayonet. Then came the *Hartford* head on, but at the last moment Johnston veered the ram and the vessels scraped and bumped past each other. *Tennessee* got off only one shot, which exploded on the *Hartford*'s berth deck, killing five and wounding eight. *Hartford* unleashed a 12-gun broadside, but the rounds bounced harmlessly off the ram's casemate with no more effect, one observer noted, than "a popgun pellet might be expected to produce on a buffalo's skull." Leaning over the rail,

Drayton thought he saw Buchanan through a gunport and hurled his binoculars, yelling, "You infernal traitor."[28]

The battle degenerated into a violent and unequal slugfest as Union vessels crowded the *Tennessee*. Ever determined to observe the action up close and direct his men, Farragut climbed into the mizzen shrouds just above the stern quarter so that he could actually lean out over the *Tennessee's* casemate. Amid the smoke, noise, and chaos, the *Lackawanna* accidentally hit her own flagship, seriously damaging both vessels. Fortunately, Farragut had jumped back on deck immediately beforehand, where the blow knocked him down. When the men looked for him on his former spot and didn't see him, they feared he had fallen overboard. Cries of "Save the Admiral! Save the Admiral!" arose until Farragut once again sprang into the shrouds for all to see. At this critical stage of the fight, one thing was abundantly clear. If the *Tennessee* was to be subdued, it would have to be by the ironclads.[29]

Pushing in close, the *Manhattan* and *Chickasaw* engaged the ram. From the *Chickasaw*, Perkins "poured solid shot into her as fast as I could." A Rebel officer remembered how the *Chickasaw* clung doggedly to their quarter and fired her 11-inch guns "like pocket pistols, so that she soon had the plates flying in the air." The *Manhattan* got off fewer shots, but they were devastating. A Rebel lieutenant described one such blow: "a thunderous report shook us all, while a blast of dense, sulphurous smoke covered our port-holes, and 440 pounds of iron, impelled by sixty pounds of powder, admitted daylight through our side, where, before it struck us, there had been over two feet of solid wood, covered with five inches of solid iron." Conditions for the ironclad sailors on both sides were hellish. Perkins was "wet with perspiration, begrimed with powder, and exhausted with constant and violent exertion." Webfeet in the *Tennessee's* casemate were likewise reeking with sweat and black powder, and the continual concussions from their own guns had many bleeding from their noses. Others suffered intensely painful powder burns. The Rebel ram's armored sides effectively stopped the Federal projectiles but not so the gusts of burned powder and wadding that blew into the opened gunports. One unfortunate seaman, attempting to unjam a port, was obliterated by an explosion immediately over his position, and his remains had to be shoveled into a bucket and tossed overboard. The same shot sent an iron splinter flying into Buchanan's lower leg, badly fracturing it. Unlike the Union sailors' deep concern for their admiral, none of the common Rebel webfeet showed any interest in Buchanan's condition, and the surgeon had to hoist him up and carry him below unaided.[30]

By 10:00 a.m., the *Tennessee* was a proverbial sitting duck. Her smokestack had been sheared off, drastically reducing engine draft; her steering chains, which ran across the deck with only light protection, were broken; several of her gunports jammed shut; and her casemate was on the verge of failure under the ironclads' repeated point-blank hits. Unable to maneuver or bring any of her guns to bear, there was nothing more she could do. Johnston so informed Buchanan, who replied, "if that is the case you had better surrender." Johnston hurried topside and "with almost a bursting heart" lifted a boat hook with a white flag attached. The *Manhattan* was just about to fire when her captain saw the flag. Johnston cried, "For God's sake, don't fire; I surrender, I surrender." When asked, "Who do you surrender to?" Johnston quickly replied, "I surrender to you, sir; for God's sake, don't fire again; we are disabled." As the firing stopped and the smoke drifted away, the white flag could be seen by other vessels in the fleet. Exhilarated blue jackets thronged rigging and decks, cheering wildly. Mobile Bay was theirs at last.[31]

Aboard the *Chickasaw*, a happy and relieved Perkins dashed off a quick note to his mother about his prominent role in the fight, boasting, "I told you I would come out all right!" Harrington, on the *Monongahela*, wrote an excited letter to his father. "We have fought this day one of the most terrific and terrible but one of the most glorious of the war. We got underway at 4 o'clock this morning and steamed in. We had a horrible fight with the fort. After coming in and beating off the rebel gunboats, the rebel ram *Tennessee* attacked us. *This ship* led the way into her, ramming her twice." He admitted that their loss was "severe" but declared that he had never seen "such glorious bravery in my life. I am proud of this day." The cost had indeed been high. One hundred and forty-five blue jackets were dead, ninety-three of those aboard the *Tecumseh*, 170 wounded, and four captured. Ironically, given that Farragut's captains insisted the *Hartford* go in second, she suffered the most casualties of any other vessel, except the *Tecumseh*—twenty-five killed and twenty-eight wounded. Little wonder that Farragut called the Battle of Mobile Bay "the most desperate I ever fought." By contrast, the Confederates suffered only twelve men killed and twenty wounded, but they had lost the bay, and now their forts stood vulnerable and surrounded.[32]

Farragut wasted no time in turning his attention to these bastions. Several light-draft gunboats shelled Fort Powell from the west while the indefatigable Perkins moved his *Chickasaw* toward the eastern face and opened fire. Writing to Lizzie on August 7, Williams described the result. "The shells exploding in the face of the work displaced the sand so rapidly that I was convinced unless the iron-clad was driven off it would explode my magazine and make the bomb-proof untenable." Sensibly worried that his entire garrison would soon be blown to smithereens, Williams telegraphed Col. Charles Anderson at Fort Gaines that he couldn't hold out much longer. Anderson told him to save his men when "your fort is no longer tenable." Williams decided that there was no time like the present, and under cover of darkness with the advantage of a low tide, he marched his men over to the mainland, leaving a detachment to blow up the fort. The explosion was spectacular and reduced Powell to a "heap of rubbish and ruins." Farragut now had an open supply route to New Orleans through the Mississippi Sound.[33]

Fort Gaines was next. Once again, the *Chickasaw* played the lead role, pummeling the brick walls while Union soldiers advanced on the western side, steadily harassing the garrison with artillery and small arms fire. Convinced that the situation was hopeless, several of Anderson's officers presented him with a petition to surrender at once. He agreed and sent a small boat bearing a flag of truce out to the *Hartford* to request terms. Standing on the walls of Fort Morgan three miles distant, "Ramrod" Page could clearly see the white flag. Furious, he signaled Anderson to hold his fort but got no answer. On the morning of August 8, the Stars and Stripes fluttered over the bastion to more Union cheers. Page angrily telegraphed the news to General Maury in the city, who had the "painfully humiliating" task of notifying Richmond.[34]

With more resolve and a better fort, Page held out longest. After Fort Gaines' surrender, he faced the full attention of Granger's troops, who were ferried across the bay and opened siege operations from the east, and Farragut's fleet, including the *Tennessee*, now a United States vessel. Day and night the Yankee bombardment progressed, sometimes, wrote Page, "of several hours duration" and at others more "desultory." The Confederates replied when they could in an effort to stave off the inevitable. On August 12, Wilkinson recorded in his diary that "the casemates are not safe; the shells have no respect for them." Two days later, he wrote: "Our flag staff was shot away and a rifle 32 in. in the lunette battery dismounted. The Yanks make it pretty hot for us in here." The men were in "good spirits, apparently, and hard at work," but a "perfect rain of balls" from the Yankee sharpshooters, combined with the "flying bricks," made any movement above the parapets suicidal.[35]

Satisfied that matters were well under control, Farragut decided to reconnoiter up the bay and inspect the city's defenses for himself. On August 15, he took several light draft vessels, including the indispensable *Chickasaw*, to within 3 miles of the city proper. Stationed in Battery Gladden just off the southern tip of Pinto Island where the Mobile River spills into the head of the bay, Lt. William Mumford noted a "clear, warm day" in his diary. "Seven of the enemy's gunboats came within sight of the city during the morning," he continued, "and at 10 minutes to 2 o'clock, p.m. opened fire upon the bay batteries. About thirty shots were fired." The Confederates returned fire from their batteries and the gunboat *Morgan*, now anchored behind the obstructions. Sporting a patched hole at her waterline acquired during her escape after the bay fight, the *Morgan* barked "like a little dog," according to one observer. A brisk cannonade continued for some time with no harm done by either side. Amid all the booming, Farragut carefully studied the works through his glass and later informed Welles, "until these obstructions can be removed, there will be no possibility of our reaching Mobile with any of our light draught vessels." Watching from the shore, a local carpenter remarked that "so effective was this water line . . . that Farragut's fleet might as well have attempted to sail through the Green Mountain Range." Mobile was safe for the present, but deprived of her outlet to the wider world.[36]

Down at the forts, the bombardment thundered on. "At daybreak on the 23rd, accompanied by an engineer, I inspected the fort to determine the condition for further defense," Page later wrote. The situation was hopeless. The water battery was untenable, the brick casemates breached, and "another shot . . . would bring down the walls"; numerous guns were dismounted; frequent small fires started by the constant explosions had forced the garrison to flood the powder supply; and overall the fort was "a mere mass of debris." Incredibly, casualties were minimal, only one dead and a few wounded, but that number

Figure 27. Fort Morgan after the siege. The walls clearly show artillery and fire damage. A Federal warship is visible upper right. Courtesy Library of Congress.

was likely to rise drastically very soon. At 6:00 a.m., Page ordered a white flag displayed, and at 2:00 p.m. his proud garrison formally surrendered. Frustrated and angry, some Rebel officers broke their swords or, in Page's case, appeared at the ceremony without one. Farragut was miffed at this breach of military propriety, but in the scheme of things it was nothing. The Stars and Stripes was raised over the rubble, the fleet responded with a 100-gun salute, and Mobile Bay was well and truly a Union lake. As a British newspaper noted, "Now neither can cotton go out nor goods run in, and Mobile, its inhabitants, and garrison, are thrown on the resources of the impoverished and hard-pressed Confederacy."[37]

Reaction to Farragut's victory ran from joy in the north to shock and dismay in Rebel territory. The *New York Times* called it "glorious news" and devoted most of a front page to eyewitness accounts. The *Daily Ohio Statesman* praised Farragut, predicting, "this latest achievement of the 'old salamander' will place him at top of the list of all Naval commanders of the world." The *Boston Weekly Transcript* agreed, "Commodore Farragut's exploits in Mobile Bay are on such a grand scale that it is not surprising the Richmond chivalry are mortified and confounded." Welles declared that the news "sent a thrill of joy through all true hearts" and personally informed Lincoln. In Montgomery, by contrast, a correspondent reported that recent events had "an almost stunning effect on our community" and "almost banished Richmond and Atlanta from our thoughts."[38]

Not for long. On September 2, General Hood evacuated the Georgia capital. The following day, Lincoln issued a proclamation of thanks for the "signal success that Divine Providence has recently vouchsafed to the operations of the United States fleet and army in the harbor of Mobile . . . and the glorious achievements of the army under Maj.-Gen. Sherman in the State of Georgia." The president requested that on the following Sunday "thanksgiving be offered," and "prayer be made for divine protection to our brave soldiers and their leaders in the field." He closed by hoping that the Almighty would "continue to uphold the Government of the United States against all efforts of public enemies and secret foes." Thanks to Farragut and Sherman, his reelection was assured, and complete Union victory was finally in sight.[39]

# 7

## Wilson's Raid, 1865

Selma was ours and fairly won.
—Gen. James Harrison Wilson

Bad news kept coming for Confederate Alabamians through the fall and into the winter. In distant Virginia, Lee's hard-pressed and steadily shrinking army was desperately fighting from entrenched positions at Petersburg, only 24 miles outside Richmond. Closer to home, Hood had marched his diminished force into middle Tennessee in an attempt to cut Sherman's supply line and draw him away from Atlanta. After a brief pursuit, the Ohioan reversed course and launched his devastating March to the Sea instead, leaving subordinates to deal with Hood's ill-considered invasion. This they did and handily. The Confederates were badly bloodied at Franklin on November 30, where they lost 5,000 irreplaceable infantrymen and five generals, and two weeks later they were thoroughly smashed at Nashville. The broken remnants scattered into the Deep South. Many deserted, fed up with the war. Of those left, infantrymen were sent into the Carolinas to oppose Sherman there, artillerymen to Mobile to man the city's big guns, and cavalrymen into Alabama and Mississippi to recuperate and forage. As if prospects weren't already bleak enough, the first weeks of 1865 saw the steady assemblage of the largest cavalry force ever on the North American continent, and it was pointed straight at the state's vital industrial heartland. The *Chattanooga Daily Rebel*, publishing at Selma after fleeing its home city, grimly assessed the situation. "The day of trial for this portion of Alabama has arrived," it announced February 5. "The miseries and desolations of war are brought to our own doors."[1]

The bearer of this misfortune was one of the youngest generals to wear the

MAJ. GEN. VOLS.

Figure 28. Gen. James Harrison Wilson
was a careful planner and an aggressive
fighter who dealt Confederate Alabama
its death blow in the spring of 1865.
Courtesy Library of Congress.

Union blue. James Harrison Wilson, Harry to his intimates, was only twenty-
seven years old but possessed a long combat record in both the eastern and
western theaters and a reputation as a crack administrator and gifted problem
solver. He stood five feet ten inches tall, wore a drooping mustache with a
long goatee, and had, despite his youth, the hardened features that came with
sustained and active service in all weathers. A native Illinoisan and an 1860
graduate of West Point—sixth in a class of forty-one—he was decisive, sol-
dierly, and serious. Besides his organizational talents, Wilson was a close and
careful student of how best to employ cavalry, until then the Union army's
least appreciated and utilized arm. As he surveyed the broader picture from
Alabama's Tennessee Valley, Wilson was convinced that a strong mounted raid
on Selma would serve several strategic goals at once, hastening the war's end.
These included destroying central Alabama's war-making industries, second
only to those at Richmond, which continued to turn out guns, ammunition,
uniforms, and supplies, and diverting enemy attention from General Canby's
upcoming attack on Mobile. From Selma, Wilson's force could then either
march for the coast to bolster Canby, slash west into Mississippi, or pivot east

into middle Georgia. This broad swath of the Deep South had been relatively untouched by the war thus far, and the Rebel high command viewed it as a defensible "last ditch" or, failing that, a safe corridor into the Trans-Mississippi Department where the war could be continued should Richmond fall. Wilson's Raid promised to not only gut the Confederacy's industrial capacity but also to deprive it of this "last ditch" as well.[2]

General Grant had long hungrily eyed central Alabama, of course, and needed little persuasion to authorize such a raid. That winter he wrote to Wilson's immediate superior at Nashville, Gen. George Thomas, to make it so. What Grant and Thomas had in mind was a contingent somewhat larger than Rousseau's the previous summer. This didn't suit Wilson at all, who wanted overwhelming strength when he rode south. In order to convince the "Rock of Chickamauga," Wilson invited him to a massive review outside Gravelly Springs in Lauderdale County. "The valley was full of moving horsemen," one witness wrote, "companies abreast and every rider at attention. . . . It was truly a grand sight." Thomas got the message, and enthusiastically told Wilson to take the largest force he could muster, potentially over 25,000 sabers.[3]

Wilson steadily amassed his "army of cavalry," instituted strict discipline, and drilled the men daily. This included teaching them how to ride double, rather than single file, as previously. Given the number of men he planned to take, double files meant significantly shorter columns, improving speed and efficiency. Additionally, the men were taught how to better maneuver and jump their horses, always diverting exercise for energetic youngsters, such as these troops mostly were. One Iowa trooper, E. N. Gilpin, wrote that he rarely saw Wilson, but when he did, "he is sitting straight in the saddle and riding hard. He is a superb horseman, and his soldiers like him." When not training or doing scut work, the men lounged about, swapping jokes and stories, playing cards, writing letters, or thoughtfully puffing pipes. Gilpin observed the Third Iowa in camp, "Mess kits burnished, and blankets fluttering in the wind," and betrayed no little pride when he declared, "Our fellows can do anything, from running a locomotive to a prayer meeting; they are masons, stokers, lawyers, farmers, engineers, store-keepers, horse-doctors, gamesters, and not a few can play the fiddle o'nights, or could before we broke them of it." Capt. Lewis M. Hosea, a young West Point graduate who would soon perform a vital mission for Wilson, agreed, writing later that immediately be-

fore the raid the "entire command" displayed "an *esprit du corps* hitherto unknown among them."[4]

Other than Wilson and a few select officers at headquarters, nobody knew
the line of march or intended destination, only that something big was in the
offing. Confederate spies and scouts haunted the Yankee camps and gleaned
what they could, but on February 11 the *New York Times* removed any uncertainty, announcing a "Great Cavalry Campaign," and boasting that "Clouds
of Cavalry" would soon sweep all the way to the Gulf. "It is by far the largest expedition of this character of the war," the paper reported, "and its conditions and prosperity have been so thoroughly canvassed in advance, that
no doubt whatever is entertained of its complete success." Southern papers
were reporting much the same. The Columbus (Mississippi) *Republic* correctly
concluded that the Yankee concentration was "for the purpose of moving on
Selma and Montgomery as soon as the roads are in suitable condition." The
Mobile *Tribune* was convinced that after cutting through central Alabama,
Wilson would drive for the coast to help Canby overthrow that "great commercial city of the Gulf."[5]

Roughly 75 miles to the southwest of Wilson's brigades, a Rebel private
named J. P. Young waited "quietly in camp" with his comrades, "refitting and
shoeing horses." His outfit, the Seventh Tennessee Cavalry, rode with Forrest
and had covered Hood's recent retreat. Despite their hard usage, these butternuts were still full of pepper, and on February 21 "held a mass meeting to
give expression to their determination to fight to the bitter end the common
enemy." They drafted a series of resolutions to that effect, one stating, "That
we have every confidence in our ability to defeat the efforts of our enemy, ex-
pel his armies, frustrate his purposes, and ultimately gain liberty and independence." Another called on the "fair women of the South" to continue their
selfless sacrifice "and frown upon those of our countrymen who have deserted
our cause, or refused to come to its defense in this hour of peril." Lastly, on
the hotly debated issue of blacks being allowed to fight for the South, these
die-hards resolved that "although we are not fully convinced of the expedi-
ency of enlisting and arming slaves for the service, we will nevertheless, cheerfully acquiesce in the policy of our government." This confidence and spirit
was by no means universal among Forrest's men. Frank A. Montgomery, a
Mississippi colonel, later recalled that, "The romance of the war was indeed

gone, only a sense of duty sustaining the cause, both in the army and among those citizens who had not yet yielded to the spirit of submission, which was spreading abroad and casting its baleful influence over the army like a dark shadow presaging our coming doom."[6]

Wilson knew that his force would likely be larger, better mounted, armed, and equipped than Forrest's threadbare ragamuffins, but he wasn't about to underestimate his enemy. Nor were the ordinary bluecoats in the saddle. "Forrest is a dangerous foe," Gilpin wrote, "quick, daring, resourceful, and whoever tackles him will find his hands full." The gaunt cavalryman with the thick, dark goatee and intense eyes had long before proven himself one of the Confederacy's most gifted and determined field commanders, "the very devil" according to Sherman. By the time of Wilson's Raid, Forrest had chalked up a series of impressive victories, including that over Streight almost two years previously, but accusations that his men slaughtered surrendering black troops and white Unionists at Fort Pillow, Tennessee, in April 1864 stained his reputation.

Despite this, many Southerners invested their hopes in his bravery and skill, practically worshipping him. Whether they reviled or lauded, nobody North or South ever made the mistake of thinking Nathan Bedford Forrest wasn't dangerous.[7]

Thanks to his own scouts, Wilson knew where Forrest was, and in an effort to "study his frame of mind," dispatched Captain Hosea under a flag of truce, ostensibly to negotiate a prisoner exchange. On the evening of February 23, Hosea and six troopers of "fine physique," beautifully mounted and fully kitted out, trotted into Rebel lines where the young captain dismounted and presented himself to the Rebel commander. The subsequent interview was both friendly and frank. Fully aware of his interlocutor's fierce character and daunting reputation, Hosea was surprised to find himself charmed by the man in the flesh. Forrest was tall and handsome, his face notable for its "dignity of expression." As they talked by flickering candlelight, Hosea admitted that he was "frequently lost in real admiration." Engaging in a little light one-upmanship, the young bluecoat informed the Rebel general that Wilson was a West Point graduate. Unimpressed, Forrest replied, "Wal, I never rubbed my back up agin a college, an' I don't profess to know much about tactics, but I'd give more for fifteen minutes of the 'bulge' on you than for three days of tactics." Hosea took careful note, as he should have. If anyone knew the value of fifteen minutes, it was Forrest, and if the Federals wanted to avoid a humiliating defeat they had best move fast, keep the famed gray paladin guessing, and hit hard.[8]

Wilson hardly needed the lesson, but events kept conspiring to reduce his force and delay his departure, originally scheduled for March 5. To begin with, persistent chilly rains soaked the command and raised area streams above their banks. As Gilpin accurately noted, "This is a country of rivers. The little wriggles of ink down the page of our military map are mountain streams flowing by stately pine woods, through hemlock bordered ravines; some clear and colorless, others shaded blue and green, that when falling in sunlit cascades are very beautiful." The problem that winter was too little sunlight, however, and day after day, week after week, the rain came down in torrents. The majestic Tennessee crested and then overflowed to a width of 4 miles in places. According to one bluecoat, "I seen a boat out in a cornfield. The river is higher than it has been for forty years, so the citizens say." At least one Union supply depot was swept away, along with dozens of valuable wagons and numerous boxes and barrels of rations and supplies. Men took ill and filled the hospitals, coughing and shivering. There were occasional breaks in the weather, but streams remained up and the roads were a sloppy mess. Just before his scheduled departure, Wilson regretfully informed Thomas that because the Tennessee was still rising, "It will be several days before I can begin to cross my command." As it turned out, the blue columns would not get away until March 22.[9]

The rain delay was frustration enough, but Wilson became even more irritated when orders arrived to send 5,000 men and good mounts to New Orleans. These were meant to reinforce Canby, but Wilson doubted the Kentuckian needed them given the resources already on the coast. This reduction, plus his inability to procure enough horses for some of the men still on hand, meant that he would march south with about 13,000 sabers, considerably less than planned. Still, skies were clear when buglers awoke the troops on the second day of spring, and optimism was high. Wilson proudly noted their "magnificent condition" and averred that he was "in the best of spirits and health."[10]

The men cheerfully spurred forward at last on their great mission. "Never can I forget the brilliant scene," Hosea later recalled, "as regiment after regiment filed gaily out of camp, decked in all the paraphernalia of war, with gleaming arms and guidons given to the wanton breeze." They were equipped similar to Rousseau's raiders—Spencer carbines, Colt revolvers, shiny sabers, and supported by twelve cannon. The mounted force consisted of three divisions—the First officered by Gen. Edward McCook, who Wilson described as "strong and vigorous"; the Second by Gen. Eli Long, a former Indian fighter; and the Fourth by Gen. Emory Upton, younger than Wilson at twenty-five but considered "an incomparable soldier." Besides the cavalry, there were 1,500 infantry in support of the supply train—250 wagons loaded with rations, coffee, sugar, salt, and extra ammunition. Lastly, given Alabama's abundant streams, Wilson deemed it wise to bring along a ready-to-assemble pontoon bridge, thirty canvas boats hauled aboard fifty, six-mule-team wagons. Once across the Tennessee, Wilson directed his columns along "divergent routes for the purpose of confusing the enemy." It helped considerably that a strong Union force had been reported marching north from Pensacola. Although this column would ultimately turn to strike against Mobile, Forrest didn't know that and had already started south to meet it when he received word that behind him Wilson was underway at last. Forrest's command included two divisions under Gen. James Chalmers and Gen. William "Red" Jackson respectively, a few thousand men each, as well as a couple of brigades under the capable General Roddey, but these officers and their men were strung out and divided by swollen creeks and rivers. Concentrating them for a cavalry battle of the ages would be a challenge. Forrest had been compelled to watch over "a vast extent of country," Wilson observed, "and was nowhere strong."[11]

As a result, Rebel opposition was nonexistent to light all the way to Jasper, where Wilson's columns congregated on the twenty-seventh. Informed that Forrest was now intent on blocking him as soon as possible, Wilson ordered the men to cross the Black Warrior and drive for Elyton. To speed up the advance, he unloaded the supply wagons and placed the parcels onto the mules, leaving the wagons behind. Even so, getting 13,000 men and a dozen heavy cannons across the roiling, rain-swollen stream proved to be the most difficult obstacle up to that point. To make matters worse, it had rained again, and the river was becoming less fordable by the hour. "The Black Warrior is about one hundred and fifty yards wide," Gilpin explained, "with rough bottom of shelving rock, and runs very swiftly." Eager to get across, General Upton steered his horse into the current, his men gingerly following. Quite a few fell or were swept off their saddles, "some swimming, others clinging to the rocks, and some plunging far down where the channel ran between precipitous banks at the mercy of the foaming waters." According to Indiana Sgt. Benjamin McGee, four men in his outfit were drowned after being tumbled "over and over" in the turbulence. One trooper's horse survived and was pinned against some rocks. The poor animal managed to clamber on top of them, and stood there trapped, "groaning most piteously," too traumatized to plunge into the water again. Rescuing a horse in such circumstances wasn't worth "a man's life," McGee wrote, and they regretfully left the animal "to its fate." Fortunately for Gilpin, he and his mount, "Charley," negotiated the passage successfully, "the waves surging angrily away, followed by a dark green ripple." Dripping water and relieved to be across, McGee, Gilpin, and their comrades quickly covered the 8 miles to the Warrior's Locust Fork, which they forded more easily, and on the twenty-ninth pushed into Elyton.[12]

Birmingham's predecessor gave no hint of its future growth and prosperity. Rather it was an uninspiring gaggle of buildings nestled in the Jones Valley. One bluecoat called it "miserable," and Wilson agreed, remembering it decades later as "a poor, insignificant Southern village, surrounded by old field farms, most of which could have been bought at five dollars an acre." Its importance stemmed from the surrounding industrial assets—mines, foundries, rolling mills, collieries, and other "valuable property," all going full tilt. Since secession, Alabamians had worked feverishly to develop their state's natural advantages. Wilson's troopers knew what they had to do. After flushing a few Rebel skirmishers out of Elyton, they fanned into the countryside. Wilson had issued strict orders against molesting civilians or destroying personal property, but excited and loosely supervised scouts could and did sometimes go too far. Gilpin's outfit wandered around the house and outbuildings of "a rich old Southerner" ogled by "a little army of negroes." Personal property didn't include foodstuffs or useful supplies, and the men helped themselves to "chickens, butter, eggs, hams in the smoke houses, thousands of bushels of corn in the barns, and forage of all kinds on the place." Several enterprising troopers discovered the wine cellar and rolled out barrels of peach and apple brandy "from among the musty cobwebs into the light of day." Eagerly crowding around, Gilpin and his comrades filled their dented tin cups with the liquor, "lest it might give aid or comfort to the enemy." Elsewhere, other units were more focused and went to work with a vengeance, wrecking tramways, burn-

ing wooden structures, and blowing up stone furnaces at Oxmoor and Iron-
dale. McGee's outfit, farther back than Gilpin's, passed some of this destruction a day later and found the fires "still burning." Hundreds of blacks, who
had been working when the Yankees arrived, sat or wandered about, "utterly
lost and dumbfounded. Like bees without a hive they did not know where to
go or what to do." When he bedded down that night, McGee contemplated
an apocalyptic scene, "the sky was red for miles around, caused by fires burning cotton-gins, mills, factories, &c, by our scouts and the 4th division, which
was just ahead of us."[13]

From Elyton, Wilson dispatched 1,500 men from McCook's First Division, commanded by a twenty-eight-year-old native Kentuckian, Gen. John
T. Croxton, with orders to head for Tuscaloosa. Their mission was to "destroy
the bridge, factories, mills, university (military school), and whatever else may
be of benefit to the Rebel cause." This foray also promised to shield Wilson's
right flank and slow down any Rebel pursuers in that vicinity. Rebels were certainly there, mostly Red Jackson's men, and Croxton had a brisk skirmish with
them at Trion, generally getting the worst of it before the Confederates disengaged and reversed direction in an attempt to meet the larger enemy force.
Free to move unimpeded, Croxton pushed on to Tuscaloosa while Wilson's
main columns headed for Montevallo and Selma. During the coming weeks,
Croxton's column, dubbed the "Lost Brigade," was destined to meander for
hundreds of miles across Alabama from Bridgeville to the Georgia line before it
reunited with Wilson at Macon after almost a month on its own. Throughout
its course it would wreck railroads and military assets and never be in any real
danger, though Wilson certainly worried about its fate.[14]

All of that was to come, of course. Croxton's first step was to tackle Tuscaloosa, and that meant securing the lightly defended bridge over the Black
Warrior River, which the Yankees reached the evening of April 3. Charles
Wooster, a twenty-two-year-old Michigander, was one of two men to volunteer for an attempt to capture the sentries. Wooster and his companion
quickly shucked all their equipment but for a pistol each, and crept onto the
span. "Who's there?" came the challenge. "Friends!," Wooster answered, but
at that instant a lurid muzzle flash and a roar split the darkness and the ball
zipped through the crown of the young Michigander's hat. The Yankees returned fire, wounding one of the guards. The other Rebels huddled behind

a cotton bale barricade and there followed a brief skirmish before the blue-coats poured across the bridge and succeeded in seizing two small field pieces that hadn't even been unlimbered. Meanwhile, at the nearby military college, the youthful cadets, most in their middle to late teens, had been mustered. Called "Katydids" for their likeness to the insect when fully uniformed, these youngsters were all that stood between Croxton and the campus. "When the corps arrived opposite the Methodist college," one of them later wrote, "we saw the flashes of the guns and heard the firing between the business part of the city and the bridge and were moved at the double-quick and in perfect order to the middle of the block next east of Greensboro Street and halted." The cadets managed to fire a few volleys, which slowed the Yankees a little. Fortunately, the faculty officers saw no point in sacrificing their charges in a stand-up fight with hardened veteran bluecoats, and so the youngsters were pulled out and marched away from the action. Their Civil War was over.[15]

That night the Yankees occupied the town. According to Wooster, "all stores, government houses &c. were given up to indiscriminate plunder; but I heard of no private dwelling houses being disturbed. Nigger[s] of all sorts and sizes and poor whites could be seen from morning till night carrying away all manner of dry goods and provisions." The following morning the troopers burned or destroyed everything that could be of any use to the Confederacy—cotton warehouses, foundries, a tannery, nitre works, and a hat factory. Nearby, a 200-man detachment marched onto the university campus and proceeded to fire its distinguished brick buildings. Incredibly, the elegant Rotunda with all of its books was included. Anxious to prevent needless cultural vandalism, several professors met the raiders and begged that the building be spared. A courier was sent to headquarters to ask, and soon returned to report that the men were to follow orders. According to legend, one of the Federal officers quickly ducked into the building to take one book as a souvenir. Clutching an 1853 English translation of the *Quran* he rejoined his comrades, and the building was torched. A small powder magazine on campus was also blown up, and falling debris set several neighboring houses ablaze. The president's mansion and the little observatory were ignored, but otherwise the destruction was considerable and heartbreaking. By the time Croxton's bluecoats exited town, smoldering ruins and ashes littered the riverbank, lanes, and groves of what had theretofore been a pleasant and handsome center of commerce and learning.[16]

Trusting Croxton to complete his task and rejoin the van at Selma, Wilson pushed on toward Montevallo. Red Jackson had hoped to reach the Cahaba River, flowing between Elyton and Montevallo, before the Yankees and destroy the bridge there, but his tussle with Croxton made that impossible, and during the thirtieth and thirty-first Wilson's men crossed the stream. McGee remembered the experience as only slightly less harum-scarum than that at the Black Warrior. The span was a rickety railroad bridge 300 feet long and 100 feet high.

Working quickly, dismounted troopers ripped up cross ties and placed them between the rails as tightly together as possible, making a primitive bridge for the horses. "To stand at the end and look across, it appeared to be suspended in the air, as you could not see that there was a thing supporting it," McGee later wrote. The horses sensibly balked, rearing "back from it in the wildest fright, and it was with the utmost difficulty that we got them started across it." The men compensated by forming the animals up head to tail so they couldn't look down, each trooper walking alongside his mount, murmuring encouragement. The only thing that would have made it more difficult, perhaps impossible, would have been Rebel skirmishers taking potshots at them all the while.[17]

Upton's Fourth Division galloped toward Montevallo first, where it encountered some of Roddey's cavalrymen. According to Gilpin, the bluecoats "fought them into town and charged them out." More destruction followed—rolling mills, foundries, and the like, including the Bibb Naval Furnace at nearby Brierfield. "The day was beautifully bright and perfectly still," McGee remembered, "and the smoke from a burning factory or mill would rise straight into the air 500 feet high, and as the country was comparatively level we could see all of these from the column, and 20 of these vast domes of smoke might have been counted at a single view, some of them 20 miles away." Surely, McGee thought, "the end could not be far away." Just south of town resistance stiffened as several hundred butternuts were now between the Federals and Selma. Musket and Spencer discharges rattled and cracked over the fields and through the woods at an increasing rate, but nowhere near the undifferentiated roar familiar to these men from big battles. "This is the first time we have met any rebels to amount to anything," McGee declared. There were a few spirited butternut sallies before a mounted saber assault by Iowa troopers swept the way

Figure 29. Ruins of Bibb Naval Furnace photographed during the 1930s. Courtesy Library of Congress.

clear again. Forrest and his personal escort of seventy-five hard-riding fighters heard the racket, but weren't able to link with Roddey until Randolph, less than 40 miles north of Selma. For his part, Wilson was highly pleased. His men had "fairly 'got the bulge' on Forrest," and they weren't about to lose it.[18]

Wilson was already holding most of the cards, and on April 1 luck dealt him another ace. Upton's men captured a Confederate courier carrying dispatches to Red Jackson. The information they contained was golden—Croxton was okay, Jackson was in Wilson's rear, and Chalmers was south and west of Forrest, the Oakmulgee Swamp between them. As Wilson later wrote in his memoirs, "I now knew exactly where every division and brigade of Forrest's corps was, that they were widely scattered and that if I could force the marching and the fighting with sufficient rapidity and vigor, I should have the game entirely in my hands." Which is just what he did. Wilson immediately dispatched the First Wisconsin to seize a critical bridge at Centerville and barricade the Tuscaloosa Road. That would block Jackson. Meanwhile, the rest of the command pushed the Rebels south in a running fight that left the route dotted with dead and wounded horses and men. McGee recalled the nature of the combat. "Company A fell back to their horses and company F dismounted and pushed on after the rebels, who would take advantage of every fence corner and turn, thus giving us a volley about every five minutes, while our shooting at them was more constant and regular, as we kept them moving so constantly that we could see some of them nearly all the time."[19]

Uncharacteristically on his heels, Forrest tore about like a madman, issuing orders, urging his men up, and desperately looking for a place to make a stand. With scarcely time to breathe, much less thoroughly inspect the terrain, he demonstrated his military mastery yet again by quickly choosing a strong defensive line situated along Bogler's Creek 25 miles north of Selma. The stream flowed past a little country crossroads, anchored by Ebenezer Baptist Church. From here Forrest's troopers took advantage of higher ground to cover the Alabama and Tennessee River Railroad, a handy interior supply line, as well as the wagon roads leading to Maplesville and Selma. Working quickly, Forrest positioned Alabama State Troops on the right, Roddey's men in the center, and a contingent of Kentuckians on the left. Some of Chalmers's men trickled into the lines soon after, but nowhere near enough. At most there were two thousand Rebels strung through the woods. Already dog-tired and dust covered, they began throwing up rail and brush defenses and sighted eight cannon to cover the roads. It was a good position, but too lightly defended. Would it hold? The answer wasn't long in coming.[20]

Writing years later, Wilson judged Forrest's plan at Ebenezer Church "brilliant," but stated that "it came too late and took too long to carry it out." War is full of "vicissitudes," he wrote, "and Forrest was now in the midst of them." His forces were scattered and divided by brimful rivers and extensive swamps, and most of the men that could be brought into action had already been harried across miles of hill and dale. There was nothing the Wizard of the Saddle could do, Wilson declared, "but to curse and fight, and he did both with characteristic energy and desperation."[21]

At Randolph, Wilson shuffled his columns, sending Upton's Fourth Division west to the Maplesville Road and putting Eli Long's Second in the lead on the Plantersville Road. The two columns would converge at Ebenezer Church and then push for Selma together. Rebels feebly contested the advance, until Long's bluecoats came in view of the little crossroads around 4:00 p.m. They immediately attacked, forcing the skirmishers back, but when they attempted to press their advantage met more determined opposition. This was Forrest's main defensive line. "We did not fire until the battery had commenced plowing up the road," one butternut recalled. "Then we turned loose on the poor fellows." McGee was among the surprised troopers who realized they were facing something serious. "Just then we heard a volley," he remembered, "and more than a dozen bullets came tearing down the road, and we lost no time in getting out of that, and as we ran we felt a heavy lick, and a sharp stinging pain just above the right knee. A ball had torn through our pants and cut a crease three inches long." McGee and his comrades took shelter behind a frame house and started banging away at the Rebels. Capt. James D. Taylor, a young Indianan whose company charged the skirmishers headlong yelling and waving sabers in the air, wasn't so lucky. He and his men rode through the retreating skirmishers easily enough, but then encountered the barricade. One trooper's momentum was so great that he couldn't avoid smashing into a field piece, killing his horse and breaking one of the gun's heavy wooden wheels. At once the troopers were engulfed in a vicious melee. Swinging his saber, Taylor bore down on none other than Forrest himself and the pair fought a running duel for almost two hundred yards. Forrest carried a saber and knew how to use it, but he preferred six shooters that could be easily handled in the saddle at a trot. The Indianan whaled away on his famed opponent, cutting the Rebel general's hand. But as Emerson famously wrote, "When you strike at a king, you must kill him." The diminutive Taylor wasn't getting the job done, and Forrest was able to spur his beloved mount, King Phillip, and surge ahead. This provided just enough room for him to swing around and drill the Yankee with a fatal pistol shot. Forrest later told Wilson, "If that boy had known enough to give me the point of his saber instead of its edge, I should not have been here to tell you about it." The surviving Federal cavalrymen had to desperately cut their way back out, leaving seventeen killed and wounded behind.[22]

Long quickly assessed the situation and threw multiple regiments, mounted and afoot, into the action. The volume of fire and noise increased—cannon booming, muskets roaring, Spencers cracking, Colts popping, the Rebel ordnance train blowing its whistle—and billows of white smoke rose over the landscape. Wilson later wrote that the "resistance was determined." The Confederates held for almost an hour, when Upton's men suddenly arrived on the field yelling and cheering. Nine thousand bluecoats were now assaulting the line, tongues of flame rippling along their front as they rapidly discharged their repeaters. The unsteady Alabama State Troops wavered and then gave. Despite fierce fighting by Forrest and his better soldiers, the entire Rebel line crumbled, broke, and fled south, the ordnance train furiously backing along with them. "The enemy, completely demoralized by the attacks of Long and Upton, fled in confusion, throwing away all impediments to flight," Hosea recalled. Gilpin described a road "strewn with guns, belts, cartridge boxes, coats and hats. 'Too fast for their *goods!*' the boys would say."[23]

The scrape at Ebenezer Church cost Wilson twelve dead and forty wounded. Among the wounded was Sgt. John Wall, who was carrying a guidon when a Rebel ball smashed into his hand and embedded itself in the wooden staff. Undeterred, Wall had fought on, capturing an enemy officer in the process. Other troopers suffered the kinds of freakish close calls familiar to most combat veterans, whatever the war. One man was spared when his molasses-filled canteen stopped a bullet, another when his brass belt buckle took the hit instead of his gut, and a third when a ball spent its force on his saddle flap rather than his thigh. Gilpin acknowledged, "Bullets play some very funny tricks." There is no estimate of Rebel casualties, but the Yankees took three hundred prisoners and three field pieces. That night, the troopers bedded down at Plantersville, an unimpeded road ahead. Gilpin was quartered in a nearby house, and from the window contemplated the army at rest. There was no sound, he wrote, "and only the light of campfires glimmered in the sky, away south toward Selma."[24]

Buglers roused the men at 6:00 a.m. on Sunday, April 2, and by that afternoon they at last beheld their goal on the plain below. "The sunlight streamed in radiant splendor over the scene," Hosea recorded, "and danced in diamond flashes on the distant river winding away to the south-west. Bodies of troops in motion, with clouds of dust pierced by flashes of light from glistening bayonets, indicated the state of busy preparation within the works, and foreshadowed the carnage of the coming conflict." In yet another stroke of luck for Wilson, an English engineer who had helped the Confederates design the city's defenses deserted and was immediately taken to Federal headquarters. He readily agreed to sketch the works for the assembled generals, and explained their construction and armament in detail. Wilson was sobered, and knew "that we were confronted by a problem of great difficulty and complexity," one that would require "hard work and desperate fighting" to overcome.[25]

Selma had begun to be fortified in 1863, and within Alabama was second only to Mobile in the extent and quality of its defenses. Many years after the war, Selman William Oliver Perry, who had been nine years old in 1865, recalled their construction. "The labor was all done by slaves," he told a newspaper reporter. "The natural embankment from the river up Valley Creek to the intersection of Pettus and Gary Street was used." Young Perry visited the earthworks on several occasions, hauling provisions for his father's slaves, who were in the labor gangs. "The embankment was ten feet wide at the base and about seven feet tall," he remembered. "The dirt was gotten at the base of the embankment, making a ditch for further protection. It was topped by a picket fence." The line stretched almost completely around the city, with the river serving as a natural barrier along the south. Along the eastern and western sides of town, the works were fairly plain dirt ramparts with interspersed gun emplacements and rifle pits. But across the northern front, straddling the Summerfield and Range Line roads and facing the Yankees, they were stronger, with various obstacles including felled trees with the branches left on and sharpened, pointed stakes and trip wires littering the open ground out front. Hosea studied them carefully and counted thirty-two pieces of artillery "of large caliber" that pointed "grimly from the embrasures, placed to sweep every point of attack and concentrate a fire upon the roads forming the only approaches to the city." Wilson later declared that from what he could see, "nothing had been left undone to make the place impregnable."[26]

Selma was in an uproar. Untested state troops and jaded regulars raised clouds of dust as they tramped toward the defenses with worried expressions on their faces. Panicked civilians and black servants ran hither and thither among braying mules and impatient horses, hiding valuables and loading wagons for evacuation. All along the riverfront, Confederate authorities worked frantically to get as many military assets as possible loaded onto trains for shipment out on the Alabama and Mississippi Railroad, only recently completed to Meridian. J. J. Thomas, a civilian train engineer, later recalled his hectic work on the tracks backing locomotives and coupling cars, "whistles blowing and bells ringing." He stole a few moments to hurry over to a boardinghouse and gather up his wife and new baby, whom he put in a caboose "with our few household goods." Forrest didn't calm matters any when he clattered into town covered in blood and bellowing that every able-bodied man who didn't report for duty would be thrown into the Alabama River. There were hundreds of white male civilian workers in town, but with little to no military training, and only whatever weapons they could beg, borrow, or steal, nobody expected much out of them. These scenes of disorder and desperation were all the more surreal given the splendors of the season. One local woman, Sarah Ellen Phillips, remembered the "golden glories of the jasmine," "dogwoods arrayed in robes of white," and "bursting buds and blossoms" scenting the air. "How rude the shock that called us from the boundless enjoyment of all the beauties of Spring in Alabama!" she wrote in her diary.[27]

About a mile north of town, Lieutenant Colonel Montgomery hurriedly manned the defenses with his Mississippians. Studying the broad plain to his front, he saw several riders appear on the crest of the far ridge. He thought they might be Confederate pickets. The sun had begun to sink, and suddenly hundreds more appeared, "moved slowly for a while, and then broke into a cheer and charged, full three thousand men." The suddenness of the attack stunned many on both sides. Despite some limited and ineffectual artillery dueling, the Confederates did not expect any real fighting until the next morning, while Federal soldiers had been told to prepare for a night assault. At Plantersville Wilson had switched his columns once again, and now Long was on the right, advancing astride the Summerfield Road, while Upton was on the left, marching down the Range Line Road. Events accelerated when some of Chalmers's men finally caught up to the Yankees and attacked Long's rear guard. This was one of Forrest's favorite tactics, meant to discombobulate enemy plans. Unfortunately for the Rebels, there were too few of them, and their ruckus was nothing the Federals there couldn't handle. Long didn't know that, however, and decided to launch the attack on Selma at once lest the entire Union scheme be disrupted.[28]

The Yankee troops, most dismounted for the attack, had almost 600 yards of open ground to cover. They started at a walk, then a trot, and finally ran forward in a great charge. "From the entire line of defense flashed the musketry till all was shrouded in the smoke of battle, and only the red blaze of musketry and artillery could be seen," McGee recalled of the terrible moments.

Montgomery wrote that "as the enemy came nearer I could plainly see the deadly effects of our fire." Men and horses were hit all up and down the line. Long was struck in the forehead by a nearly spent ball, suffering a concussion that would incapacitate him for several weeks. This potentially demoralizing event was unnoticed by most bluecoats immersed in the dust, smoke, and confusion of battle. McGee and his comrades quickly reached the Rebel works and began milling about in the ditch, attempting to hide from the enfilading fire. Montgomery described stepping up and emptying his weapon "five times into the struggling mass." The Federals weren't delayed long, however. According to Hosea, they "opened a withering fire" with their Spencers, and "as boys play leap-frog, the more active 'boosting' their comrades, surged through the ditch and sprang up the parapet with wild cheers." Hosea resorted to an elaborate but effective Homeric simile to describe the scene: "As when a huge sea wave rolls along the shore with gathering strength, meets an opposing crag, mounts up the steep ascent, and white with fury, sweeps resistless over the topmost crest, so the surging wave of gallant men swept over the parapet at Selma." Equally determined, some Confederates met their assailants hand to hand, clubbing their muskets and grappling with the onrushing bluecoats. But they were hopelessly outnumbered and their efforts were futile. "I knew all was lost," Montgomery admitted, as butternuts broke and fled all around him. In the words of one Rebel, "we simply had to skedaddle from there."[29]

Others surrendered, or attempted to, and some were shot for their trouble. McGee related one episode when a "man in citizen's dress, gun in hand," cried out, "I am a minister, don't kill me." A Yankee captain retorted, "Do you preach with that gun?" In the next moment the preacher dropped, "pierced with Spencer balls." This unfortunate clergyman might have been the Reverend Arthur M. Small. According to an old Alabama legend, when his body was borne back to the manse after the battle, a rose bush arching over the entrance dropped all its petals. The bush blooms anew every April, as a reminder of his sacrifice. Montgomery told the sad story of Henry Elliot, a mere youth who when wounded tried to surrender, "but the man who first got to him shot him again and again and left him for dead." After lying helpless overnight with a broken back, legs, and an arm, Elliot was finally taken to a hospital where shortly thereafter he died.[30]

Those Confederates still in the fight retired to a less substantial inner defensive line, where Forrest attempted to rally the others. But they were quickly overwhelmed, and the Rebel general and a small contingent fought their way out of town. Eager to get in on the action and inspire his men, Wilson himself thundered toward this inner defense line astride his big gray, Sheridan, flanked by his blood-red battle flag and personal escort. He later described the experience as a "whirlwind of battle." As his animal leaped into the works Wilson heard someone yell, "Shoot that man on the white horse." Instantly, Sheridan was hit in the chest and tumbled forward, throwing Wilson into the dust. The horse immediately regained its feet, and Wilson inspected it, carefully holding its mane. The animal, head held high and "eyes blazing as though they were balls of fire" seemed okay. Wilson detected a trickle of blood, but with no other mount at hand, rode the horse throughout the eventful day. Incredibly, Sheridan survived until wounded again some weeks later in Georgia, after which it died.[31]

There now began a pell-mell race for town, Rebels and Yankees, black laborers, riderless horses, bouncing caissons, and barely controlled wagons, all mixed together in the gloaming. "Everything was in the wildest confusion," a young planter's wife recalled, "wounded horses and broken wagons blocked the streets, and the dust was blinding." Phillips and her family had listened to the sounds of battle, fearing the worst, when their servants suddenly started yelling, "The Yankees are coming! The Yankees are coming!" Terrified, the family found their home engulfed in the chaos. Troopers galloped up to "our very doors," Phillips wrote, "ran up the steps and through the house, upstairs and down." In her mother's room the soldiers ransacked the bureau drawers, searching for "hidden treasures." Out in the backyard she described "chickens flying, turkey running, dogs barking and Yankees shooting." Wilson had issued strict orders against looting, but the increasing darkness and tumult provided handy cover for anyone with criminal intent. To add to the hysteria, retreating Confederates blew up the nitre works, sending flames and debris high into the night sky and set fire to thousands of cotton bales riverside. Rogue troopers looted a liquor store, and immediately got drunk, sharing the spirits with ecstatic newly freed slaves. Not surprisingly, other fires were set throughout the evening, consuming the Episcopal Church and several private homes. Gilpin shuddered at the memory, "Of all the nights of my experience, this is the most like the horrors of war—a captured city burning at night, a victorious army advancing, and a demoralized one retreating." Civilians who had managed to flee town before the battle could see the red glare for miles.[32]

"Selma was ours and fairly won," Wilson later wrote, "but it was not till well into the next day that we realized the full extent of our victory." Or the cost. Forty-six troopers were killed, 300 wounded, and thirteen missing. Among the dead were Corporal Booth of the Fourth Ohio, the first Union solider to gain the parapet, who was shot through the head, and Lt. Col. George W. Dobb, the unit's commanding officer. The wounded, Union and Confederate, were settled in a hospital where they received the best care that Union surgeons, local doctors, and ministering angels could offer. There is no accurate estimate of Confederate casualties, though Wilson thought they were somewhat less than his own, and a trooper reported a similar number of dead on each side of the parapet after the fight. Almost 3,000 Rebels were captured, including Montgomery, and were herded into a makeshift prison pen, where they were loosely supervised. Montgomery was even allowed to visit the battlefield under guard.[33]

Several days after the attack, Wilson met with Forrest under a flag of truce at Cahaba to discuss a prisoner exchange. It was his first face-to-face meeting with his renowned foe. The two men sat down to a "bountiful Southern dinner" and chatted "like old acquaintances, if not old friends." Looking depressed and with his arm in a sling, Forrest stated, "Well, General, you have beaten me badly, and for the first time I am compelled to make such an acknowledgment. I have met many of your men, but never before one I did not get away with, first or last." Wilson was conciliatory, "Our victory was not without cost. You put up a stout fight, but we were too many and too fast for you." On the matter of an exchange, Forrest claimed he didn't have the authority and would have to check with his superior. Wilson's greatest benefit from the interview came when the Rebel general inadvertently revealed that Croxton's command was still alive and well in the field.[34]

No sooner was the sun up on April 3 than Wilson established firm control over his men and the civilian population, posting guards to prevent further looting. He then set about the serious work of wrecking Selma's war-making capabilities. This was an enormous task. Among the assets were twenty-four buildings at the Selma Arsenal containing fifteen siege guns, ten field pieces, sixty field carriages, sixty thousand rounds of artillery ammunition, one million rounds of small arms ammunition, three million board feet of lumber, three hundred barrels of resin, and several large engines and boilers; five buildings at the Naval Foundry containing three engines, thirteen boilers, twenty-nine siege guns, and assorted machinery; five buildings at the Selma Iron Works with foundries, engines, and machinery; the Horseshoe Factory with one engine and 8,000 pounds of horseshoes; a shovel factory with one engine and eight forges; the Alabama and Mississippi Railroad roundhouse with one engine, machinery and tools, and over twenty passenger, box, and platform cars; and on the tracks of the Alabama and Tennessee River Railroad, five locomotives and numerous cars. The troops went to work with a will. On April 4, McGee and his outfit "fixed up a spout on an inclined plane that led down to the river," with a wooden platform below. Soldiers and freed slaves rolled artillery shells down the chute, which then hit the platform below and bounded some 50 feet out into the Alabama. "This tickled the darkies wonderfully," McGee chuckled, "and for two days they just kept the river boiling." Local toughs and street urchins were supplied with hammers and allowed to break up locomotives, and hundreds of former slaves were hired to gather up "wagons, ambulances, caissons, limber-chests, blacksmith's forges, and artillery wagons," and pile them all in the arsenal, "preparatory to burning them." This took days, but at last on April 6 the arsenal was fired. "The rattle of exploding rifle and musket cartridges was deafening," McGee wrote, "we have not heard such a constant roar since the battle of Chicamauga." Even though the workers had been admonished not to leave any artillery shells in the complex, dozens of rounds had been carelessly ignored or overlooked, and these began exploding in spectacular fashion, shooting sparks and shrapnel everywhere, sending one and all running for cover. "The scene was hideous and unearthly beyond anything we had ever imagined," McGee recalled. "The explosions continued for three hours, much louder than any we had ever heard, and of sufficient violence to shake the earth for miles around, making the whole city a perfect pandemonium." Had it not been for a steady rain, McGee averred, Selma would have been completely consumed. Lastly, in a final indignity, all the horses and mules in town not needed by the invaders were slaughtered to deprive the Rebels of their use. Many of these unfortunate animals were dispatched and tossed into the river, but dozens of others were left to lie where they had been killed, rotting in stables, intersections, and along roadsides, adding their stench

Figure 30. A sketch of Selma made May 24, 1865, by a Federal soldier. Gutted buildings are visible, as are still extant landmarks. Courtesy DePauw University Archives and Special Collections.

to that of charred wood, and burned powder. Little wonder that the psychological trauma of Selma's fall would reverberate for generations.[35]

At last, on April 10 the Yankees departed. Reasoning that matters on the coast were under control, Wilson procured a skiff and sent a black man down the Alabama River to inform Canby of his intention to turn east for Montgomery. Because the state capital was on the opposite side of the river, the pontoniers threw an 800-foot bridge across the stream and the bluecoats marched over it and out of town. Hundreds of rejoicing blacks followed. Their long-sought day of Jubilo had come. Although no one in Alabama knew it yet, the war was all but over. Richmond had fallen April 2, and Robert E. Lee surrendered to General Grant April 9. Jeff Davis was on the run with a few trusted aides, fleeing deeper into a last ditch that thanks to Wilson was no longer tenable. Unfortunately communications were poor to nonexistent across much of the South. Opposite Mobile, at Blakeley, thousands of Yankees and Rebels were about to clash in the war's last major infantry assault. News of Lee's surrender would arrive too late to prevent even more senseless destruction, suffering, and death in the Heart of Dixie.

# 8

## The Mobile Campaign

It appeared to me that all hell had turned loose.
—Pvt. William Kavanaugh, CSA

Protected by her earthworks, artillery, channel pilings, torpedoes, water batteries, and skeleton navy, Confederate Mobile awaited the hammer blow. Grumpy
doomsayers, or "croakers" as they were called, ominously predicted defeat
and desolation. Lieutenant Mumford, buffeted by high winter winds, soaked
by rain, and sprayed by breaking waves at Battery Gladden, conceded in his
diary, "The prospects of the Confederacy look gloomy." Official voices were
more sanguine. In early March, General Maury reassured the *Advertiser and
Register*'s readers, "Our fortifications are strong—our stores are abundant and
good—our troops are veterans—and with the cordial support of the people in
all measures required for public safety, and, with the blessing of Almighty God,
are confident of victory." In an effort to prepare Mobile for siege, authorities
ordered civilians evacuated, barrooms shuttered, and all cotton turned over to
the military. Williams, now stationed at one of the batteries ringing the city,
informed Lizzie that the intent of the dictate to turn over all the cotton was
to burn it if Mobile fell, saving it from "the Yankee maw."[1]

The press endorsed these moves and encouraged the people to acquiesce.
"Women, children and slaves, if there be means of sending them away, had
better go without delay," the *Mobile Telegraph* exhorted. "It is no pleasant thing
to have bomb shells falling around our houses." Despite the urgency, compliance was limited to nonexistent. While some fled with all the valuables they
could carry, most simply waited—unable to leave, too war-weary to care, or

hopeful that the defenses would hold. Tavern keepers and merchants similarly ignored the barroom order and continued plying the thirsty troops with all the whiskey they could drink, at three to five dollars a glass. Predictably, arrests for carousing and drunkenness were commonplace. Lastly, no one wanted to surrender their cotton if they had any. Citizens viewed the commodity as a valuable liquid asset and very practically and reasonably concluded that its possession would be a signal advantage once the war ended. Authorities were determined, however, and Williams informed his wife that every house in town "is being rigidly searched and cotton is discovered where no one suspected its existence." In some cases, he wrote, "it has been found under floors or buried in cisterns—I heard of one who had a single bale disguised as a bed-covered with sheets and blankets with an innocent pillow at the head."[2]

Despite the increasing austerity, Mobile struck many observers as profligate and carefree even as Union forces marshaled for the coup de grâce. A member of New Orleans' famed Washington Artillery, Philip D. Stephenson, later recalled that "a semblance of the ways of peace still existed there. Coffee houses were in full blast where 'coffee' could be bought for a dollar a cup, with an 'ironclad' pie thrown in." James Maxwell, an artilleryman assigned to the city defenses, delightedly discovered that fish and oysters "were plentiful, as well as eggs and vegetables." Kate Cumming, depressed by her months of hospital work, remarked disapprovingly that the city "never was as gay as it is at the present; not a night passes but some large ball or party is given. Same old excuse: that they are for the benefit of the soldiers; and indeed the soldiers seem to enjoy them." Maxwell and some of his comrades even got to pay a visit to local literary celebrity Augusta Jane Evans, noted for her ardent Confederate patriotism and intimidating vocabulary. "We were in our new gray jeans jackets and pants and linsey shirts," he wrote. Nonetheless, Maxwell and his companions felt underdressed amid so many senior officers "rigged out in their best uniforms." It mattered not. "We were welcomed, introduced all around, entertained on equality." While the officers clustered around the writer and her father, the enlisted men chatted amiably and played "back gammon checkers and cards" with Evans's younger sisters. When the soldiers left, Miss 'Gusta, as she was affectionately called, referenced the stormy weather, saying, "I hope you gentlemen will not form an opinion about the meteorology of Mobile, by what you have seen since your arrival." "Yes Madam," they politely replied as they left the porch. But as they walked away one of the men asked, "what in the mischief she said? Meteor—meteor, what?"[3]

When not guzzling coffee or whiskey, slurping oysters, or making social calls, soldiers like Stephenson, Mumford, and Maxwell worked hard at buttressing Mobile's already formidable defenses and drilled at their posts. Across the bay at Spanish Fort, Stephenson and his comrades labored on a 16-by-20-foot bombproof. "We cut down great trees," he explained, "rolled the trunks over the mouth, then put a layer of brush and dirt; then came another layer of heavy logs crosswise, then a layer of brush and dirt, until the roof was six to eight feet thick." At Battery Gladden, Mumford and his crew fought against constant erosion. On January 9, he wrote: "Strong southeast wind blowing all day, accompanied by heavy rain. Tide rose very high, the waves washing the water in the quarters. The parapets were injured considerably." And at Battery B, one of the forts on the city's land side, Maxwell and his comrades practiced with small mortars and "big cast iron siege guns," blasting away "at targets out in the marsh."[4]

Maury made every effort to get as many soldiers as possible into these defenses, but the Confederacy's dwindling manpower and bedrock racism made it an exercise in frustration. Stephenson wrote that every man "who could carry a gun was in the ranks." Even at that, the most optimistic estimates of the troops on hand numbered less than 10,000 muskets: "odds and ends," Stephenson remarked, "fragments of other commands, boy militia, etc.; a few were veteran troops." One theretofore willing source of recruits was conspicuously absent—Mobile's free Creoles. Some of this distinctive community's young men had volunteered to serve as early as 1862 and were used as a home guard. A year later, Maury wanted to enroll them in an artillery unit, but he was rebuffed by Richmond. Perplexed, he tried to give the government a little history lesson. "When Spain ceded this territory to the United States in 1803," he explained, "the creoles were guaranteed all the immunities and privileges of the citizens of the United States, and have continued to enjoy them up to this time." He admitted they had "negro blood" but insisted they wanted to serve and would make good soldiers. James Seddon, secretary of war, was unmoved: "Our position with the North and before the world will not allow the employment as armed soldiers of negroes." But by mid-February of 1865, with the Confederacy pressed on every side, Richmond was singing a different tune, even debating out of desperation whether or not to emancipate and arm slaves throughout the South. Mobilians held a public meeting and endorsed the plan, but it was too little, too late. The gray-coated rank and file was cynical and unimpressed. "The time for *big talk* has passed," one man grumbled. "Disguise the fact as we may, the *real sentiment* of this brigade and this division is for peace on almost any terms."[5]

Mobile's prospects certainly looked bleak. The only meaningful questions were, from which direction would the Yankees ultimately attack, and how many of them would there be? Throughout the winter and spring of 1865 Union forces steadily increased from Pascagoula to Pensacola. The *New York Times* reported, "Dauphin Island and Mobile Point glisten with Federal bayonets." Monitors and light-draft gunboats dotted the upper bay, and warships and transports regularly hove into and out of the lower bay. On March 12, at Battery Gladden, Mumford reported "twelve vessels in sight," and the troops were kept at their guns day and night. With a better prospect and perhaps keener eyesight, Laura Roberts Pillans counted twenty-one watercraft including five monitors. "It is supposed that our trial is approaching," she glumly wrote in her diary.[6]

The overall Federal commander of the Mobile campaign was a capable if plodding and uninspiring officer. General Canby, or "Sprigg" as he was sometimes called, graduated next to last in his West Point class of 1839. Rather slumped, plain looking, and clean shaven (a rarity for Civil War generals on either side), his army service included battling the Florida Seminoles, holding New Mexico for the Union, putting down the New York City draft riots, and coordinating with Farragut in the attacks on Forts Morgan and Gaines. He had been wounded in the buttocks in November 1864, hardly an edifying *badge d'honneur* for a military man, and was still limping four months later. Grant considered him a better administrator than fighter, but Sprigg was now the top army man on the Gulf Coast. Grant, eager to employ every force in the field to crush the reeling Confederacy, ordered him to drive north and help Wilson topple Selma and Montgomery. Mobile could be safely bypassed, Grant suggested, but if Canby was uncomfortable leaving an intact garrison in his rear, Grant was willing to let him deal with it if he did so speedily. "Take Mobile and hold it," he gruffly informed the Kentuckian, "and push your

Figure 31. Gen. E. R. S. Canby. From
C. C. Andrews, *History of the Campaign of
Mobile; Including the Cooperative Operations
of Gen. Wilson's Cavalry in Alabama* (New
York: D. Van Nostrand, 1889).

forces to the interior." Instead, Canby dithered. Grant expressed his vexation
to Secretary of War Edwin Stanton on March 14: "I am very much dissatisfied with General Canby. He has been slow beyond excuse."[7]

But Canby had not been entirely idle and, within days of Grant's com-
plaint, was finally underway with a well-conceived operation. Reasoning that
Mobile's land defenses were too strong, he determined to attack from the east,
reducing the Rebel bastions at Spanish Fort and Blakeley, and then using the
delta's labyrinthine streams to invest the city via its swampy back door. His
offensive consisted of four elements. First, several thousand troops would conduct a feint from Cedar Point in southern Mobile County to make the Rebels think the main attack was coming from there. Second, the Thirteenth
and Sixteenth Corps (roughly 16,000 men in each), under Generals Granger
and A. J. Smith respectively, would advance from Forts Morgan and Gaines
up to the Fish River in Baldwin County, where they would regroup prior
to the attack—Granger's men marching east across the elongated peninsula
and then north, and Smith's sailing by troop transport across the bay. Third,
13,000 men under Gen. Frederick Steele would conduct a strong feint toward Montgomery from Pensacola, taking Pollard and cutting the vital Alabama and Florida Railroad, before swinging west to Blakeley. Lastly, the navy
would provide vital support in ferrying the troops, clearing torpedoes, and

shelling enemy positions. It was a solid strategy, and as noted in the previous chapter, Steele's feint fooled Forrest long enough to give Wilson the "bulge" upstate. All told, 45,000 Union troops and several hundred sailors were involved. Significantly, more than 5,000 of these soldiers were black, mostly former slaves from Louisiana. They were intensely motivated, not least because capture meant reenslavement. They were good troops, hardy and brave, and according to one officer were "burning with an impulse to do honor to their race." This augured poorly for the Rebel defenders in light of the smoldering Fort Pillow outrage.[8]

Canby's primary theater of operations was Mobile Bay's Eastern Shore, extending from the mouth of Weeks Bay, a small, shallow body of water in southwestern Baldwin County, north 22 miles to Spanish Fort, and east roughly 7 miles to the Fish River. Today this area encompasses some of modern Alabama's most beautiful and desirable real estate, noted for tan beaches, gentle surf, sandy soil, moss-hung live oaks, and tony communities like Point Clear, Fairhope, and Montrose. During the Civil War, however, it was lightly settled and its streams, ravines, swamps, tangled thickets, piney woods, and primitive roads presented significant obstacles to a large army on the move. Canby's chosen rendezvous point for Granger's and Smith's troops was Dannelly's Mills, a semiruinous collection of frame buildings and an old ferry 6 miles up the Fish River. The elevations around Weeks Bay are at or near sea level, but moving northward, the ground rises to upwards of 100 feet at the head of Mobile Bay and along the Tensaw River, where Spanish Fort and Blakeley are respectively situated. Little wonder that the Confederates chose to erect their defenses there, with sweeping views of the bay, delta, and rolling woodlands.

The works at Spanish Fort were the strongest, a mile and a half long and shaped like "a horseshoe pressed open," in the words of one Confederate general. Christopher Columbus Andrews, a Union brigade commander who would write a history of the Mobile campaign immediately after the war, described them more thoroughly. Andrews started with the "Old Spanish Fort," the mother work believed to have been a colonial outpost, "built on a bluff whose shape projects abruptly to the water." Overlooking the delta, this position had been much improved by the Confederates and included big guns meant to support Batteries Huger (pronounced *Hu-gee*) and Tracy below. Huger sat at the northern end of one of the delta's distinctive lobster-claw-shaped islands, where the Blakeley River splits from the Apalachee, and contained eleven guns. Tracy, with five guns, was situated upstream on the Apalachee's marshy western bank. Combined with pilings and torpedoes in the channels, these forts and the big guns on the bluff thoroughly commanded Mobile's eastern riverine approaches. On the land side encircling the revamped Spanish fortress was "a continuous line of breastworks and redoubts," Andrews explained, with a ditch in front "five feet deep and eight feet wide." This line was bordered at each end by swampy ground and felled timber. Its southern anchor was Fort McDermott, a giant earthen affair with a sally port, embrasures, heavy cannons, field pieces, mortars, bombproofs, and a magazine. It could easily hold four hundred men. From McDermott a trench ran several hundred yards up to the "Red Fort," named for the vermillion-hued clay the Rebels had spaded over the parapets. This position contained eight artillery pieces, including a formidable Columbiad christened the "Lady Slocomb" for the battery captain's wife. From there the line continued north and west for 600 yards, "striking the marsh on Bay Minette at a point about a mile above old Spanish Fort." All along the front of this main line were rifle pits and obstacles like chevaux-de-frise (logs driven through with long sharpened stakes meant to deter cavalry), abatis (felled timber with sharpened branches), debris, trip wires, and dreaded subterra torpedoes, or land mines. The land mines were considered fiendish by the Federals, a "mean way of fighting," as one of them expressed it.

Impressive as all of this was, the Confederates hedged their bets and, unknown to the Federals, provided themselves a handy escape route—a narrow wooden treadway below the bluffs across 1,200 yards of marsh to a point opposite Fort Tracy. From there, steamers could evacuate the garrison in an emergency. This turned out to be inspired foresight. "We felt ourselves to be in a trap," Stephenson declared as soon as he and his comrades occupied the defenses.[9]

Five miles to the north, Blakeley had once been a thriving county seat, but by 1865 was practically a ghost town with only a few dwellings, the old courthouse, and a river landing. It was and is a beautiful place, with ancient Indian shell middens, sandy streets, and enormous live oaks. The Confederate defenses wrapped around the village in a 3-mile-long trench punctuated by formidable redoubts and redans, though none were as dominating as McDermott. As at Spanish Fort, there were rifle pits and obstacles out front. Maury's problem

Figure 32. The site of the town and Battle of Blakeley is a state park today. Enormous live oaks shade the old streets, and Civil War earthworks thread through the area. Courtesy Library of Congress.

was not the physical quality of the Eastern Shore's defenses, of course, but rather the number and worth of the troops to man them. Just like at Selma, they were far too few. Blakeley was defended by less than 3,000 soldiers, a mix of Hood's veterans, old men, and young boys. Their commander was Gen. St. John R. Liddell, a native Mississippian who had seen extensive action in the western theater and lost a teenage son at Murfreesboro. Figuring the main attack would come at the center of the line, Liddell placed stalwart Missourians there, veteran Mississippians on the left, and untested Alabama State Troops in the center and on the right. It was a woefully thin gray line to be sure, the men spaced 10 feet apart. One of the Missourians cynically assessed the situation, "Our brigade could hold its lines, but we also knew that the old men and boys to our right . . . would get excited when the assault came, and shoot the tops of the trees off, and the Yanks would bulge right in on them." At Spanish Fort, fewer than two thousand graycoats were commanded by Gen. Randall Lee Gibson, a Louisiana planter's son and Yale graduate whom Bragg had labeled an "arrant coward" for his failure to take the "Hornet's Nest" at Shiloh. Being held in low esteem by Bragg, who was one of the Confederacy's worst generals, was hardly damning, and Gibson had steadily advanced in rank. Many of his men at Spanish Fort were fellow Louisianans who had proved their mettle in the Tennessee campaign, but they were depleted and war-weary. Gibson sympathized but exhorted them nonetheless, "You must dig, dig, dig. Nothing can save us here but the spade."[10]

Before Canby could attack he first had to get his thousands into position, and in that the very landscape and elements were against him. The easiest parts of the plan were the feint in southern Mobile County and the transport of Smith's troops across the lower bay, both of which went smoothly. On March 18, two thousand bluecoats used a rickety pier to debark at Cedar Point and admired the abandoned oyster shell revetments the Rebels had erected. "The oyster-shell fortifications displayed something of a Yankee ingenuity," a member of the Ninety-Fifth Illinois wrote, "and to us who were accustomed to a different material, presented a novel and interesting appearance." With no opposition, the men camped on the point and were soon "skirmishing not with rebels, but after oysters, of which they brought skiffs-full to the shore and furnished the camps with large supplies of this luxurious article of food." The worst trial these men faced was a "large-sized, ravenous" mosquito swarm.

During the next few days the bluecoats advanced up to the Fowl River disarming subterra shells, loudly beating drums and playing music at night, lighting multiple campfires, and noisily shelling the scrub, all in an effort to create the illusion of a larger force. Other than spotting a few enemy scouts and some light skirmishing, there was little incident, and on March 22, the Federals marched back south, boarded transports, and were ferried across the bay and up the Fish to join Smith's troops. Their feint had the desired effect. Mobile newspapers reported that 6,000 Yankees were on the move from the south.[11]

The Thirteenth Corps got underway on March 17. "The march was exceedingly difficult," Granger wrote, and he wasn't exaggerating. Twenty-year-old Charles Musser, a member of the Twenty-Ninth Iowa, found the scenery dull and the going rough, "Scrubby Pine and Live Oak, roads getting worse and worse fast." Another bluecoat dismissed the peninsula as a "barren, miserable desert." The next several days brought torrential rains, and the troops encountered seemingly endless bogs and swamps as they turned north. Musser explained, "one may judge how the roads is when 8 large Horses cant move a 12 Pounder Napoleon gun." Whenever a gun or a wagon got stuck, the troops had to stack arms, wade into the slop, and try to push it out. "Then we pull the donkeys," a Wisconsin soldier wrote, "mud up to our knees, but those long-ears weren't dumb. When things didn't move, they layed down." Granger himself threw his shoulder against a wheel at one point, cheering the troops. Civilian encounters were rare, but one old slave woman clasped her hands as some Iowans trudged by, exclaiming: "Glory, Hallelujah! The Lord's done heard us. There's eight hundred of us praying for you at Mobile!" After five days the troops finally joined the Sixteenth Corps at Dannelly's Mills, regimental bands playing "Oh, Ain't I Glad I've Got Out the Wilderness." From there the combined force marched north, and by March 27, advance elements were digging in before the Rebel works at Spanish Fort. "Boys all well and full of fight," Musser reported, "just as soon fight as not."[12]

Meanwhile, at Pensacola, Steele's men began their advance on March 20, and the going was just as difficult there. "We have to drag the wagons through by ropes nearly all the way," one bluecoat complained, "they are the worst roads I ever saw." The nearby woods rang with axes and shouts as hundreds of men chopped down trees and corduroyed the forest tracks in an effort to improve the going. As if things weren't already irritating enough, mounted

Rebels harassed the advance, destroying bridges and taking potshots at the troops. They included the Sixth Alabama led by the indefatigable James Holt Clanton, the very same who had blundered into Rousseau's troopers the previous summer and gotten his coat perforated for his trouble. Clanton and several hundred men made a stand along Pringle's Creek below the Alabama line. According to Andrews, this was a shallow stream "skirted with shrubbery." The north bank gradually sloped up to a little crest, along which "was a high fence of split rails, and a few hardwood trees with heavy foliage." There the Rebels waited. "I had an Enfield rifle which was captured from the enemy," one teenaged butternut later wrote, "and when they came rushing up on the other side . . . we commenced firing. I shot at least twenty times and others did as well, but owing to the smoke we could not tell what damage we did." This was a sharp little fight, but as hundreds more Federals charged toward the creek bank, the Confederates decided discretion was the better part of valor and retreated, burning a bridge behind them. Clanton, true to form, got into more trouble than necessary when he refused to surrender to several Yankees and shot the officer. As he wheeled his horse to flee, a heavy .58 caliber slug hit him in the back, knocking him to the ground. Incredibly, he survived and later surrendered to the Federals in Pensacola. On March 26 the bluecoats finally reached Pollard, destroying railroad track and burning some abandoned warehouses. Steele then turned his column west and by April 1 reached Blakeley. Artillery and musket fire were clearly audible down at Spanish Fort, where the final act was already underway.[13]

For the next two weeks, Mobilians not only heard the gunfire but saw it and felt it, too. On March 27, twenty-year-old Mary Waring recorded in her journal, "Today the enemy commenced operations by an attack on *Spanish Fort.*" Together with friends and neighbors she listened to the fearful racket: "The firing was heavy and continuous, the booming of Artillery was heard distinctly on this side, rendering us very uneasy as to the fate of our brave and gallant boys stationed in and around the fort." Citizens jammed the "wharves and all the high places in the city . . . watching the firing." Beside herself with worry, Waring paced about "like a restless spirit, trying to compose myself" to no avail. William Rix, a Vermont carpenter who had been working in Mobile when the war began and was then unable to leave, was also awed by the bombardments but hopeful of Union victory. "The windows of our houses, six miles away, rattled as if the old buildings were in an ague," he recorded, "and people were lulled to sleep by the music of death." Each morning Rix walked down to the waterfront, where he could observe the fresh Federal trenches dug the previous night "coiling like a boa constrictor around the victim." Hunkered down at Battery Gladden, Mumford couldn't see the Eastern Shore "on account of the hazy atmosphere," but he did note Confederate steamers and gunboats threading the delta back and forth, ferrying over supplies and returning with wounded. Amid all the anxiety and uncertainty, the local press tried to buck up the population. On April 2, the *Register* wrote, "we have guns, food, powder and ball, and men enough to hold and defend the fortifications . . . against all the power the enemy can now bring against it. But Mobile is not to 'go up!'"[14]

For their part, the Union common soldiers were sobered. "We are considerably astonished at the character of the obstacles, and the determination of the opposition," one Minnesota volunteer wrote to his aunt early in the siege. "The position against which the army is now operating is a very formidable defensive work, strongly garrisoned, and held with great pertinacity." James Newton, a young Wisconsin soldier, wrote to his mother, "We are right in the midst of a siege, similar to that of Vicksburg, 'only more so.'" He told her that as soon as his regiment arrived, they were "out skirmishing . . . and we had a great time dodging around the abattis in front of the fort." His greatest fear was that his officers would order a suicidal attack. "Since our ill fated charge on the fortifications at Vicksburg hardly a man in the Regt can think of charging again without shuddering," he confessed. Happily for Newton and his comrades, Canby had no such intention. The days of ruinous frontal assaults across open ground were over. Instead, the Federal strategy involved sappers methodically excavating zigzag approaches and long parallel trenches, which the main force could occupy. Advance parties scooped out rifle pits in front of those for sharpshooters, who endeavored to keep the Rebel defenders pinned down. The process was then repeated—more zigzags, another parallel, more rifle pits—until the besieged works were no longer tenable. The Rebels attempted to disrupt this seemingly inexorable enemy advance with deadly accurate artillery fire, sharpshooting, and limited sorties by small parties to drive back Federal work parties. To better protect themselves in their works, both sides placed head logs that they colorfully called "skull crackers" along the forward edge and scooped out a little dirt underneath so that they could fire from below the log and not be exposed.[15]

Canby concentrated his artillery and efforts on reducing Spanish Fort first. But during the early phase of the siege, the Confederates generally held the upper hand. Their guns were well protected and sighted in, and they enjoyed additional support from the gunboat *Morgan* and the hulking ironclad *Nashville*, whose shells smashed through the treetops, raining debris and iron fragments down on the scurrying bluecoats. According to one Yankee soldier, these rounds were often visible for their entire trajectory "rolling end over end way up in the air," compounding the terror. Gibson proudly reported, "For the first ten days my artillery, aided by well-trained sharpshooters, was able to cope with that of the enemy, sometimes silencing his guns, and often broke up his working parties in handsome style." But as more Union cannon were brought to bear, punishing artillery duels became routine. The Lady Slocomb was especially effective for the Rebels. She was positioned so that she could be pivoted to fire from one of three embrasures. When these openings were not in use, butternut artillerymen blocked them with large iron panels. Yankee sharpshooters kept an eye out for any movement of these panels and, the moment one was shifted to run the big gun out, poured in a hail of musket fire. It was nerve-racking for both sides and kept up until two direct artillery hits killed three of the Slocomb's gunners and disabled the gun. On April 4, Canby had seventy-five big guns situated and opened a sustained two-hour bombardment. Before ducking into a bombproof, one graycoat observed, "the entire length of their works was one blaze of artillery."[16]

Fortunately for the beleaguered Confederates, the Union navy wasn't able to effectively add its muscle to the contest. Torpedoes were the reason. Adm. Henry K. Thatcher, a forty-nine-year-old native Mainer who had resigned from West Point to join the old navy, called them "the only enemy we regard." He knew whereof he spoke. Again and again Union vessels came to grief because of these devices, which the Confederates liberally sowed in the river channels every chance they got. The monitor *Milwaukee* was the first, blasted on March 28 when she steamed into the mouth of the Blakeley River. She opened fire on a Rebel steamer in the delta and then trained her guns on Fort McDermott. According to Andrews, "when the first shell came screeching up the bay, there was immense cheering all along [the] line." But Union

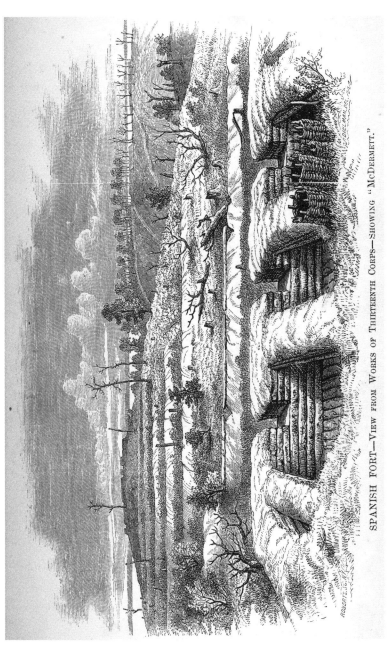

SPANISH FORT—VIEW FROM WORKS OF THIRTEENTH CORPS—SHOWING "McDERMETT."

Figure 33. Union siege works at Spanish Fort. The protective head logs, or "skull crackers," are clearly drawn. The name derived from the fact that the logs were continually knocked onto the soldiers' heads by hostile fire. Still, that was better than a bullet to the brain. From C. C. Andrews, *History of the Campaign of Mobile; Including the Cooperative Operations of Gen. Wilson's Cavalry in Alabama* (New York: D. Van Nostrand, 1889).

celebration was premature. Although the area had been previously swept for torpedoes by Union vessels dragging big chains, one apparently drifted into the monitor. "Just then a shock was felt on board," Andrews explained, "and it was known at once that a torpedo had exploded on her port side, abaft the after turret, and about forty feet from the stern." She slowly sank, giving the crew time to get safely on deck, and was some time longer fully settling, her flag and turrets easily visible above the surface. The single-turret monitor *Osage* took a hit the next day, sinking in 12 feet of water and losing four sailors. On April 1, the tin-clad steamer *Rodolph* struck a torpedo while she was salvaging the *Milwaukee*. A 10-foot gash was torn in her starboard bow, three men were killed, and eleven were wounded. Horrified, Thatcher backed his vessels into the upper bay, where they steamed around, fired shells that landed short, and attempted to concoct a strategy for dealing with the deadly torpedoes.[17]

Meanwhile, Confederate vessels ran between the city and the fortifications at will, though it was sometimes a dicey experience. George S. Waterman recalled one such episode decades later in an article for *Confederate Veteran* magazine. He had been hit on April 5 and that night boarded the *Heroine*, a former blockade runner transporting "a 'goodly fellowship' of the dead and wounded" to Mobile. Mixing past and present tense to give his account immediacy, Waterman wrote, "It was now time to make the run under forced draught. Pointing her sharp nose into the teeth of the wind, the *Heroine* passes the batteries with a rush, her wheels beating a devil's tattoo as they plow up the green water. All at once there is a flash, followed by a shell whizzing over our heads." They had been spotted, and "the fireworks began to play. Clippity clip! That shot grazes a stay and makes it sing. The vials of Uncle Sam's wrath burst forth so long before his breakfast hour. The sky is scored and blistered with the shells and balls, the heavens shine like the ceiling of a circus tent." As the wounded hugged the deck, the captain and pilot fearlessly stood at the helm, enemy shot splashing all around. The *Heroine* stayed her course, and eventually Waterman heard the pilot quip, "we ain't in any more danger now from sparks . . . than a maiden of two and forty summers." At last the vessel glided into the harbor, and the wounded were removed to private homes for treatment. "Luck did favor us," Waterman gratefully concluded.[18]

Because of this functioning water route, not only were Spanish Fort's wounded defenders quickly evacuated, but also those still in the trenches enjoyed frequent shipments of food, supplies, ammunition, and morale-boosting letters and care packages. On April 4, a Louisianan expressed his gratitude in a letter to the *Register*. "Many thanks to the kind ladies and gentlemen of Mobile for their liberal donations of hams, eggs, coffee, milk, bread, cakes, pies, etc.," he wrote. "I can assure the fair ladies of Mobile, in behalf of the regiment which I represent, that their kindness is highly appreciated by the officers and men of the Eastern Shore." He went on to state that these treats inspired them to "greater deeds of valor in driving back the hateful Yankees from Alabama's soil." He then concluded with a little poem, "Fair ladies of Mobile, / 'Tis with rapture that we feel, / That no more glorious cause / E'er won world's applause, / Than that we *fight for thee*."[19]

The siege of Spanish Fort included many highly localized incidents common to all historic events. The Yankees conducted much of their digging at night to escape detection, and this often placed them uncomfortably close to the Rebel lines. Andrews related the scary experience of some Iowans led by Capt. J. L. Noble. On the night of March 28, Noble was out in front of a Union battery with three hundred unarmed bluecoats digging new works. A small armed detachment accompanied the work party, but some of them had "stuck their guns with the bayonets on into the ground" in order to help their comrades dig. Around midnight it began to rain, and unbeknownst to Noble and his men, some Rebels crept up close. The graycoats sprang for the muskets and for a "few minutes the combat was hand to hand," Andrews wrote. "Capt. Noble called for his men to stand by him, which they did, with spirit, and kept their assailants out of the work." There was gunfire, and one Yankee and seven Rebels were killed. Noble's hair was clipped by a ball before the enemy retreated. Even more heart-stopping was the experience of Union Capt. L. K. Myers and six unarmed ammunition carriers who got lost between the lines on the night of March 29. Some men in a rifle pit directed them, and as they approached what they thought was their line, Myers hailed, "Boys, I am coming back again." A voice answered, "Come on," and the bluecoats soon came "face to face with a reb in gray, with sword at his side, and at his left about twelve men (butternut clothing) with arms at a ready." The two groups cautiously studied each other through the darkness as best they could. "Do you know where you are—do you belong to us?" the Confederate officer asked. Equal to the frightening moment, Myers replied, "Of course we belong to you, ain't you Confederate soldiers?" The reply was yes. Myers explained, "We are bringing out ammunition and wish to pass down the line with it, if you will direct us the way to the next post." But the Rebels were suspicious and after some verbal fencing in an attempt to remove any doubt, offered to accompany them. Myers realized then that his adversary "knew what we were" but wanted to hold any reaction until he could double his force at the next position. Fortunately for Myers, his men kept quiet, "trusting me to manage affairs." But then one of the butternuts exclaimed, "Hold on, these are not our men!" Each side fled from the other, the Rebels discharging their weapons into the gloom, and several balls snapped by Myers's head. Incredibly, Myers then decided to personally give chase, brandishing his revolver, and shot one Confederate soldier dead before a bullet smashed into his leg. He crawled back to his squad and was sent to the regimental hospital. For the next several days Rebel sharpshooters called out to his men, "How is Capt. Myers?" and the bluecoats taunted back, asking after their officer who had fled an unarmed party.[20]

By April 8, it was clear to Gibson that he couldn't hold much longer: "all my artillery was about silenced; . . . the enemy had largely increased his; . . . his working parties, greatly re-enforced at every point and carefully protected against sorties were pushing forward upon my flanks . . . at a rate that would bring them up to our main works; . . . and, finally, . . . there was unusual activity and movement in his lines." As if all of that weren't enough, the men were completely used up by the constant digging and battling, and there were no reinforcements to be had. It was time to get out, a conclusion considerably emphasized by a tremendous one-hundred-gun Union bombardment that night. Stephenson and his comrades cowered beneath the barrage. "The din was so great it distracted our senses," he wrote. "We could hardly hear each other speak and could hardly tell what we were doing. The cracking of musketry, the unbroken roaring of artillery, the yelling and shrieking of the shells, the bellowing boom of the mortars, the dense shroud of sulphurous smoke thickening around us—it was thought the mouth of the pit had yawned and the uproar of the damned was about us." Across the bay in town, citizens crowded the waterfront to watch the awesome display. Nearby, Rix climbed onto his rooftop, "among the slates and tiles," to watch the spectacle in private. He lamented his lack of poetic ability but then, in some of the most beautiful writing to come out of Civil War Alabama, described what happened when the firing suddenly ceased around midnight. "It seemed as if some omnipotent foot had stamped out the fire of the fight as you would a blazing match," he wrote. "The instantaneous arrest of the battle was positively sublime. I could not go down to my bed yet. I wanted to peer into the darkness and see if a finger of light would write on the black scroll the result—and it did." There before him, "beautiful rockets" ascended, "and ere long, miles below, the fleet sent up its brilliant response; and so for an hour the conversation went on in rainbow hues, pleasantly suggestive of peace."[21]

Rather than follow up that night, Canby waited until morning. In what must rank as one of the war's most impressive orderly withdrawals, Gibson took advantage of the interim to evacuate almost the entire garrison. Removing shoes and carrying their muskets on their left shoulders to hide any metallic glare, the troops, officers, and several hundred slave laborers clad in cast-off Confederate gray, filed down onto the treadway. Spanish moss had been spread over the boards to muffle their footsteps, and high marsh grass helped hide their movement from advanced Yankee pickets, whom they could actually hear conversing. At the end of the long walk, Stephenson could just discern "the dusky forms of several gunboats waiting to carry us away." The men were ferried up to Blakeley, then over to Mobile, where shocked citizens witnessed their arrival. "Still I had to believe the evidence of my own eyes," Waring wrote, "for our soldiers were passing by in squads, from an early hour, dirty, wet, and completely worn out." One boy who saw the bedraggled defenders "all along the wharves" described them as "shoeless, hatless, coatless and hungry."[22]

"Spanish Fort is ours at last!" James Newton exulted to his parents. Several hundred Confederates had been captured in the final days of the siege, and because they had regularly seen the Mobile newspapers, one of them informed Newton that Richmond had fallen. "They all seem to be heartily sick of the war," he continued, "some of them go so far as to say that the principal portion of inhabitants of Mobile are praying for our success." The intensity of what those men, blue and gray, endured at Spanish Fort may be gleaned by a Union ordnance report from May 5 that listed the "amount of both small-arm and artillery ammunition expended during the siege." Overall, the Federals discharged 498,715 musket rounds. The Twenty-First New York Battery expended 1,102 artillery shells; Battery K of the Sixth Michigan Heavy Artillery, 495 rounds; and so on unit by unit into the thousands of rounds. Yet for all of that, casualties were surprisingly low, a tribute to both sides' skill at siege warfare and good tactical sense. The Confederates lost ninety-three killed, 395 wounded, and something over three hundred captured. Canby lost fifty-two killed, 575 wounded, and thirty missing.[23]

Blakeley now stood alone, and Canby turned all his attention to it. Throughout the fighting down at Spanish Fort, the Thirteenth Corps had kept up the pressure on the Rebels in their front where the opposition was just as obstinate. "These Rebels here are the most determined and quarrelsome that we have ever battled with," Samuel Crawford of the Twentieth Iowa wrote to his parents. "Vicksburg or Fort Morgan Rebels are not to compare with them, for they will not let the least chance of hurting someone slip." Cpl. Carl Hatch of the Eighty-Third Ohio agreed. "Lying under the Rebel guns for three days," he informed his sweetheart, Susie, on April 5, "the novelty has worn off. 'Tis true the bursting of shells in close proximity to our dear selves is not as agreeable as we would wish, neither is the whizzing of a bullet the best music in the world." Three days later, the enemy fire was just as effective. "Shells have been promiscuously among us, tearing through tents, breaking guns, etc.," Hatch wrote. "Our tent was favored with one rascally piece weighing about two pounds, that, as the boys say, would *show daylight* through some of us if we sat in its way."[24]

During lulls there would sometimes be truces between blue and gray, and the men met halfway, according to one Yankee, "to swap lies for the ten minutes, and at other times to trade coffee for a Mobile paper and a plug of tobacco." There was no such fraternization between black Union troops and the Rebels. But one of the former, Sgt. Cassius M. Clay Alexander, reported a quirky exchange. "Say, Blacky, let's stop and eat some Dinner," a Rebel called out to him after they had been firing at one another all day. "All right," Alexander agreed. There was a period of quiet, and then Alexander shouted, "Hello, Reb?" "What do you want?" "Are you ready?" "No, not yet." After a bit longer, Alexander "cried for a chew of tobacco." A musket banged, and the Rebel snarled, "Chew that!"[25]

The final Federal assault came late in the day on April 9. Black troops began moving forward first on the Union right. "Lay low and mow the ground," a butternut officer shouted to his men when he discerned the attack, "the damned niggers are coming!" Undaunted, the Federals rushed forward, leaping over obstacles and debris, ducking into natural declivities for cover, dashing onward, driving Rebel skirmishers, and clambering into the main line. Finally, at 5:30 p.m. the entire Federal line surged forward, 16,000 strong. "There seemed to be a constant blaze of musketry along the breastworks," Andrews declared. Hatch wrote to Susie that "we rushed on, scrambling in the brush, jumping over logs, now stumbling over sharpened stakes, at another tripping up with the telegraph wires that were laced through here and there, knee high." Clearly, the Rebels were prepared. Hatch remarked that "such a storm of grape shells, canister, etc. I never wish to see again." The subterra torpedoes also proved to be frighteningly effective. An officer with the Ninety-Seventh Illinois stepped on one at the edge of the Rebel trench. The explosion blew off his leg and mortally wounded two soldiers. "It was no happy augury," Andrews admitted, "and as the wounded were borne along the trench and approach to the rear, the spirits of the beholders seemed depressed. Such is the terror of concealed dangers." Capt. F. M. Lollar charged forward with his men and suffered a humiliating incident. "The ground was rough, and in jumping off a log my sword scabbard got tangled up with my legs and threw me headlong," he sheepishly admitted. Loading and firing as fast as he could, twenty-year-old Rebel William Kavanaugh called the assault an "imposing sight." Tongues of flame darted along the lines, acrid smoke rolled across the battlefield, cannon boomed, men cried out, and hearty Yankee cheers rose above the din. "It appeared to me that all hell had turned loose," Kavanaugh recalled, "and that every man in the U.S. was practicing on us with repeating rifles." Despite dogged resistance by veteran graycoats like Kavanaugh, the green Alabama State Troops melted before the onslaught, and within minutes it became clear that the entire line would crumble. "We could see heavy masses of the enemy crossing the works on the right," one Missouri butternut recalled, "where the Alabama 'boy-reserves' were stationed, and wheeling to the right and left, firing down our line as they advanced. We saw in a moment 'the jig was up.' A few hundred men in an open fight could do nothing with the twenty-two thousand who had made that charge. Our first thought was 'escape.'"26

On the Rebel left, black troops poured into the works. A Union officer wrote, "As soon as our niggers caught sight of the retreating figures of the rebs the very devils could not hold them. Their eyes glittered like serpents and with yells and howls, like hungry wolves, they rushed for the rebel work." Crawford remembered that the "excitement among the Negroes . . . was fierce and revengeful. Their battle cry was 'Fort Pillow.' Their officers had to draw their revolvers and hold them to their faces to keep them from ending the days of the cowering rebels on their knees begging mercy." Other Confederates attempted to find white Yankee soldiers to surrender to, some ran for the river, and small pockets kept fighting. One butternut lieutenant feared that he and his men "were to be butchered in cold blood" and ordered them to "die fighting to the last." Two white Union officers attempting to restore order were shot down by their own troops. Andrews admitted that some prisoners were murdered but claimed that such acts were far from universal among the black Federals. "A colored soldier of the Fiftieth regiment found his former young master among the prisoners," he wrote. "They appeared happy to meet, and drank from the same canteen." In the parlance of the day, the bottom rail was now on top.[27]

The final assault on Blakeley was Alabama's largest land battle and one of the last of the entire Civil War. That it came only hours after Lee's surrender at Appomattox Courthouse did not lessen the pride of the Union veterans who made the charge nor of the Confederates who held to the last moment. General Grant was another matter, and in his memoirs he expressed frustration about how Union strategy against the Port City unfolded. "I had tried for more than two years to have an expedition sent against Mobile when its possession by us would have been of great advantage," he wrote. "It finally cost us lives to take it when its possession was of no importance, and when, if left alone, it would within a few days have fallen into our hands without any bloodshed whatsoever." Federal casualties at Blakeley were 116 killed and 655 wounded. Confederate losses were never accurately tallied, but were probably slightly less. Most of the garrison was taken prisoner, however, including General Liddell. "I suppose now slavery is gone," he sadly remarked to Canby the following day. Only a handful of men managed to escape. Forts Huger and Tracy held out a little longer, but were abandoned on April 11, and Mobile lay open to the Federals.[28]

With less than 5,000 men to defend the city, and now vulnerable to Union naval might from the rivers, Maury reluctantly abandoned Mobile. Church bells pealed, and anxious citizens thronged the streets and wharves as the remnant Rebel navy steamed upstream for Demopolis and the weary infantry marched out of town along the Mobile and Ohio Railroad tracks. In a last act of defiance, cavalry set fire to the confiscated cotton on the riverfront, but ever-practical locals rushed in to douse the flames, preserving at least some semblance of an economy.

There was now a power vacuum, and with no official restraints in place, hundreds went wild. "The streets were filled that morning as in the season of Mardigras," Rix later wrote, "and the tide in the different thoroughfares set in one direction, converging on the government warehouses on Water Street." Men smashed the heavy locks and pushed open the doors, and crowds surged after them to loot the contents. "All day long," Rix continued, "like a colony of ants, men, women and children were rushing through the streets in jealous fear of not getting their share." People of all classes partook of the opportunity. Rix witnessed one woman, "once of the better sort," pushing home a heavy flour barrel, while a stout Irishwoman with beefy forearms marched resolutely along with "a side of bacon balanced on her head and as many hams as her arms can clasp." Coffee, sugar, and rice disappeared quickly, and then people began stealing weapons, "loads of sabers, and bayonets and Springfield rifles, which were found in the original cases." Lastly, the maddened throng found boxes of signal rockets and began setting them off in glee. "The wonder was that the mob was not self-quelled by being blown to atoms," Rix marveled.[29]

Fortunately for Mobile, the chaos didn't last long. Admiral Thatcher ferried 8,000 Federals commanded by Granger across the bay, landed them two miles south of town, and then moved a gunboat and several river monitors "directly in front of the city." He and Granger dispatched a brief note to Mayor R. H. Slough. "Sir," they wrote, "your city is menaced by a large land and naval force. We demand its immediate and unconditional surrender." Desperate to avoid catastrophe by out-of-control citizens or by Federal bombardment, Slough raced out to meet the bluecoats in a rattletrap carriage drawn by two white horses and flying a large white flag. "The city has been evacuated by the military authorities," he informed Granger and his staff. "Your demand has been granted, and I trust, gentlemen, for the sake of humanity, all the safeguards which we can throw around our people will be secured to them."[30]

Federal troops marched into town early in the evening of April 12, flags fluttering and drums beating. Citizens disappeared into their houses, sullenly watched, or openly celebrated. "I have a sad tale to tell you," one man wrote to his sister. "At about 4 o'clock the advance of the Yankee army reached the city at the same time as their boats arrived at the foot of Govt St. As soon as the negroes and puerile white people saw the boat at the wharf they rushed down the street shouting and hurrahing." Another citizen recalled that the city "was resonant with every patriotic refrain from the 'Star Spangled Banner' to 'John Brown's Soul Is Marching On.' Every one realized for the first time, as he listened to the 'tramp, tramp' of orderly files, that 'the boys' had come." Rix headed for the Custom House, where he just missed a speech by General Granger. "O, it is all rose-color," a man nearby quipped. "Granger says it is a free country—do as we damn please—only we must not show our noses on the street after dark." The Federal soldiers bivouacked at various places— Bienville Square downtown, Choctaw Point, and out the Stone Street Road. The sight of armed black soldiers upset many whites, and the new social order was a profound shock. "We came across a number of negro children," Kate Cumming fumed, "and I politely asked them to let us pass, but they very rudely said, 'The middle of the road is for you and the sidewalk for us.'" There would be adjustments for everyone to be sure, some pleasant, others painful, but at long last Mobile's war was over. Not so Alabama's. Upstate, Harry Wilson was still on the march.[31]

# 9

## Montgomery Falls

*Lawd! I didn't know there was so many Yankees in the world!*
*—a Montgomery boy*

On Sunday April 2, 1865, twenty-five-year-old Ellen Blue of Montgomery made her way to church. She had been ill for days and was happy to get out of the house, "a blessed privilege." Upon entering the sanctuary, she found many of the pews empty. "There is so much anxiety felt about the proximity of the raiders that many people did not go to Church," she wrote in her diary. The following day Blue and her neighbors learned of Selma's fall, and though some hoped the Yankee force would head south, most feared Montgomery was next. "I have found it hard to analyze my feelings today," Blue wrote. "I do not feel alarm or any great excitement but a stirred feeling deeper than the surface which renders me unfit for any employment."[1]

Montgomery was not an industrial hub like Selma, though it did have an arsenal, a foundry, various machine shops, and government warehouses and hospitals. Its primary importance was as a railroad center and the state capital. But as the Cradle of the Confederacy, its capture would represent a powerful symbolic victory far in excess of its limited military significance. Municipal and Confederate authorities knew this and moved quickly to prepare as best they could. Just as at Mobile, Governor Watts ordered all saloons closed, cotton confiscated, and every able-bodied man into the ranks. He also began making plans to evacuate the state government to Eufaula. Meanwhile, the treasurer whisked all of the state money to nearby Coosa County where he stacked the bills into canvas sacks, wired the sacks tightly shut, weighted them with chains, and submerged them into a muddy creek. Whatever happened at

Montgomery, the state of Alabama would at least have access to funds in the aftermath. Brig. Gen. Daniel Adams, a thrice-wounded, one-eyed officer who had battled Wilson north of Selma, and Brig. Gen. Abraham Buford, a West Point graduate and veteran of many fights, took command of the city defenses and vowed to hold them. Since Rousseau's raid the previous summer, much had been done to fortify Montgomery. A semicircular line of trenches, redoubts, and redans looped around the city. There was some artillery but nowhere near as much as at Selma or Mobile, and only 1,800 troops were available, the usual late-war assemblage of jaded veterans, convalescents, old men, and boys, with a fire company thrown into the mix. No one, least of all Adams, should have expected to slow down, much less to defeat, Wilson's blue columns.[2]

West of Selma, the Yankees encountered rolling prairie land alternating with swamps and creeks. "We were at last within the richest planting district of the South," Wilson wrote. "The roads, bordered by hedges of Cherokee roses, were redolent with spring perfumes." The men were in high spirits and, despite the occasional Confederate scout or skirmisher on their flanks, remained confident of success. The good feelings were augmented by the large numbers of black people who were continually joining the column, singing the men's praises. In an effort to manage them, Wilson had the able-bodied males formed into military companies and marched along at the rear by white officers. He attempted to discourage women, children, and the elderly by ordering them away and burning bridges, all to no avail. Freedom had come. It was grand, and the euphoria spread. McGee and his comrades decided to observe one slave celebration up close and personal. The grinning bluecoats crowded into a 16-foot-square log cabin where fifty black men and women were "jumping up and down, clapping their hands (patting juber), puffing and blowing like steam engines, and sweating like race horses" to the accompaniment of fiddles, tambourines, banjos, and a man "rattling the bones." Eager to get in on the fun, McGee pushed in to the middle of the room where he bumped up against a 200-pound "buxom form of a wench." Overjoyed to be dancing with a Yankee soldier, she redoubled her exertions, stomping McGee's toes, scraping his shins, and showering him with sweat.

Freedom had come, the auction block and the lash were now things of the past, and it was a memorable day for all.[3]

On April 10 and 11, the troopers rode through Lowndesboro, then and now one of Alabama's most beautiful little communities. Legend has it that they didn't stop because a local doctor told them there was a smallpox epidemic raging. As they trotted down the town's sandy street after dark, a member of the Fourth Iowa was beguiled by the scene. "It was past midnight," he wrote. "No living creature appeared in the town, not a light was seen, not a sound was heard except the subdued rattle of arms in the columns. . . . It was a dream world, through which the war-worn soldiers march silently in the deep shadows of the oaks." While Lowndesboro's lovely houses were spared pillage, nearby plantations didn't fare so well. Among them was that of Judge John Bragg, Gen. Braxton Bragg's brother. Before the war, John Bragg divided his time between Mobile and his wife's native Lowndes County. In one of the war's many little ironies, the family had transferred most of their furnishings, silver, china, and mirrors to the Lowndes County locale in the belief that Mobile would fall after New Orleans. This put them and their treasures directly in Wilson's path. Knowing of the judge's relationship to General Bragg, Yankee raiders broke into the house and terrorized the family. They seized the judge and lifted him onto the polished dining room table where they secured a noose to a ceiling hook and placed it around his neck. This was fine fun for coarsened soldiers, and they made a great show of getting ready to hoist the judge off the table. The Bragg children went into hysterics, which fortunately moved the bluecoats enough to spare him. Down he came into the arms of his family. They were then roughly hustled outdoors and the mansion torched. Wilson had strictly forbidden this kind of behavior, of course, but loosely supervised raiding parties committed numerous depredations along the march, scarring the memories of Alabama's planter elites and their descendants for generations.[4]

Wilson fully expected a "sharp fight" at Montgomery. But at the last minute, the Confederate departmental commander at Meridian, Gen. Richard Taylor, ordered Adams and Buford to burn the cotton, evacuate the city, and retire to Columbus, Georgia, an important manufacturing city on the Alabama line. According to the *Advertiser*, Montgomery's citizens greeted the abrupt change "with stupor and no little dissatisfaction." A delegation of leading residents called on General Adams for reassurance and an explanation. The interview was unsatisfactory. To begin with, the delegation asked if the Confederate authorities intended to defend the city or not, as it had been earlier assured, and Adams replied that the "query was based on the most idle curiosity, which he would not gratify." Stunned, the citizens then begged him not to burn the cotton for fear the city would be destroyed. Adams rebuffed them, saying his orders were to burn the cotton and that was what he planned to do. Forty-one-year-old Sarah Follansbee, a native New Englander and schoolteacher, reported that "great consternation spread over the whole city." Besides the thousands of cotton bales riverside and stuffed into warehouses downtown, there were cotton barricades across the streets, including one near Follansbee's house where the bales actually abutted wooden picket fences. Despite the fears and protests, Adams was as good as his word, and retreating Rebels started firing the cotton on April 11. "The scene which followed beggars description," the *Advertiser* wrote. "Dense columns of gray smoke piled above the city and almost shut out the light of the sun. Women with frightened countenances were seen running hither and thither, crying and wringing their hands, and hundreds of excited persons were endeavoring to secure the furniture from adjacent houses." In contrast to the newspaper's description of hysterical women flitting about, Follansbee and some of her female friends determinedly approached the Confederate soldiers about to torch the bales on their street. Much argument ensued, until an officer acquainted with one of the ladies happened by and ordered the men away. "A number of us sat perched on the bales till long after midnight," Follansbee wrote, "fearing another cohort would come for the same purpose." Downtown the fire companies endeavored to contain the infernos. "The members of the negro fire company especially deserve great praise," the Montgomery *Daily Mail* reported. "The brave fellows, reckless of life and limb, met the furious flames at every advance, and kept the conflagration in check." And so those who had had no say in Alabama's disastrous decision to secede from the Union played an instrumental role in saving its capital city from destruction by the very men theretofore sworn to defend it.[5]

Freed of Confederate military authority, Montgomery's mayor and several leading civilians rode west under a flag of truce. During the wee hours of April 12 they encountered Union troops at Catoma Creek, delighting the commander with their surrender offer. Troopers of the Fourth Kentucky Cavalry were the first into town, clopping up to the capitol steps where they dismounted and awaited the main van, which arrived around 8:00 a.m. "With perfect order in column of platoons," Wilson wrote, "every man in his place, division and brigade flags unfurled, guidons flying, sabers and spurs jingling, bands playing patriotic airs, and the bugles now and then sounding the calls, the war-begrimed Union troopers, batteries, ambulances, and wagons passed proudly through the city." One little boy gaped in open-mouthed wonder, "Lawd! I didn't know there was so many Yankees in the world!" The mayor formally surrendered Montgomery, and General McCook assured the gathered citizens that order would be preserved and that they would be protected. One gratified Yankee major took note of the momentous occasion: "The Stars and Stripes are floating over the capitol of Alabama." It had been four long years.[6]

Sarah Follansbee was awakened that morning when her servant Milly dashed into her room shouting, "Come! Come see the Yankees!" Throwing on some clothes, Follansbee and her neighbors gathered along the streets where they beheld the Federals "looking brilliant with buttons and '*accoutrements*.'" At last able to express her native Union pride, Follansbee thought the galloping men "fine looking" with their clean linen "as if right fresh from the laundry," bright brass buttons, and "sabers drawn and clashing." An officer assured the ladies that the streets would be patrolled and that they could have guards for their homes if they wanted them.[7]

The *Advertiser* was less enamored of the spectacle, particularly the reaction of local blacks, "grinning and rejoicing" and shaking hands with their new friends. "The deluded wretches thought the day of Jubilee had come," the paper reported, "and they were going to have things their own way." The press was not a little satisfied to add that instead Union officers ordered them to go home and that some troopers even used the flats of their sabers to drive off loiterers. This did little to dampen their enthusiasm. While black children and women rejoiced, hundreds of young men were eager to join up and wear the Union blue. Unable to take them all, the Federals were bewildered about which ones to choose. One bluecoat hit upon the idea of having them compete in foot races for the privilege to enlist. This proved entertaining to the white soldiers, and Hosea joked that the winners soon comprised the "crack athletic corps in the army."[8]

The Federals did not long delay in Montgomery. They destroyed the arsenal, some steamboats, and railroad rolling stock but otherwise left the town alone. Wilson bivouacked his men on the eastern outskirts and decided on

his next move. Captured newspapers reported Richmond's fall and Lee's retreat. Canby needed no support on the coast. Therefore a continued march
east seemed best. The war was all but over, but Wilson wanted to ensure that
retreating Rebels couldn't regroup in Georgia for a bloody last stand. "The
situation as I still saw it," he wrote, "made it my duty to continue 'breaking
things' along the main line of Confederate communications through central
Alabama, Georgia, and the Carolinas." Columbus was next, where a frenzied
populace and ragtag Confederate force prepared for the worst.[9]

All across the southern half of Alabama, Federal troops were moving. On
April 12, at roughly the same time that Wilson's troopers were making camp
outside Montgomery, Canby wrote to chief of staff Maj. Gen. Henry Hal-
leck, informing him that 10,000 soldiers had occupied Mobile. "A. J. Smith,
with 14,000 men, moves tomorrow for Selma and Montgomery by land," he
continued. "[Gen. Frederick] Steele, with 10,000, in a day or two by water.
[Gen. Benjamin] Grierson with 4,000 cavalry, will operate on the east of the
Alabama, and [Gen. Thomas J.] Lucas, with 2,000 west of the Tombigbee."
Thatcher's light-draft steamers and gunboats would convey Steele's force and
secure critical points on the rivers.[10]

What was left of the Confederate command structure in the Deep South
frantically tried to cobble together a coherent defense against these multiple
forces. On April 14, Taylor wrote to Maj. Gen. Howell Cobb at Columbus
that matters about Mobile "will occupy me for several days in this quarter, and
the enemy will require watching from Eastport, Tuscaloosa, and Vicksburg."
He vainly hoped Canby would swing his army's attention west of the Mississippi, "as we have our hands full without it." From Chunchula, in northern
Mobile County, D. W. Flowertree, an assistant adjutant general, sent a hurried message to Gibson, then fleeing Mobile with the remnants of his command. "Impress on Spence [a cavalry officer] the importance of destroying
the bridges and trestles as he retires." In a separate missive to Spence, Flowertree instructed, "You had better place the section of light artillery, which you
have, beyond Eight Mile Creek without necessary delay." From Demopolis,
the local military commander hurriedly ordered a cavalry colonel to "retain
sufficient mounted men to scout the river south of Demopolis." From Meridian, yet another officer alerted Forrest that enemy cavalry "is reported mov-

Figure 34. In this remarkable image, Federal steamboats moor at an Alabama River landing in the spring of 1865. A columned mansion is visible on the bluff above. Marshall Dunham Photograph Album, Mss. 3241, Louisiana and Lower Mississippi Valley Collections. Courtesy Louisiana State University Libraries, Baton Rouge.

ing up the river on Claiborne. We should resist his crossing the river . . . as long as possible."[11]

None of these and countless other communications made any difference. The few remaining Rebel soldiers and webfeet were beaten, demoralized, and on the run. Mississippian W. P. Chambers had managed to escape from the debacle at Blakeley but wandered for days with a "burning fever and delirium." By April 12, he and a few comrades had reached Suggsville, where they slept in a Presbyterian church. "We had about a half inch of candle," he later recalled, "and finding a 'note-book' convenient we sang a few old pieces of music before going to sleep." That and the cushioned pews comforted them considerably, but the exhausted men were of no use for further military service. At nearby Claiborne, a contingent of the Fifteenth Alabama Cavalry clashed with some of Lucas's Federals. One graycoat described what happened. "Colonel Myers then gave the command to charge, and at the same time the 'Rebel yell' went up. We drove the advance guard back about one-fourth mile, when we came in full contact with the enemy consisting of about 3,000 men." This was considerably more than they had bargained for, and after a brief skirmish they fell back toward Choctaw Bluff. The butternuts fared no better to the west. Cavalry attempting to slow the Union pursuit of Maury's remnants confronted the Yankees at Eight Mile Creek in northern Mobile County. "Quite a brisk skirmish occurred at the bridge," an Ohio correspondent reported to the readers back home. The Rebels were brushed away before they could burn the crossing. "Night coming on, the enemy being mounted, and we without cavalry, the pursuit was not continued, and our forces encamped at Whistler. We buried four of the enemy's dead. Our loss was three wounded."[12]

Meanwhile, the hodgepodge Rebel navy steamed northward to Nannahubba Bluff, where the Alabama and Tombigbee Rivers converge to form the Mobile. Learning that Selma had fallen, Commander Ebenezer Farrand ordered his pilots to steam up the Tombigbee for Demopolis, which was still in Confederate hands. His vessels consisted of steamboats, ironclads, blockade runners, and a range of other craft that joined them en route. There would eventually be eighteen vessels, including the *Nashville, Baltic, Morgan, Southern Republic, Heroine, Black Diamond*, and *Marengo*. The ungainly flotilla must have been an extraordinary sight to the backcountry children who no doubt witnessed it. One can imagine the fireside scenes decades later, when they regaled their grandchildren about when the big ships and ironclads chuffed up their muddy and familiar waters. William Lochiel Cameron was a young officer on the *Nashville* who was at first frustrated by the river but eventually became soothed by it. "Although the river was deep, it was narrow and crooked," he later wrote. "Our vessels were long and wide and every once in a while we were into the bank, first on one side and then on the other." At night, tied to a tree riverside, he and his mates were lulled to sleep by the water sluicing along the sides, and during the following days they made "a pleasure journey" out of their retreat. After all, it was springtime in Alabama, and war now seemed very far away. "The trees along the banks of the river were just covering their limbs with a lovely green," he wrote, "and the birds were singing merrily as they flew from bough to bough."[13]

The Confederate fleet soon reached Demopolis, where it created a sensation. Local belles showered their attentions on the sailors and marines. Cameron and several others were invited into one woman's parlor where her two daughters served a scrumptious dessert. Cameron later enthused, "Just think what it was to us to eat strawberries and cream out of real china plates with silver spoons and to drink cool lemonade from cut glass tumblers offered by lovely maidens who had beautiful eyes, rosy lips and altogether engaging manners!" It was a young man's dream, and Cameron lingered long after most of the others had returned to the fleet. Not all of the Rebels felt so duty bound, however, and with news of Lee's surrender desertions spiked. The local army commander complained to a fellow officer, "I am reliably informed that some of the pilots, engineers, and others of the crews of the steamboats now at this post are deserting and going down the river in boats and skiffs of various kinds, with a view of getting to Mobile." Scouts were ordered to arrest them but proved just as apt to abandon the service. The Confederacy was rapidly evaporating.[14]

In the midst of these tumultuous events, word of Lincoln's assassination arrived, further agitating civilians, soldiers, and ex-slaves. In Mobile, Rix was one of the first people in the state to hear the news. He had gone for an evening walk down on Front Street to contemplate the river and take the air. The waterfront was practically deserted, with only a few fishermen nearby. "I saw on the distant water a boat approaching," Rix later recalled, "and knew by the regular lift of the oars, as they flashed in the setting sun, that it was a man-of-war's yawl." An officer stood in the stern, one hand on the tiller and the other holding a sheaf of papers. At his command, the sailors tossed the oars (lifted them out of the water and held them perpendicularly). The craft gently glided to the wharf, where firm sunburned hands made it fast, and the officer hastily clambered out with a touch of his hat to Rix. As he dashed into town, the sailors informed the Vermont carpenter that Lincoln had been shot. Fearful of possible retribution by the occupying force, Rix hurried home as fast as he could go. "The next morning the news had spread through the town," he wrote. To his wonder most Mobilians seemed genuinely sorry. As for the bluecoats, the event affected them "like the cold pattering of a rain." Officers bustled about, "wrapped in official reserve."[15]

At the opposite end of the state, in Huntsville, Mary Jane Chadick heard the news on April 15, a Saturday. The mails being subject to censorship, she had gone to see the provost marshal to get some letters approved. "While examining them, he remarked to me, 'We have just got some news that I fear will be worse for you Southern people than anything that has yet happened. President Lincoln was shot last night, at the theatre in Washington, and died this morning. Seward was stabbed, but it is thought will recover.'" Stunned, she asked if a "Southern man had done the deed." No, he replied, "It was done by Booth." Like many Southerners, she especially feared what would happen now that Andrew Johnson, known to be much less conciliatory toward the South, was president. Clement Clay, the former Confederate senator, could only cry, "God help us!" when he learned of the tragedy.[16]

Three days later, Federal authorities in Huntsville held official observances to mark the solemn occasion. "All business was suspended," Chadick wrote, "and the business houses draped in mourning." A procession of troops filed through the downtown streets "with arms reversed, and flags tied with crepe and the band playing a funeral dirge." Most citizens were respectful or at least chose to remain indoors, but some few were foolish enough to manifest joy. One young man was seen laughing with some belles, and soldiers searched his home, threatening to burn it. Two young women were arrested for celebrating and were harshly lectured before being released. Throughout the state, the pro-Union newspapers, now to the fore, registered regret. In Montgomery, the *Daily Mail* wrote that Lincoln's death "is lamented by Union men of the South quite as much as those of the North; and it is a calamity in which we of the South are far more deeply interested, even than our fellow-citizens of the Northern States of the Union." In Mobile, the *Daily News* echoed Rix's observations, writing that a "general gloom seemed cast over the brave officers who have fought so long and well the battle of the Union." Reaction among former slaves was equally sorrowful. In Mobile they wore black armbands, and one man in Selma expressed the sentiments of many when he declared, "Mr. Abraham Lincoln died a warrior for this country." As for those Rebel soldiers still in the field, they were simply sick of all the killing and worried that Lincoln's conciliatory gestures toward the South would now be replaced by draconian persecution.[17]

It was obvious that the war was ending, but intact Confederate forces were still confronting the Federals, albeit feebly. And, unfortunately, men were still dying. East of Montgomery, Wilson pushed hard for Columbus, with only light resistance. McGee described one brief clash during which several Rebels were captured. When the butternuts anxiously inquired what was to become of them, a Union officer dismounted, "took their guns and broke them around a tree, and told them to go home and stay there." As the Yankees trotted away, "the rebels hallooed after them, 'Good bye, boys; that's much better than we expected.'"

If the enemy wasn't providing serious trouble, the Alabama landscape certainly was. On April 15, the command reached Line Creek and had to traverse what McGee called "the worst swamp we ever saw." Horses became bogged down and had to be stripped of saddles and pulled out by hand. Then it began raining. One Iowa sergeant shuddered at the memory of the ordeal. "Alligators of immense size we saw—in large numbers, sleeping on logs, and snakes of all kinds and size, and other kinds of reptiles we never saw before were all around us. It gave us the Horrors." This was the brooding, sinister South of novelists and storytellers, home to maroons, haints, and maddened animals, far scarier than scattered Rebel cavalry.[18]

On Easter Sunday, the troopers reached Tuskegee. McGee thought it "a most beautiful place, containing a court-house, a college, several churches, and some of the finest evergreens we ever saw." A Wisconsin major agreed. "It is one of the finest towns I have ever met with in the South. The most exquisite taste is manifested in the ornamentation of the ample grounds around each dwelling." Indiana private Alva Griest likened the town to a "flower garden, a paradise on a small scale." One of Upton's officers admired the "fine homes, beautiful lawns, and pretty girls." It was springtime, and given the presence of comely ladies and the absence of much real fighting, young men's thoughts were understandably wandering. The Yankees only tarried a few hours, long enough to provoke anxiety among the students at the Female College. Carrie Hunter expected the bluecoats to burn the town and was amazed when they didn't. Still, her fears were not wholly allayed. Several of her friends had their jewelry filched by the enemy in what she termed an act of "yankeefied yankeeism." When the troopers spurred east again, the usual crowd of black people excitedly followed. McGee described "men, women, and children on horseback, ass-back, mule-back, cow-back; in carts, wagons, wheel barrows, and every other way you could think." Clattering and rejoicing, this improbable cavalcade followed behind the increasingly exasperated Federals.[19]

Shortly thereafter, the Yankees reached the state line, and Columbus was visible below them. "There were some forts west of the river well filled with artillery and well manned with rebel soldiers," McGee observed. The southern half of Alabama is divided from Georgia by the Chattahoochee River, and Columbus lies along the old Fall Line, where a drop in elevation meant tumbling water and a good power source. Like Selma, the city was a critical Confederate manufacturing center with extensive war-making industries. Besides all of the foundries, machine shops, rail yards, and warehouses with their armament, ammunition, uniforms, supplies, and railroad stock sitting around, two Confederate warships lay in the river under repair, the nearly finished ironclad *Jackson* and the gunboat *Chattahoochee*. These vessels were especially attractive prizes.

West of Columbus on the Alabama side was the small suburb of Girard. Three bridges connected the two towns, one of them that of the Columbus and Western Railroad. In order to protect these crossings, the Confederates had erected a series of earthworks on nearby hilltops, as McGee and his comrades saw. The works were extensive and well made, but again there were too few troops to man them. There was yet another good river crossing 35 miles north of Columbus where the Montgomery and West Point Railroad had a bridge. The Rebels had thrown up a square earthwork there on the Alabama side known as Fort Tyler. Wilson decided he would attack both West Point and Columbus, the bulk of his force devoted to the latter place.[20]

The Yankees targeted Fort Tyler first, and it fell after a brisk fight that cost the Union twenty-nine casualties. But the big show was downriver, where Wilson ordered a night assault for April 16. Almost 3,000 bluecoats participated, and according to an Iowa trooper, the enemy "at once opened every gun they had on us, and the rattle of their muskets was steady and regular." Another Federal described enemy projectiles "leaving a fiery streak behind them" as they hurtled overhead. Happily for these men almost all of the gunfire was too high, and casualties were remarkably light. Wilson remarked that though the flashes and roars were frightening, "it was far more noisy than destructive." In a rush the Federals mobbed the Franklin Street Bridge where desperate Southrons met them hand to hand on the Alabama side. Gilpin described how a Rebel colonel spurred into the melee, attempting to inspire his men. "He raised himself in the saddle and cried, 'Rally round your chief! Rally!' and just then, whack, one of our boys hit him over the head with his carbine, and off the old fellow tumbled among his staff." Another butternut attempted to burn the bridge and was knocked down just as he struck the match.

The Federals poured into Columbus where chaos and destruction followed. In the aftermath, McGee tallied their trophies—the two war ships, five steamboats, fifteen locomotives, 250 railroad cars, fifty-two field guns, 100,000 rounds of artillery ammunition, 115,000 bales of cotton, and 1,200 prisoners. At long last, Wilson's men were gone from Alabama soil. They proceeded on to Macon with no opposition and captured Jefferson Davis a few weeks later in southern Georgia. The *New York Times* lauded Wilson's Raid as an "astonishing sweep" that accomplished much at little cost, demonstrating "the utter hollowness of the Confederacy." Whether or not the raid helped conclude the war, as its advocates argued, or was simply gratuitous destruction when it no longer mattered, as Southern partisans claimed, is a pointless argument. Until there was a formal surrender, the fighting and destruction would continue.[21]

Federal troops marching up from the coast got word of a possible conclusion to hostilities in late April. Lucius Hubbard wrote to his aunt about their reaction: "The heat, dust and fatigue were forgotten; the weary became rested and the footsore suddenly cured. Officers and soldiers abandoned themselves to the most extravagant demonstrations of joy." The men broke ranks and fired into the air against orders, threw down their weapons, and laughingly wrestled each other in the dirt like little boys. Down at Mobile Bay, naval salutes thundered across the water. Years later, an ex-slave named Gus Askew recalled the war's end at Eufaula. He told an interviewer for the WPA that as a lad he saw General Grierson's troops march into the area with flags snapping and drums beating. The big soldiers were intimidating to Gus and his pals. "But we went away from the so'jers and had a good time 'mongst ourselves like we always done when there wasn't any cotton pickin.'"[22]

Further evidence that the war was finally over came with the large numbers of paroled Confederate soldiers returning to the state. Wales Wood of the Ninety-Fifth Illinois was camped at Montgomery where he and his comrades witnessed some of these parolees. "Day after day, a continuous stream of Southern officers and enlisted men . . . were now coming back, defeated, crest-fallen, satisfied with war, glad that it was ended, and apparently no longer of rebellious spirit." Among those Wood saw were Generals Bragg and Pillow and Adm. Raphael Semmes.

The wives and families of these beaten graycoats were relieved and thankful. In Huntsville, Chadick recorded feelings of "great joy, mixed with sadness"

Figure 35. Gus Askew, interviewed in his
eighties, vividly recalled the day the Yankees
marched into Eufaula seven decades earlier.
Courtesy Library of Congress.

when her husband returned. So much had been endured "for the sake of the cause," to no avail. In Barbour County, Victoria Clayton saw a man approaching her house on horseback. "Wondering who this stranger was, and watching him closely until he reached the house, I found to my delight that he was our beloved lost one returned to us." Henry DeLamar Clayton, her husband, had been a major general and fought in every western battle from Perryville to Franklin. She thought his survival "a miracle" and praised God in heaven. Many other Southern women were not so lucky. As April gave way to May, there remained some active Confederate forces—General Maury's skeleton infantry at Meridian, Forrest's diminished cavalry in west Alabama, and Farrand's ungainly fleet at Demopolis, all under the command of General Taylor. The formal surrender of these forces followed rapidly.[23]

On April 22, Taylor wrote to Canby requesting that they meet soon. Canby was not able to reply until four days later, when he expressed a willingness to do so anywhere near Mobile. They finally came face to face at the Magee Farm, a plain wooden house 12 miles north of Mobile. The contrast between the two men's circumstances was stark. Taylor and an aide arrived in much-faded uniforms aboard a creaky railroad handcar pumped by two black men. Canby awaited them in a bright blue coat with shiny brass buttons, backed by a full brigade and a regimental brass band. The musicians greeted the Rebels with a rousing rendition of "Hail! Columbia," but Canby instantly intervened and ordered "Dixie" instead. Taylor thanked him but said that the former tune was more appropriate. The interview was cordial, and champagne corks popped to mark the occasion. Taylor later quipped that these were "the first agreeable explosive sounds I had heard in years." The men arranged a formal surrender to take place in Citronelle on May 4. It would include all of Taylor's forces, the last active Confederates east of the Mississippi River. Canby's terms were generous, and Taylor was properly grateful. Ex-Confederate officers could keep their sidearms and were promised transportation to their homes.[24]

At Meridian on May 7, General Maury released his infantry into civilian life with a brief and unapologetic address that hinted at the Lost Cause Cult to come. "Our last march is almost ended," he told them. "But we will never forget the noble comrades who have stood shoulder to shoulder with us until now, the noble dead who have been martyred, the noble Southern women who have been wronged and are unavenged, or the noble principles for which we have fought." The following day, Gibson bade his Louisianans who had struggled so bravely at Spanish Fort goodbye. "For more than four years we have shared together the fortunes of war," he said. "Hereafter you shall re-count to your children, with conscious pride, the story of these rugged days, and you will always greet a comrade of the old brigade with open arms. . . . May God bless you." Forrest, who was rumored to be considering a run to Mexico with disgruntled ex-Rebels, stood before his faithful troopers on May 9 at Gainesville, not far from the Mississippi line. His surrender speech was penned by a trusty adjutant but fully expressed what he felt, and it is one of the war's most eloquent. "That we are beaten is a self-evident fact," he stated, "and any further resistance on our part would be justly regarded as the very height of folly and rashness." Their cause was lost, he admitted, but the na-tional government had manifested "a spirit of magnanimity and liberality" that should be met with "faithful compliance." He professed admiration for his men's bravery and urged them to forget past humiliations and defeats. "You have been good soldiers," he closed, "you can be good citizens. Obey the laws, preserve your honor, and the Government to which you have surrendered can afford to be and will be magnanimous." To the relief of many, there would be no border dash led by the Wizard of the Saddle.[25]

Farrand's fleet steamed back downriver to Nannahubba Bluff for its formal surrender. Cameron wrote that they found several Union gunboats awaiting them. On May 10, 112 Confederate officers, 285 sailors, and 24 marines were paroled. The formal surrender document stated, "We, the undersigned, prisoners of war belonging to the Confederate naval forces . . . in the waters of the State of Alabama, this day surrendered by Commodore Ebenezer Farrand to Acting Rear Admiral Henry K. Thatcher, United States Navy." The men agreed not to serve in any military capacity against the United States ever again. George Waterman, who had recovered from his wound and accompanied the fleet aboard the *Heroine* ever since, described the emotional scene. "The officers and crew assembled on deck, and our colors came down and were saluted with raised caps, while tears flowed freely." Union prize crews took over the vessels and headed back downstream. The Confederate Navy was no more. Formalities concluded, the men mixed together, exchanging tobacco and stories. "I know that I found myself in the quarters of the young officers on board the *Cincinnati* drinking iced wine and smoking Havana cigars," Cameron noted satisfactorily. All in all, it wasn't a bad ending for him, considerably better than for most ex-Confederates.[26]

The American Civil War was over. Alabama's human and material losses were catastrophic, shattering its social, economic, educational, and political structures. Out of at least 81,000 Alabamians who wore the gray, 16,000 died of disease or battle, a 20 percent loss. Most, like the gallant John Pelham, perished far away, but others, like the unfortunate mechanic obliterated at the *Tennessee*'s gunport during the Battle of Mobile Bay, or young Henry Elliot cruelly shot and shot again at Selma, died practically within shouting distance of home. Thousands more were wounded or suffered debilitating psychological trauma that would never heal. Some turned to drink or opium for relief, little discussed due to Victorian reticence. Widows, orphans, and one-armed men became fixtures of the age. A few high-ranking and prominent Alabamians were arrested by Federal authorities—Governor Watts at Union Springs on May 1, Admiral Semmes and Senator Clay later—but none were held very long. Those who had waged war on the United States were generally let alone to remake their lives as best they could.

That would be difficult given that the state's economy was a shambles. To begin with, emancipation meant that $200 million in capital investment simply disappeared. Many of the state's cities and towns bore evidence of some destruction, Selma most of all, and on May 25, 1865, an accidental magazine explosion at Mobile leveled eight city blocks, killing and maiming hundreds in the theretofore intact Gulf city. Railroads, depots, warehouses, bridges, and river landings all over the state had been destroyed or damaged, and the Mobile harbor was a silted-up mess of sunken wrecks, pilings, and still-active torpedoes that would hinder maritime traffic for months to come. Vast tracts of the state's prime farmland in the Tennessee Valley and Black Belt were scoured as if by locusts, and abandoned farms and burned barns dotted the lonely rural landscape. "The Yankee hordes, like an avalanche, have swept over our land," the *Montgomery Daily Advertiser* wrote, "leaving ruin and desolation to mark their track." Even those counties spared direct military activity suffered. In south Alabama, Clarke County's tillable land declined by over 30,000 acres between 1860 and 1870, and its production levels on the remaining farmland plummeted due to labor shortages, missing livestock, broken equipment, and lack of seeds. Bands of deserters and ne'er-do-wells lurked in the north Alabama hills and coastal swamps, committing crimes and terrorizing helpless civilians. Large numbers of destitute whites and blacks overwhelmed authorities and were it not for Federal intervention would have died. In Dallas County, one Yankee soldier described women "who have the air of having once lived genteely" coming into the camps begging "for washings to do to keep them from starvation." Meanwhile, Union soldiers settled down to a long occupation, and the Freedmen's Bureau was established to help shepherd the former slaves toward full citizenship. What kind of place Alabama would become remained to be seen in the spring of '65. But as one ex-slave said over half a century later, "A'ter de Surrender nothin' neber was de same."[27]

# Epilogue

## *White Columns and the Gun That Won the Civil War*

It stands regal and serene just off County Road 23 in Wilcox County's Possum
Bend community. White Columns, or more formally the Tait-Starr-Woodson
House, is the kind of plantation home outsiders picture when they think of
the Old South—grand, two stories, a stunning architectural gem fashioned of
local materials by sophisticated talent. The house consists of two large wings
joined in an L-shaped footprint, one facing south and the other west. Each
is capable of standing alone as the principal facade and features soaring, full-
height octagonal columns made of 12-inch-wide pine planks joined along the
edges, flat-sawn balustrades, elegant eave brackets, and metal downspouts em-
blazoned at the tops by brass eagles and the 1860 construction date. A low
hip roof caps the ensemble. The interior includes eighteen rooms, the largest
24-feet-square with 14-foot ceilings; crown molding; beautifully grained doors
in eared-architrave surrounds; and, most impressively, intersecting cross halls,
each measuring a commodious 24 by 55 feet. Unusually, though the west facade serves as the main entry, the primary staircase is located in the south
hall. In their charming 1942 volume *Deep South*, Caldwell Delaney and Frank
Kearley were especially smitten by the staircase, a mahogany wonder they described as possessing "massive grace."[1]

My own introduction to White Columns came several years ago, courtesy of a Black Belt Ramble hosted by my friend and colleague Cartledge
Weeden Blackwell III. Cart, as he's more familiarly known, is a native Selman
who has nourished a love for Alabama's historic architecture since he was old
enough to fit Lincoln Logs together into imitations of the rustic outbuild-

Figure 36. White Columns, as photographed by the Historic American Buildings Survey during the 1930s. Courtesy Library of Congress.

ings and tenant houses he encountered in the countryside. As it turns out, he comes by this passion honestly, being a direct descendant of the talented ante-bellum architect Alexander Bragg, who erected Greek Revival masterpieces in both North Carolina and Alabama. Cart went on to obtain degrees from the College of Charleston and the University of Virginia and currently works as the assistant director of the Mobile Historic Development Commission. Al-ways eager to share his knowledge and enviable access to some of the state's most gracious historic homes, Cart twice annually hosts Black Belt Rambles for a clutch of like-minded historians, architects, and friends, including my-self. Our headquarters for these jaunts is located at Cook Hill, Cart's Wilcox County family seat. This is a lovely 1839 I-house hard by the Alabama River west of Camden. Within comfortable driving distance are numerous architec-tural treasures, some lovingly restored and maintained, others neglected, over-grown, and looking like they could illustrate the cover of a Faulkner novel. These tours are always wonderful excursions, full of busy sightseeing by day and stimulating conversation on a commodious front porch or around a blazing fire pit by night.

Cart took us to White Columns on a fall ramble. We pulled up to the house on a splendid November morning, admiring the sun-dappled grounds and spreading fields beyond. We were ushered inside the west wing by a young man who had obviously been hard at work painting. As any owner of a frame historic house will testify, there are always a thousand and one things that need doing, and White Columns is certainly no exception. We were met in the enormous hallway by the current owner, Ouida Starr Woodson, who, though wheelchair-bound and on oxygen, was pleased to see us and freely offered her extensive knowledge about the place and the families that have lived there.

According to Mrs. Woodson, White Columns was built by a Mexican War veteran and planter named Felix Tait. Cart's ancestor, Alexander Bragg, was the architect, and, indeed, the house displays a comfortable blending of the Greek Revival and Italianate styles that only a master of both could achieve. Like many of his Black Belt neighbors, Tait served in the Confederate army as an officer and was later in the state legislature. The war combined with compulsive gambling ruined him, and shortly thereafter he sold White Columns to a well-heeled native Englishman and Camden resident named Samuel Tepper. On New Year's Day 1880, Tepper presented the house to his daughter, Molly, and her new husband, Dr. Lucius Ernest Starr, as a wedding present. Mrs. Woodson is a descendant of that couple, and her residence at White Columns represents a generations-long rootedness familiar to many Alabamians and astonishing to some outsiders. The young man who met us in the yard is Mrs. Woodson's grandson, and numerous other current family members practically ensure that the house will remain in the family for years to come.[2]

Mrs. Woodson said that we were free to explore the downstairs, where not barred by closed doors. The magnificent staircase was blocked by a giant potted fern. My first impression inside White Columns was the chill. Although it was a balmy Indian summer morning outside, the cavernous plastered interior was significantly cooler, a delight in summer but no doubt a harbinger of winter discomfort in difficult-to-heat spaces. As our eyes adjusted to the gloom, we admired the many historic maps, portraits, and foxed pictures hanging along the walls. While Mrs. Woodson remained where she was to field questions, the rest of us began to explore. To the right of the hall was a room that apparently had served as Dr. Starr's study. It included a fireplace, a secretary full of leather-bound books, a fascinating old medical contraption for stress relief resting in a wooden box with the elaborate instructions on the lid, and, in one corner, an antique rifle. Curious, I walked over and picked up the weapon. Just as my father had instantly known that Chuck Hogue's find was a Spencer carbine, I recognized this gun as a Spencer rifle, a slightly heavier and longer version of the carbine, but still remarkably easy to handle. It was blackened with age, and every moving part was rusted shut, but it was clearly a Spencer, from the distinctive lever and hammer to the metal ammunition tube frozen into the wooden butt. One of the other ramblers, Luke Adams, and I studied it together. Could it have been left by one of Wilson's raiders, we wondered? Or a Yankee occupier immediately after the war? Surely there was a story here—a white-columned Black Belt mansion plus a Yankee rifle propped in a corner had to equal a Civil War connection of some sort. We asked the young man nearby, but he merely shrugged, "It came with the house." Luke then took the gun out into the hall and queried Mrs. Woodson. She did not disappoint. "That's the gun that won the Civil War," she said and proceeded to share the colorful story.

Like Tait, Dr. Starr had enlisted in the Confederate Army, in his case at Bibb County as a sergeant and cavalryman in Hilliard's Legion. This outfit saw considerable action in the western theater, and Starr was wounded through the knee during Bragg's 1862 Kentucky maneuverings at a place called Flat Lick. Placed in a Confederate hospital near Barbourville, Kentucky, he was soon captured by the Federals and held in the vicinity for several months. According to Mrs. Woodson, there was a good deal of ribbing between the Yankee guards and their prisoners as to which side had the best marksmen. To settle the matter, they decided to have a shooting contest, and Starr was chosen to represent the Southern boys. The match consisted of attempting to hit a penny at some distance using a Spencer repeating rifle. The guards' man fired first and missed, but Starr's shot hit the coin and bent it for all to see. Shortly after this good-natured contest, Starr was paroled and later rejoined the Confederate Army as a surgeon, serving out the war in that capacity. Fifteen years later, he married Molly Tepper and moved into White Columns, hobbling about with an honorable wound and enjoying life as a respected physician.[3]

Frequent visiting has always been an endearing feature of Black Belt life, enlivening isolated households, and Dr. and Mrs. Starr no doubt enjoyed their fair share of such episodes. But one in particular proved more memorable than most. It began with an unexpected knock at the door, and there on the threshold was none other than the Yankee prison guard of years before, bearing good wishes, the bent coin, and the winning Spencer rifle. One can imagine the reunion and the old veteran talk that must have filled the study long into the night, with curious family and servants peeping around corners and hanging on every word. And so there the rifle had remained, quietly in its corner, its work of fighting, marksmanship, and reconciliation done, gently rusting with the passing seasons. We warmly thanked Mrs. Woodson for the story and reverently returned the gun to its accustomed spot.

As we left White Columns, I gloried in the incredible richness just experienced, and wondered how many more Alabama Civil War stories have been sadly forgotten. The past is all around us, sometimes in unexpected corners, waiting to be unlocked. Where there is documentation or knowledge handed down—continuity—there is illumination. But where story is forgotten or neglected there are only relics devoid of real meaning. As any archaeologist will readily explain, context is everything. The Civil War and its passions recede, but we owe it to ourselves and our heirs never to forget the remarkable men and women who endured those rugged days ever so long ago.

# Notes

Prologue

1. The marker stands in Reynolds Cemetery, located down Reynolds Cemetery Road off the highway. This site ceased to be the official center of the state in 1953 when Congress approved the Submerged Lands Act, extending the state's borders into the Gulf, thereby shifting the center to Chilton County. None of us was aware of this during the 1960s, however, and I doubt that if we were it would have bothered us in the least. After all, we still had the marker! See *Mobile Register*, November 25, 2013.

2. Jones, *Yankee Blitzkrieg*, 63–66; 66 ("I am satisfied").

3. Armes, *Story of Coal and Iron in Alabama*, 24.

4. I learned this saying from my father. The Confederates also applied it to other repeaters of the time, like the Henry rifle.

5. Windham, *Odd Egg Editor*, 147 ("noted for"), "Psychological Test," 1–2.

6. Strange to say, I never heard Ta Ta speak of the momentous civil rights events that gripped Selma during my childhood, and I have no idea what she thought of the turmoil. She may have preferred the distant romantic past to a modern controversy, or she perhaps simply thought the topic inappropriate for a youngster.

7. Jeanne Sledge, personal interview, May 7, 2015.

8. It was only years later that I learned that the engineer, J. J. Thomas, had written a memoir titled *Fifty Years on the Rail*, published in 1912. He describes the running fight and the fall of Selma on pages 33–35 of his book. He was eighteen during the raid and lived in Selma in later life, where Ta Ta no doubt interviewed him.

9. *Selma Times-Journal*, July 23, 1986.

10. The painting is titled *The Lyons Sisters at Arcola Plantation* and was done around 1861 by William Carroll Saunders, a native Alabamian who later worked out of Columbus, Mississippi. See Black, *Art in Mississippi*, 68.

11. Sledge, "Summerfield," ii ("To Octavia"); Fitzgerald, *Rubaiyat of Omar Khayyam*, n.p.

12. For the actions noted in the *Official Records*, see Letford and Jones, "Military and Naval Activities," 189–206; Wilson, *Under the Old Flag*, 2: 229 ("a whirlwind"); Shingleton, *High Seas Confederate*, 54 ("daring and gallant"); O'Brien, *Mobile, 1865*, 182 ("one of the best").

Introduction

1. *Montgomery Weekly Advertiser*, January 2, 1861; Cumming, *Gleanings*, 20–21 ("The city"); Denman, *Secession Movement in Alabama*, 92–93 (convention date).

2. Baldwin and Thomas, *New and Complete Gazetteer*, 25.

3. *DeBow's Review*, February 1855, 157; Brewer, *Alabama: Her History, Resources*, 80; Cline, *Alabama Railroads*, 46 ("one vast garden"); *DeBow's Review*, April 1859, 468 ("wildest").

4. Royall, *Letters from Alabama on Various Subjects*, 40 ("Fancy is inadequate"); Watkins, *King Cotton*, 150 (1859 yields); Gosse, *Letters from Alabama*, 277 (cotton field like snow).

5. *DeBow's Review*, November 1855, 611 ("The pine").

6. Baldwin and Thomas, *New and Complete Gazetteer*, 26.

7. Thornton, *Politics and Power*, 292–93 (literacy); Center, "Burning of the University of Alabama," 42 (the University); "Astronomical Observatories," 42 (the observatory).

8. Ormand, Bagby, and Goldthwaite, *Code of Alabama*, 239.

9. Danielson, *War's Desolating Scourge*, 9–11 (north Alabama slavery); Sledge, *Mobile River*, 130 (Creoles).

10. Sledge, *Mobile River*, 271 (Zeno Chastang); Olmsted, *Journey*, 560; Lane, *Architecture of the Old South*, 132 (Whitfield).

11. Patillo, *Carolina Planters*, 319–20 (McKenzie Mill Place); Keller, "Alabama Plantation Life in 1860," 219–24 (Oak Grove).

12. Griffith, *Alabama: A Documentary History*, 170–71 (Proctor); Gosse, *Letters from Alabama*, 40 (slave women); Rogers et al., *Alabama: The History*, 109 (slave girl).

13. Olmsted, *Cotton Kingdom*, 2: 125.

14. Milner, *Alabama: As It Was*, 4 (overall agricultural wealth); Brewer, *Alabama: Her History, Resources*, 83 (agricultural output); Hoskins, "Best Southern Patriots," 151 (acreage devoted to cotton); Amos, *Cotton City*, 21 (cotton production), 20 (routes to Mobile and New Orleans); *DeBow's Review*, January 1855, 23 (disconnect).

15. Brewer, *Alabama: Her History, Resources*, 84 (livestock numbers); Wiggins, *From Civil War to Civil Rights*, 113 (open range).

16. On industry, see Thornton, *Politics and Power*, 280–81, and *Census of 1860*, Manufactures, 13–14; "Manufacturers in Southern States," *Hunt's Merchants' Magazine*, 38 (April 1858): 509 (Bell Factory); Cloud, "Day with Daniel Pratt," 156 (Prattville).

17. *DeBow's Review*, March 1859, 342 (railroad mileage); Thomas, *Iron Way*, 216 (depots); Cline, *Alabama Railroads*, 42 (map of lines).

18. Gabel, *Rails to Oblivion*, 11–12 (track); Cline, *Alabama Railroads*, 24 (Lyell), 42–43 (rules).

19. Olmsted, *Journey*, 574–75 (towns); Evans, *Sherman's Horsemen*, 123 (Talladega); Jordan, *Antebellum Alabama*, 39 (Marion); Gamble, *Alabama Catalog*, 5 (Huntsville population); Sterling, *Belle of the Fifties*, 159 (Huntsville); Besson, *Eufaula*, 3; Olmsted, *Journey*, 574.

20. *DeBow's Review*, January 1859, 117 ("correct idea"); De Leon, *Four Years*, 23; Russell, *My Diary*, 165.

21. Shippee, *Bishop Whipple's Southern Diary*, 88 ("sailor just on shore"); Russell, *My Diary*, 191 ("mulattoes"); Sledge, *Mobile River*, 90 (waterfront, women's hoops); Meriwether, "A Southern Traveler's Diary," 136 ("city of cotton"); Phillips, *Plantation and Frontier*, 286 ("receptacle").

22. Oldmixon, *Transatlantic Wanderings*, 154 (architecture); Cumming, *Gleanings*, 18.

## Chapter 1

1. McMillan, *Alabama Confederate Reader*, 22–23; Childress, "Mount Vernon Barracks," 126.

2. "Andrew B. Moore (1857–1861)," http://www.encyclopediaofalabama.org/article/h-1454 (accessed July 5, 2015); Webb and Armbrester, *Alabama Governors*, 79, 80 (quotes).

3. Maffitt, *Life and Services of John Newland Maffitt*, 215–16.

4. Goodheart, "Caught Sleeping." See also *New Orleans Bee*, January 8. 1861.

5. Goodheart, "Caught Sleeping."; US War Department, *War of the Rebellion: Records of the Union and Confederate Armies*, series 1, vol. 1: 327 (hereinafter cited as OR; all references are to series 1 unless otherwise noted), (Reno's excuse); *New Orleans Bee*, January 8, 1861.

6. *New York Times*, January 8, 1861; McMillan, *Alabama Confederate Reader*, 23 (quoting Moore's letter to Buchanan).

7. McMillan, *Alabama Confederate Reader*, 26–27; Denman, *Secession Movement*, 117–18 (on north Alabama).

8. Denman, *Secession Movement*, 131 (resolution).

9. Rogers, *Confederate Home Front*, 19–21.

10. McMillan, *Alabama Confederate Reader*, 34 (ordinance), 36 (Clemens letter).

11. Jones, "Letters of W. H. Mitchell," 183–84; Thornton, *Politics and Power*, 460 (Tuscaloosa delegate).

12. *Montgomery Weekly Advertiser*, January 12, 1861; Tenney, *Military and Naval History of the Rebellion*, 9–10 (Mobile); Sexton, *Southern Woman of Letters*, 29 (Evans letter); Denman, *Secession Movement*, 150 (US flag); Bunn, *Civil War Eufaula*, 78.

13. McMillan, *Alabama Confederate Reader*, 49–50.

14. McMillan, *Alabama Confederate Reader*, 48 (government); Foote, *Civil War*, 1: 7 (Davis's eyes).

15. Rogers, *Confederate Home Front*, 25 (Davis's arrival); *New York Times*, February 17, 1861 (Davis's remarks); McMillan, *Alabama Confederate Reader*, 56–57 (Yancey's speech).

16. Capers, *Life and Times of C. G. Memminger*, 307 (weather, decorations, procession); Rogers, *Confederate Home Front*, 1 (Market Street), 28 (procession).

17. McMillan, *Alabama Confederate Reader*, 59–62 (Davis's speech); Capers, *Life and Times of C. G. Memminger*, 309 ("In uttering the words") Jones, "Contemporary Account of the Inauguration of Jefferson Davis," 273–74 (Mrs. Jackson); Woodward and Muhlenfeld, *Private Mary Chesnut*, 3 ("I do not allow myself").

18. Brannon, "Stars and Bars," 434 (Committee quotes); Bradley, "Tattered Banners," 14–15 (Stars and Bars); United Confederate Veterans, *Confederate Women of Arkansas*, 175 (Nicola Marschall story).

19. Bradley, "Tattered Banners," 14, 16 (flag construction, Miles quotes); *Montgomery Weekly Advertiser*, March 6, 1861 (flag raising); Owen, "Raising the First Confederate Flag, 199 (Tyler quotes).

20. Lawler and Schaefer, *American Political Rhetoric*, 257 (Corner Stone Speech); McMillan, *Alabama Confederate Reader*, 95 (Alabama ME Church); *Harper's Weekly*, July 13, 1861

(Russell witnesses auction); Woodward and Muhlenfeld, *Private Mary Chesnut*, 15 (Chesnut witnesses auction).

21. Russell, *My Diary North and South*, 165; Capers, *Life and Times of C. G. Memminger*, 310–11 (Treasury office).

22. Jones, *Rebel War Clerk's Diary*, 36 ("overwhelmed"); Rogers, *Confederate Home Front*, 32 (officers); Maffitt, *Life and Services*, 220 (Maffitt interview).

23. Rogers, *Confederate Home Front*, 33 (Cobb), 34 (Varina Davis); Woodward and Muhlenfeld, *Private Mary Chesnut*, 29 (Mallory); Russell, *My Diary North and South*, 177 ("ladylike").

24. McMillan, *Alabama Confederate Reader*, 88 (telegram); Woodward and Muhlenfeld, *Private Mary Chesnut*, 59 ("shells bursting"); Rogers, *Confederate Home Front*, 36–37 (bombardment, Lincoln).

25. McMillan, *Alabama Confederate Reader*, 42–45 (capital moved).

26. Gay, *Life in Dixie*, 18 ("It was a beautiful sight!"); Stevenson, *Thirteen Months in the Rebel Army*, 195 (Selma ladies); John W. Henley et al. to Governor Moore, January 19, 1861 (Canebrake Cadets); McMillan, *Alabama Confederate Reader*, 98 (north Alabama and Bowie knives).

27. Maxwell, *Perfect Lion*, 47 (Pelham).

28. *Mobile Daily Advertiser*, April 24, 1861 (departure); Hotze, *Three Months*, 6–8 (river trip).

29. Burnett, "Letters of Three Lightfoot Brothers," 389 ("A soldier is worse"); Marcus A. Worthington to Sister, June 28, 1861, Worthington Family Letters; Nelson, *Hour of Our Nation's Agony*, 30 (Mississippian in Mobile).

30. Cutrer, *Oh, What a Loansome Time I Had*, 22 ("You know not my feelings"), 28 ("It is so lonsome"); Mrs. P. E. Collins to Governor John Gill Shorter, April 5, 1862.

31. Cumming, *Gleanings*, 32 (defenses); Browning, *Lincoln's Trident*, 19–20 (blockade, *Aid*); US War Department, *War of the Rebellion: Official Records of the Union and Confederate Navies*, vol. 4, 201 (hereinafter cited as *ORN*; all references are to series 1 unless otherwise noted) (*Aid* seized).

32. Cumming, *Gleanings*, 32 (New England ice); Benners, *Disunion, War, Defeat, and Recovery*, 70 ("The Yankees are threatening").

33. Folmar, *From That Terrible Field*, 10 (December 9 episode), 14–15 (Christmas Eve duel, "The most magnificent"); *ORN*, vol. 17, 11–12 (Cicero Price), 13 ("The activity").

## Chapter 2

1. Konstam, *Mississippi River Gunboats*, 6–7.

2. Maxwell, *Perfect Lion*, 61 (Pelham).

3. Foote, *Civil War*, 1: 173–74.

4. Hughes and Stonesifer, *Life and Wars of Gideon J. Pillow*, 325 (Scott on Pillow); *OR*, vol. 7, 694–96 (Alabama and Mississippi delegation).

5. Moore, "Expedition to Florence, ALA.," 119 (Foote's orders); Johnson, "Confederate Defenses and Union Gunboats on the Tennessee River," 51–52 (gunboat raid).

6. Black, *Railroads of the Confederacy*, 139 ("vertebrae"); Jones, *Rebel War Clerk's Diary*, 110 ("Three of the enemy's gun-boats"); Moore, "Expedition to Florence, ALA.," 120 (Phelps report).

7. Bradley and Dahlen, *From Conciliation to Conquest*, 13–15 (conciliation policy).

8. *OR*, vol. 7, 154–56 (Phelps's report); Slagle, *Ironclad Captain*, 172 (*New York Times*).

9. Groom, *Shiloh 1862*, 358 (Shiloh and casualties); McMillan, *Alabama Confederate Reader*, 134 (Cumming).

10. McMillan, *Alabama Confederate Reader*, 144–46 (Mitchel); "Civil War Days in Huntsville," 195, 201 (Chadick); *Mobile Register*, May 18, 1862 (letter from Huntsville).

11. *OR*, vol. 10, 641–42 (Mitchel and quote); McMillan, *Alabama Confederate Reader*, 146 ("His movement").

12. Danielson, *War's Desolating Scourge*, 81 ("unwinking," quote is by John Hay, Lincoln's private secretary); "Civil War Days in Huntsville," 201 ("Truly our town"); Beatty, *Citizen Soldier*, 144 ("The men of Huntsville").

13. *OR*, vol. 10, 165–66 ("bitterest feeling," "Armed citizens"); "Civil War Days in Huntsville," 207 (Chadick); Danielson, *War's Desolating Scourge*, 46 ("Unorganized bodies").

14. Beatty, *Citizen Soldier*, 139.

15. Bradley and Dahlen, *From Conciliation to Conquest*, 101 (Athens), 103 ("On the whole"); Langella, *Haunted Alabama Battlefields*, 118 (Donnell House).

16. Bradley and Dahlen, *From Conciliation to Conquest*, 104.

17. Ibid., 105–6; Danielson, *War's Desolating Scourge*, 75 ("throwing filth").

18. Bradley and Dahlen, *From Conciliation to Conquest*, 106–7.

19. Ibid., 18–19, 24 ("having imbued").

20. Ibid., 110 ("the soldiers"), 111 ("a 'Goddam Bitch'"); Danielson, *War's Desolating Scourge*, 76 ("chief delight"); Bradley and Dahlen, *From Conciliation to Conquest*, 112 ("sidewalks").

21. Bradley and Dahlen, *From Conciliation to Conquest*, 114 ("Colonel Turchin"); Danielson, *War's Desolating Scourge*, 75 ("No worse order").

22. Bradley and Dahlen, *From Conciliation to Conquest*, 132 ("One of the most"); Danielson, *War's Desolating Scourge*, 61 ("rebels as if"), 77–78 (soldiers' quotes); "John Basil Turchin," *Encyclopedia of Alabama*, http://www.encyclopediaofalabama.org/article/h-1652 (accessed August 5, 2015).

23. "Civil War Days in Huntsville," 204 ("horse panic"); Saunders, "War-Time Journal," 451 ("destroying and burning"); Danielson, *War's Desolating Scourge*, 133–34 (Sherman).

24. "Civil War Days in Huntsville," 209 ("many of the negroes"), 223 ("playing the mischief"), 220 ("So they are arming blacks"); Beatty, *Citizen Soldier*, 138 (Beatty quotes); Horrall, *History of the Forty-Second Indiana*, 133 ("marvelously wonderful," "Bress Mars Abraham"); McGee, *History of the Seventy-Second Indiana*, 235 ("We had 500 hogs").

25. *OR*, vol. 16, pt. 2, 309 (Rousseau); "Civil War Days in Huntsville," 216 (Monte Sano); Jones, *Artilleryman's Diary*, 150 (Russell Cave), 164 (snowy Huntsville).

26. *OR*, vol. 16, pt. 1, 840 ("He was overtaken"); series 2, vol. 6, 831–32 (accounts of the murder).

27. Danielson, *War's Desolating Scourge*, 72 (quotes).

28. Waters, "General Philip Roddey," 25, 26 ("Captain Roddey").

29. "Civil War Days in Huntsville," 226 ("tramping feet," "could hardly believe it"), 227 ("perfect crowd," "shut up some of the Jew stores"); Wilson, *Confederate Industry*, 184–85 (*Richmond Whig*).

30. Danielson, *War's Desolating Scourge*, 112 (Vasser and Lowe quotes), 113 (Fennell), 126 ("a miserable condition").

## Chapter 3

1. Foreman, *World on Fire*, 114 ("very dark, sallow"), 146 ("most dangerous"). On Bulloch see "James D. Bulloch (1823–1901)," http://www.georgiaencyclopedia.org/articles/history - archaeology/james-d-bulloch-1823–1901 (accessed August 29, 2015).

2. Owsley, *The CSS* Florida, 17–18 (Fraser, Trenholm); Bulloch, *Secret Service*, 51 ("No funds").

3. Owsley, *The CSS* Florida, 19–20 (contracts); Bulloch, *Secret Service*, 57 (quotes).

4. *ORN*, series 2, vol. 1, 252 (ship specifications); Hoole, *Four Years in the Confederate Navy*, 30 (sailing speed and quote).

5. *ORN*, vol. 1, 766 ("as 'twas"); Maffitt, *Life and Services*, 253 ("There was not").

6. Bergeron, *Confederate Mobile*, 115–16 (channels).

7. Maffitt, *Life and Services*, 252–53 ("We will hoist"); Burlingame, *Abraham Lincoln*, 223 ("One war").

8. *New York Times*, September 4, 2012.

9. Preble, *Chase of the Rebel Steamer of War* Oreto, 3 (Preble quotes); Maffitt, *Life and Services*, 253 ("Had their guns," "rapid and precise," "entering among the berth deck"), 254 ("re-rove," "Dixie flag").

10. *ORN*, vol. 1, 767 ("Our boats"); Maffitt, *Life and Services*, 256 (Buchanan), 261 ("flower garden").

11. Preble, *Chase of the Rebel Steamer of War* Oreto, 3 ("superior speed"), 4 ("mortification"); *New York Times*, September 4, 2012 ("just judgement"). After his dismissal, Preble embarked on a diligent campaign to clear his name, and though it ultimately took until 1872, he succeeded.

12. Bergeron, *Confederate Mobile*, 116 ("mail packet"), 125 (number of successful runs).

13. Wallace, *Cases Argued and Adjudged in the Supreme Court*, 343 ("at least one-half"); Bergeron, *Confederate Mobile*, 120 ("seem to drive"); *Mobile Register*, August 8, 1862 ("a fine schooner"), September 6, 1862 ("Just Run the Blockade"); Sexton, *Southern Woman of Letters*, 100–101 (on Evans); Arnold, *Denbigh's Civilian Imports*, 49 (the liquor).

14. Browning, *Lincoln's Trident*, 205 (quotes); 390 (conditions on ships).

15. Bergeron, *Confederate Mobile*, 92 ("Paris of the Confederacy"), 93 ("You are looking"); *Mobile Register*, March 1, 1863 ("rounds of heartfelt"); Ross, *Visit to the Cities and Camps*, 239 ("a capital breakfast"), 240 ("where all the beauty"), 242–43 ("created a great deal"); Fletcher, "Run through the Southern States," 505 ("oranges"), 506–7 ("anxiously").

16. *ORN*, vol. 1, 769 ("seems to fancy"); Still, "Confederate States Navy at Mobile," 129n8 ("Her steam pipes"); O'Brien, *Mobile, 1865*, 164 ("To call the *Morgan's* crew"); Symonds, *Confederate Admiral*, 183 ("vagabonds"). See also my own *Mobile River*, 124–28, on the Mobile Squadron.

17. Bergeron, *Confederate Mobile*, 82 ("rotten as punk"), 70 (*Huntsville* and *Tuscaloosa*).

18. Symonds, *Confederate Admiral*, 191 (the *Tennessee*); Friend, *West Wind, Flood Tide*, 44 (Cumming); Symonds, *Confederate Admiral*, 190 (*Nashville* and "tremendous monster" quote).

19. Bergeron, *Confederate Mobile*, 29 (Maury, "puss in boots"), Sledge, *Mobile River*, 120 (Scheliha).

20. Ross, *Visit to the Cities and Camps*, 241 ("perfect models"); *OR*, vol. 8, 153 ("If we lagged"); Bergeron, *Confederate Mobile*, 159 ("they look like"); Tenney, *Military and Naval History of the Rebellion*, 669 ("They are not bereft").

21. Corsan, *Two Months in the Confederate States*, 51–52 ("the forts").

22. Chaffin, *The H. L. Hunley*, 18–19 (on Hunley), 39–40 (on McClintock and Watson), 148 (on the machine shop, Dixon).

23. Ibid., 107–9, 232–33.

24. Ibid., 112–17. See also Bak, *CSS* Hunley, 53. Bak's title is an error, since the *Hunley* was never a government vessel and never had the CSS prefix. During the *Hunley's* recent restoration, the last crew's remains were found, including Dixon's, along with his now famous gold coin, inscribed "My life preserver."

25. *New York Times*, October 1, 1863.

26. Fry, "Life in Dallas County during the War," 216 ("Sugar was scarce"), 218 ("Each household," the dyes); Hague, *Blockaded Family*, 58 ("There was a variety"), 46–47 (medicines); Clayton, *White and Black under the Old Regime*, 118 (trading food for cloth).

27. *ORN*, vol. 1, 762 ("The Department"); Maffitt, *Life and Services*, 266 ("lead color").

28. Matthews, "Running the Blockade," n.p. ("a tiger"); Wilson and Coan, *Personal Recollections of the War of the Rebellion*, 67 ("a more sea-sick").

29. Maffitt, *Life and Services*, 267 ("light mist"); Matthews, "Running the Blockade," n.p. ("you might have thought"); Sinclair, "Eventful Cruise of the *Florida*," 420 ("Sail right ahead!," "Port your helm!," "Let fall"), 421 ("like a deer"); Wilson and Coan, *Personal Recollections of the War of the Rebellion*, 68 ("Vessel running").

30. Browning, *Lincoln's Trident*, 265 (*Florida's* depredations); Shingleton, *High Seas Confederate*, 60 ("as brave"), 54 ("daring and gallant"); Bergeron, *Confederate Mobile*, 118 ("blundering").

## Chapter 4

1. Maxwell, *Perfect Lion*, 369n27 (Custer's note), 305 (Kelly's Ford).

2. Ibid., 321–22 ("The father and sister").

3. Willet, *Lightning Mule Brigade*, 17–18.

4. Ibid., 11 ("I hope"), 21 (the goal). Garfield was later to be president of the United States.

5. McMillan, *Alabama Confederate Reader*, 174 ("Suffice it to say").

6. Faulkner, *Flags in the Dust*, 314 ("it is a known fact"); Willett, *Lightning Mule Brigade*, 31 ("We found the lower deck"), 35 ("The animals"); "Streight's Raid," http://www.encyclopediaofalabama.org/article/h-1380 (accessed October 3, 2015) ("Jackass Cavalry").

7. Willett, *Lightning Mule Brigade*, 63 ("Today we witness"); McIlwain, *Civil War Alabama*, 116 ("1,500,000 bushels of corn").

8. Willett, *Lightning Mule Brigade*, 72 ("If I succeed"), 70 ("fine, high-strung"), 89 ("We found").

9. Severance, *Portraits of Conflict*, 356 ("Defender"); Knight, *Battle of Fort Donelson*, 134 ("Get there"); Whitsitt, "Year with Forrest," 359 ("Colonel Streight").

10. Willet, *Lightning Mule Brigade*, 100 ("exhausted horses"); *OR*, vol. 23, 288 ("the boom").

11. Moore, "Streight's Raid," 342 ("skipped off"); Willet, *Lightning Mule Brigade*, 110 ("ferocious"), 112 (casualties); Whitsitt, "Year with Forrest," 359 ("brave," "practiced").

12. Willet, *Lightning Mule Brigade*, 118 ("under full"); *OR*, vol. 23, 289 ("was compelled").

13. Willet, *Lightning Mule Brigade*, 119 ("Whenever you see anything blue"); Whitsitt, "Year with Forrest," 360 ("first night battle"); Willet, *Lightning Mule Brigade*, 122 ("I find myself," "The general"), 121 ("our brave wounded").

14. Willet, *Lightning Mule Brigade*, 127–28 (Blountsville); Moore, "Streight's Raid," 342 ("took a good meal," "the rebs").

15. Whitsitt, "Year with Forrest," 360 ("It was a common sight"); Willet, *Lightning Mule Brigade*, 131–32 (Rebel sisters); Bearss, "Colonel Streight Drives for the Western and Atlantic Railroad," 173–74 (ambuscades).

16. Willet, *Lightning Mule Brigade*, 132–33 ("Boys").

17. Ibid., 136–37.

18. Ibid., 138–39 (all quotes).

19. Ibid., 139 ("He stepped quickly," "asked me my name"), 140 ("They have only wounded"), 141 (Forrest's note); Roach, *Prisoner of War*, 33 ("notwithstanding").

20. Whitsitt, "Year with Forrest," 360 ("Why should"); *OR*, vol. 23, 290 ("Many of our animals").

21. Willet, *Lightning Mule Brigade*, 146 ("throwing me," "I arrived").

22. *OR*, vol. 23, 291 ("His loss").

23. Moore, "Streight's Raid," 343 ("The boys"); Willet, *Lightning Mule Brigade*, 162 ("dead to the world").

24. Willet, *Lightning Mule Brigade*, 163 ("in order to stop"); Whitsitt, "Year with Forrest," 361 ("If he talks," "old man," "had large experience"); *OR*, vol. 23, 292 ("I yielded").

25. Willet, *Lightning Mule Brigade*, 164 ("I seen him"); Bearss, "Colonel Streight Drives for the Western and Atlantic Railroad," 85 ("Straight-neck").

26. Moore, "Streight's Raid," 344 ("At nine a.m."); Whitsitt, "Year with Forrest," 361 ("Streight had," "imaginary"); Cook, "1863 Raid," 269 ("Ah, Colonel"); Mitchell, "How Forrest Won Over Streight," 380 ("Their arms").

27. Whitsitt, "Year with Forrest," 361 ("Our victory").

28. McMillan, *Alabama Confederate Reader*, 107 ("We are satisfied"); Walther, *William Lowndes Yancey*, 367 ("prejudice and littleness"), 368 (Yancey's death).

29. Walther, *William Lowndes Yancey*, 370 ("to the politics," "a restless," "the most virulent"); *New York Times*, August 5, 1863 (quoting *Richmond Dispatch)*; McMillan, *Alabama Confederate Reader*, 252 ("We can and will").

## Chapter 5

1. Jones, *Artilleryman's Diary*, 159 ("The new year").

2. Homestead, "Publishing History of Augusta Janes Evans's Confederate Novel *Macaria*," 667; *OR*, vol. 32, pt. 2, 514 ("relative"), 515 ("a glance at the map," "such calamities," "without meeting"); Bergeron, *Confederate Mobile*, 78 (Mobile defenses); Sexton, *Southern Woman of Letters*, 93 ("not more than half").

3. Grant, *Personal Memoirs*, 388 ("Having that"); *ORN*, vol. 21, 90 ("amuse myself").

4. Browning, *Lincoln's Trident*, 417–18 (Fort Powell); Folmar, *From That Terrible Field*, 126 ("I am fixing").

5. *ORN*, vol. 21, 91 ("dilapidated"); Browning, *Lincoln's Trident*, 61 ("chowder pots"), 418 ("a train of cars").

6. Bergeron, *Confederate Mobile*, 133 ("shell grazed"); Folmar, *From That Terrible Field*, 128 (Williams quotes).

7. McMillan, *Alabama Confederate Reader*, 308 ("Our foes"); Bergeron, *Confederate Mobile*, 134 (Rebel troops in Mobile).

8. *Frank Leslie's*, April 2, 1864 ("Evidently"); Bergeron, *Confederate Mobile*, 135 ("I saw").

9. Bergeron, *Confederate Mobile*, 137 ("Not a single"); Sexton, *Southern Woman of Letters*, 96 ("twice"), 99 ("champagne").

10. Catton, *Civil War*, 441–43 (new strategy).

11. Evans, *Sherman's Horsemen*, 31 ("The expedition," "the party"). See also, *OR*, vol. 38, pt. 2, 904.

12. Evans, *Sherman's Horsemen*, 33 ("When he showed," "third rate," "drink as much"); "Civil War Days in Huntsville," 215 ("handsome").

13. Evans, *Sherman's Horsemen*, 43 (the men); Jones, *Yankee Blitzkrieg*, 18 (Spencer carbine).

14. Moore, "General Rousseau's Expedition," 190 (supplies); Evans, *Sherman's Horsemen*, 46 ("We are only").

15. Evans, *Sherman's Horsemen*, 43 ("The boys"), 45 ("I am off"); Moore, "General Rousseau's Expedition," 190 ("The bugles," "Hazardous").

16. Moore, "General Rousseau's Expedition," 191 ("the waters").

17. Evans, *Sherman's Horsemen*, 104 ("And who mout").

18. Ibid., 100–101 ("I presume," "Faster!," "seemed to dodge").

19. Ibid., 107 ("Maj. Gen."); Moore, "General Rousseau's Expedition," 191 ("In the afternoon").

20. Evans, *Sherman's Horsemen*, 108 (Curl).

21. Ibid., 111 ("Gallant"). See also *OR*, vol. 38, pt. 2, 905–6.

22. Evans, *Sherman's Horsemen*, 116–17 (the crossing); Moore, "General Rousseau's Expedition," 192 ("The ford"). See also *OR*, vol. 38, pt. 2, 906.

23. Barclay, "Reminiscences of Rousseau's Raid," 209 ("My father"), 210 ("some old silverware," "a quick," "dense clouds," "refrained," "Kentucky Gentleman").

24. Evans, *Sherman's Horsemen*, 126 ("Our road," questions, "We found"); Sherman, *Memoirs*, 69 ("Well in this war").

25. Moore, "General Rousseau's Expedition," 194 ("No force," "The long lines"); Hamilton, *Recollections*, 135 ("The railroad"). See also *OR*, vol. 38, pt. 2, 907, for a description of the railroad.

26. Evans, *Sherman's Horsemen*, 139 ("ringing"); Fretwell, "Rousseau's Alabama Raid," 538–39 ("apprehensions"); Rogers, *Confederate Home Front*, 123 (Montgomery preparations).

27. Hamilton, *Recollections*, 137 ("As yet," "Haint got time"); Evans, *Sherman's Horsemen*, 153 ("dashed in").

28. Moore, "General Rousseau's Expedition," 195 ("Both sides"); Evans, *Sherman's Horsemen*, 151 ("I shouldn't").

29. Evans, *Sherman's Horsemen*, 165 ("a pretty country town," "This was a happy find," "everything in sight"), 168 ("ransacked").

30. Ibid., 164 (Rousseau and Sherman).

31. McIlwain, *Civil War Alabama*, 192 (*Herald*); *New York Times*, August 3, 1864 ("has demonstrated"); *Montgomery Weekly Advertiser*, August 10, 1864 ("We doubt"); Evans, *Sherman's Horsemen*, 172 (success), 173 (Rousseau's message).

32. *OR*, vol. 7, 614–15 ("We ought").

33. Bryant, *Cahaba Prison*, 20 (Castle Morgan).

34. Hawes, *Cahaba*, 15 ("roosts," "packed"), 16 ("warm"), 445 ("no dry spot," "their weight," "teeth chattering"); Bryant, *Cahaba Prison*, 45 ("aquatic").

35. Grigsby, *Smoked Yank*, 74 ("wholesome," "many of the prisoners," "a young lady," "one of Scott's"), 77 ("and the conditions").

36. Bryant, *Cahaba Prison*, 65 (death toll), 67 ("the rebs").

37. Grigsby, *Smoked Yank*, 82 ("De City").

## Chapter 6

1. *New York Times*, April 5, 1864; Armes, *Story of Coal and Iron*, 135 ("The city").

2. Tucker, *Civil War Naval Encyclopedia*, 1: 333 (Jones).

3. Katcher, *American Civil War Artillery*, 20 (Brooke guns); Stephen, "Brooke Guns from Selma," 465–66 (on Selma-made guns aboard the Rebel vessels at Mobile Bay); Armes, *Story of Coal and Iron*, 144 ("massive"); *ORN*, vol. 20, 858 ("We had an explosion," "hot work").

4. Hearn, *Admiral David Glasgow Farragut*, 236 ("ram fever"), 237 ("I am in hourly").

5. Ibid., xv–xxi (Farragut's background), 250–51 ("I would sooner"); Farragut, *David Glasgow Farragut*, 208 ("God forbid"), 204 ("sticking").

6. Browning, *Lincoln's Trident*, 437 (Page, "looked to be"); Hearn, *Admiral David Glasgow Farragut*, 244 ("Ramrod," "Bombast"); Bergeron, *Confederate Mobile*, 81 ("We are very well pleased").

7. Hearn, *Admiral David Glasgow Farragut*, 244 (forts); McMillan, *Alabama Confederate Reader*, 310 (Rebel ships).

8. Friend, *West Wind, Flood Tide*, 68 ("If he won't"), 102 (ironclads).

9. Ibid., 125 (battle plan); *ORN*, vol. 21, 397 ("Strip your vessels"); Duncan, "Storming of Mobile Bay," 11 ("well written," "grandeur"); Belknap, *Letters of Captain George Hamilton Perkins*, 138 ("a lot of mechanics," "if I get killed").

10. Friend, *West Wind, Flood Tide*, 120 ("prizefighter"); Folmar, *From That Terrible Field*, 132 ("more the merrier," "fine time," "take good care").

11. Hearn, *Admiral David Glasgow Farragut*, 255–56 ("I am going").

12. Friend, *West Wind, Flood Tide*, 162 ("All hands!," "Up all," "Get under way!").

13. Ibid., 163.

14. Ibid., 165 ("some demonstration," "with intense"), 168 ("It was a grand sight").

15. Cox, "Mobile in the War between the States," 212 ("Open the fight," "instantly," "the roar"); Friend, *West Wind, Flood Tide*, 166 ("soul stirring"); Wilkinson, "Diary," 1 ("stood nobly," "yells").

16. Hutchison, "Bay Fight," 13 ("looking exactly," "with a shriek"); Duncan, "Storming of Mobile Bay," 17 ("Shot, shell"); Friend, *West Wind, Flood Tide*, 180 ("very earth").

17. The story of the boy and his father represents the only authentic "reach-back" memory of the Battle of Mobile Bay in my experience. During the summer of 1985, while conducting a historic building survey in Point Clear, on Mobile Bay's Eastern Shore, resident Carroll Rubira, then in his seventies, told me the story. As a boy, he had met an old man who had been the nine-year-old, who still recalled that distant day; Friend, *West Wind, Flood Tide*, 185 ("pandemonium," "we girls"); Burnett, *Pen Makes a Good Sword*, 142 ("will be strewed").

18. Ayto and Simpson, *Oxford Dictionary of Modern Slang*, 289 ("smoke pole," "smoke wagon"); Browning, *Lincoln's Trident*, 447 (Farragut in the rigging).

19. Friend, *West Wind, Flood Tide*, 262 ("I went up," "Never mind").

20. Browning, *Lincoln's Trident*, 448 ("The monitors"), 449 ("Tell the monitors").

21. Ibid., 448 ("Her stern"), 449 ("wildly clawing"), 450 ("Go ahead," "No, sir"); Kinney, "Farragut at Mobile Bay," 388 ("There was nothing"). The site of the *Tecumseh* wreck is marked by a buoy regularly monitored by the US Coast Guard.

22. Browning, *Lincoln's Trident*, 450 ("turned pale," "rushed from their guns," "Our best monitor"); Kinney, "Farragut at Mobile Bay," 389 ("The sight").

23. Browning, *Lincoln's Trident*, 450 ("What's the matter," "She must have"); Hearn, *Admiral David Glasgow Farragut*, 263 ("Oh God," "Go on," "Torpedoes ahead," "Damn").

24. Friend, *West Wind, Flood Tide*, 190 ("At no time," "The scream").

25. Ibid., 191 ("Well, you might").

26. Browning, *Lincoln's Trident*, 459 ("I have had").

27. Ibid., 459 ("You may pass"), 461 ("Why, that is fair").

28. Hearn, *Admiral David Glasgow Farragut*, 274 ("would turn"); Symonds, *Confederate Admiral*, 215 ("Steady," "We are alright"), 217 ("You infernal"); Rix, *Incidents of Life in a Southern City*, 3 ("popgun").

29. Hearn, *Admiral David Glasgow Farragut*, 279 ("Save the Admiral").

30. Belknap, *Letters of Captain George Hamilton Perkins*, 142 ("poured"), 144 ("like pocket pistols"), 142 ("wet with perspiration"); Symonds, *Confederate Admiral*, 217 ("a thunderous report").

31. Browning, *Lincoln's Trident*, 467 (surrender).

32. Belknap, *Letters of Captain George Hamilton Perkins*, 158 ("I told you"); Duncan, "Storming of Mobile Bay," 12 ("We have fought,"), 13 ("severe," "such glorious"); Friend, *West Wind, Flood Tide*, ix ("most desperate").

33. Folmar, *From That Terrible Field*, 136 ("The shells," "your fort"); Browning, *Lincoln's Trident*, 472 ("heap"). Williams faced a court-martial for abandoning Fort Powell, but was exonerated.

34. Hearn, *Admiral David Glasgow Farragut*, 295 ("painfully").

35. Page, "Defense of Fort Morgan," 410 ("of several hours," "desultory"); Wilkinson, "Diary," 5 ("the casemates," "good spirits," "perfect rain," "falling and flying").

36. Trickey, Holmes, and Clute, "Archaeological and Historical Investigations at Pinto Battery," (quoting Mumford's diary); Scheliha, *Treatise on Coast Defence*, 157 (Farragut to Welles); Rix, *Incidents of Life in a Southern City*, 17 ("like a little dog"); Bergeron, *Confederate Mobile*, 156 ("Green Mountain Range").

37. Page, "Defense of Fort Morgan," 410 (the inspection quotes); Browning, *Lincoln's Trident*, 476 (the surrender); Farragut, *Life of David Glasgow Farragut*, 462 ("Now neither").

38. *New York Times*, August 15, 1864; *Daily Ohio Statesman*, August 17, 1864; *Boston Weekly Transcript*, August 17, 1864; McIlwain, *Civil War Alabama*, 193 ("stunning effect").

39. Friend, *West Wind, Flood Tide*, 241–42 (proclamation).

## Chapter 7

1. *Chattanooga Daily Rebel*, February 5, 1865.

2. Jones, *Yankee Blitzkrieg*, 3–6 (Wilson), 13–14 (strategic benefits).

3. Ibid., 13–14 ("The valley").

4. Gilpin, "Last Campaign," 618 ("army of cavalry"), 625 ("he is sitting," "Mess kits"), 626 ("Our fellows"); Hosea, "Campaign of Selma," 6 ("entire command," "an *esprit*").

5. *New York Times*, February 11, 1865 (also quotes the Southern papers).

6. Young, *Seventh Tennessee Cavalry*, 132 ("quietly," "refitting," "That we have every confidence"), 133 ("fair women"), 134 ("not fully convinced"); Montgomery, *Reminiscences of a Mississippian*, 236 ("The romance").

7. Gilpin, "Last Campaign," 623 ("Forrest is a dangerous foe"); McMillan, *Alabama Confederate Reader*, 187 ("the very devil").

8. Wilson, *Under the Old Flag*, 2: 184 ("to study"); Hosea, "Some Side Lights," 9 ("fine physique"), 12 ("dignity," "frequently lost"); Hosea, "Campaign of Selma," 7 ("Wal, I never rubbed").

9. Gilpin, "Last Campaign," 629 ("This is a country of rivers"); Jones, *Yankee Blitzkrieg*, 20 ("I seen a boat"), 21 ("It will be").

10. Jones, *Yankee Blitzkrieg*, 28 ("magnificent," "in the best of spirits").

11. Hosea, "Campaign of Selma," 12 ("Never can I forget"); Jones, *Yankee Blitzkrieg*, 10 ("an incomparable soldier"), 12 ("strong and vigorous"); Wilson, *Under the Old Flag*, 2: 192 ("on divergent routes"), 194 ("vast extent").

12. Gilpin, "Last Campaign," 631 (fording the river); McGee, *History of the Seventy-Second Infantry*, 532 (McGee quotes).

13. Wilson, *Under the Old Flag*, 2: 203 ("poor, insignificant"); *OR*, vol. 49, pt. 1, 357 ("valuable property"); Gilpin, "Last Campaign," 632 (the plantation and brandy); McGee, *History of the Seventy-Second Infantry*, 534 ("miserable," the destruction).

14. *OR*, vol. 49, pt. 1, 419 ("destroy").

15. Longacre, "To Tuscaloosa and Beyond," 114 (Wooster episode); John, "Alabama Corps of Cadets," 13 (cadets).

16. Jones, *Yankee Blitzkrieg*, 151 (Tuscaloosa destroyed); *Tuscaloosa News*, September 10, 2010 (*Quran*).

17. McGee, *History of the Seventy-Second Infantry*, 535 (Cahaba crossing).

18. Gilpin, "Last Campaign," 633 ("fought them in"); McGee, *History of the Seventy-Second Infantry*, 536 (McGee quotes); Wilson, *Under the Old Flag*, 2: 209 ("fairly 'got the bulge'").

19. Wilson, *Under the Old Flag*, 2: 211 ("I now knew"); McGee, *History of the Seventy-Second Infantry*, 38 (the running fight).

20. Jones, *Yankee Blitzkrieg*, 69–70 (Ebenezer Church).

21. Wilson, *Under the Old Flag*, 2: 216–17.

22. Browne, "Forrest's Last Exploit," 492 ("We did not fire"); McGee, *History of the Seventy-Second Infantry*, 541 ("Just then"); Jones, *Yankee Blitzkrieg*, 71–72 (Taylor and Forrest's duel); Novick, *Honorable Justice*, 28 ("When you strike"); Wilson, *Under the Old Flag*, 2: 217 ("If that boy"). Decades ago, one of Forrest's gloves was given to the Alabama Department of Archives and History by two elderly sisters from Plantersville. The story was that they had treated Forrest's wounded hand and thrown away the bloodied glove. In gratitude, he gave them his other good glove, no longer needing it.

23. *OR*, vol. 49, pt. 1, 359 ("resistance was determined"); Hosea, "Campaign of Selma," 21 ("The enemy"); Gilpin, "Last Campaign," 635 ("road was strewn"); see also Folmar, "War Comes to Central Alabama," 198–202, for a good summary of the battle.

24. Gilpin, "Last Campaign," 636 (Wall's wound), 637 ("only the light"), 638 (close calls); Jones, *Yankee Blitzkrieg*, 73 (losses).

25. Hosea, "Campaign of Selma," 23 ("The sunlight"); Wilson, *Under the Old Flag*, 2: 221 (sketch).

26. *Selma Times Journal*, November 2, 1927 (Perry quotes); Hosea, "Campaign of Selma," 23 (defenses); Wilson, *Under the Old Flag*, 2: 222 ("nothing had been left undone").

27. Thomas, *Fifty Years on the Rail*, 35 ("whistles blowing," "household goods"); Phillips, "Reminiscences of War," n.p. (diary quotes).

28. Montgomery, *Reminiscences of a Mississippian*, 241 ("moved slowly"); Jones, *Yankee Blitzkrieg*, 86 (rear guard).

29. McGee, *History of the Seventy-Second Infantry*, 354 ("From the entire"); Montgomery, *Reminiscences of a Mississippian*, 242 ("as the enemy," "five times"); Hosea, "Campaign of Selma," 26 (Hosea quotes); Montgomery, *Reminiscences of a Mississippian*, 242; Pinckney, "At the Fall of Selma," 63 ("skedaddle").

30. McGee, *History of the Seventy-Second Infantry*, 554 (the preacher); Windham, *Alabama: One Big Front Porch*, 20 (the legend of the rose bush); Montgomery, *Reminiscences of a Mississippian*, 248 (Elliot story).

31. Wilson, *Under the Old Flag*, 2: 229–30 (Sheridan).

32. Woods, "Battle of Selma," n.p. ("Everything"); Phillips, "Reminiscences of War," n.p. (quotes); Gilpin, "Last Campaign," 640 ("Of all the nights").

33. Wilson, *Under the Old Flag*, 2: 234 ("Selma was ours"); Wills, "Confederate Sun Sets on Selma," 81 (casualties); Jones, *Yankee Blitzkrieg*, 87–88 (Union loss); Montgomery, *Reminiscences of a Mississippian*, 247.

34. Wilson, *Under the Old Flag*, 2: 243 (Forrest interview).

35. *OR*, vol. 49, pt. 1, 484 (assets); McGee, *History of the Seventy-Second Infantry*, 562 (spout quotes), 564 ("wagons, ambulances"), 565 (arsenal destroyed).

## Chapter 8

1. Trickey, Holmes, and Clute, "Archaeological and Historical Investigations at Pinto Battery," 55 (Mumford); *Mobile Advertiser and Register*, March 14, 1865 ("Our fortifications"); Folmar, *From That Terrible Field*, 155 ("Yankee maw").

2. *Mobile Telegraph*, March 23, 1865; O'Brien, *Mobile, 1865*, 24 (measures ignored); Folmar, *From That Terrible Field*, 155 (Williams).

3. Little and Maxwell, *History of Lumsden's Battery*, 64 ("were plentiful," "gray jeans," "meteorology"); O'Brien, *Mobile, 1865*, 25 (Cumming).

4. Stephenson, "Defense of Spanish Fort," 121 ("We cut down"); Trickey, Holmes, and Clute, "Archaeological and Historical Investigations at Pinto Battery," 55 ("Strong southeast wind"); Little and Maxwell, *History of Lumsden's Battery*, 63 ("cast iron guns," "firing").

5. Stephenson, "Defense of Spanish Fort," 119 (quotes); *OR*, vol. 2, 941 (Maury's pleas for Creoles); Bergeron, *Confederate Mobile*, 106 (Seddon).

6. *New York Times*, March 25, 1865; Trickey, Holmes, and Clute, "Archaeological and Historical Investigations at Pinto Battery," 58 (Mumford); O'Brien, *Mobile, 1865*, 28 (Pillans).

7. Grant, *Personal Memoirs*, 679 ("Take Mobile"); O'Brien, *Mobile, 1865*, 33 ("I am very much").

8. O'Brien, *Mobile, 1865*, 34 (plans), 90 ("burning").

9. Ibid., 45 ("a horseshoe"), 144 ("mean way"); Andrews, *History of the Campaign of Mobile*, 48–50 (all quotes on the defenses); Stephenson, "Defense of Spanish Fort," 110 ("We felt ourselves").

10. Tucker, "First Missouri Confederate Brigade's Last Stand," 276 ("Our brigade"); O'Brien, *Mobile, 1865*, 53 ("You must dig").

11. Wood, *History of the Ninety-Fifth Regiment*, 165 ("Yankee ingenuity"), 166 (oysters and mosquitoes); Andrews, *History of the Mobile Campaign*, 36–37 (feint).

12. *OR*, vol. 49, pt. 1, 141 ("The march"); O'Brien, *Mobile, 1865*, 37 ("Scrubby Pine"), 38 ("barren," "one may judge"), 39 ("Then we pull," "Glory"), 40 ("Boys").

13. O'Brien, *Mobile, 1865*, 61 ("We have to drag"), 63 ("I had an Enfield"); Andrews, *History of the Campaign of Mobile*, 108 (description of creek bank).

14. Holt, *Miss Waring's Journal*, 9 ("The firing"), 10 ("restless spirit"); Rix, *Incidents of Life in a Southern City*, 18; Trickey, Holmes, and Clute, "Archaeological and Historical Investigations at Pinto Battery," 59 (Mumford); *Mobile Register*, April 2, 1865.

15. Martin, "L. F. Hubbard and the Fifth Minnesota," 68 ("We are considerably," "The position"); Newton, "Siege of Mobile," 596 ("We are in the midst"), 597 ("out skirmishing," "since our ill fated"); Andrews, *History of the Campaign of Mobile*, 88 ("skull crackers").

16. O'Brien, *Mobile, 1865*, 145 ("rolling end over end"), 147 ("the entire length"); *OR*, vol. 49, pt. 1, 315 ("For the first ten days"). Today the Lady Slocomb is on display at the Confederate Memorial Hall Museum in New Orleans.

17. Perry, *Infernal Machines*, 188 ("the only enemy"); Andrews, *History of the Campaign of Mobile*, 67–68 (Andrews on the *Milwaukee*).

18. Waterman, "Afloat, Afield, Afloat," 25–26.

19. *Mobile Register*, April 4, 1865.

20. Andrews, *History of the Campaign of Mobile*, 65 (Noble episode), 73–77 (Myers incident).

21. *OR*, vol. 49, pt. 1, 316 (Gibson); Stephenson, "Defense of Spanish Fort," 123 (bombardment); Rix, *Incidents of Life in a Southern City*, 18.

22. Stephenson, "Defense of Spanish Fort," 127 (the withdrawal); Holt, *Miss Waring's Journal*, 13 ("I had to believe"); *Mobile Register*, November 1, 1914 ("along the wharves," "shoeless").

23. *Newton*, "Siege of Mobile," 599 ("Spanish Fort is ours," "They all seem"); *OR*, vol. 49, pt. 1, 153 (Ordnance report); O'Brien, *Mobile, 1865*, 182 (casualties).

24. Nerdahl et al., "Samuel Crawford, Private," 62 ("These Rebels"); Hatch, *Dearest Susie*, n.p., letters dated April 5, 8, 1865 (Rebel fire).

25. O'Brien, *Mobile, 1865*, 153 ("swap lies"), 154 (Alexander episode).

26. Andrews, *History of the Campaign of Mobile*, 200–201 ("mow the ground"), 208 ("constant blaze"), 202–3 (torpedo); Hatch, *Dearest Susie*, April 10, 1865, letter; Jones, *History 46th Illinois*, 229 (Lollar incident); O'Brien, *Mobile, 1865*, 195–96 (Kavanaugh); Bevier, *History of the First and Second Missouri Confederate Brigades*, 265–66 (line collapse).

27. "Letter of Walter Chapman," ("As soon as"); Nerdahl et al., "Samuel Crawford, Private," 63 ("The excitement"); Andrews, *History of the Campaign of Mobile*, 201 (canteen episode).

28. Grant, *Personal Memoirs*, 2: 758 (Grant); Bergeron, *Confederate Mobile*, 186 (casualties).

29. Rix, *Incidents of Life in a Southern City*, 19–22.

30. *ORN*, vol. 21, 92–94 (surrender demand); Porter, *Naval History of the Civil War*, 782 ("The city has been evacuated").

31. Delaney, *Confederate Mobile*, 192 (quoting the disgusted southerner); Bergeron, *Confederate Mobile*, 191 ("was resonant"); Rix, *Incidents of Life in a Southern City*, 24; Cumming, *Gleanings*, 259.

## Chapter 9

1. Neeley, *Works of Matthew Blue*, 389.

2. Rogers, *Confederate Home Front*, 141–43 (preparations).

3. Wilson, *Under the Old Flag*, 2: 249; McGee, *History of the Seventy-Second Infantry*, 573 (dance).

4. Jones, *Yankee Blitzkrieg*, 105 ("It was past midnight"); "John Bragg," *Encyclopedia of Alabama*, http://www.encyclopediaofalabama.org/article/h-3696.

5. Wilson, *Under the Old Flag*, 2: 250 ("sharp fight"); McMillan, *Alabama Confederate Reader*, 419–20 (all newspaper quotes, orders to evacuate); Jones, "Journal of Sarah G. Follansbee," 230 ("Great consternation"), 230–31 ("A number of us sat").

6. Wilson, *Under the Old Flag*, 2: 251 ("With perfect order"); Misulia, *Columbus, Georgia, 1865*, 19 ("Lawd!"); Rogers, *Confederate Home Front*, 151 ("The Stars and Stripes").

7. Jones, "Journal of Sarah G. Follansbee," 231.

8. McMillan, *Alabama Confederate Reader*, 421 (newspaper quote); Rogers, *Confederate Home Front*, 149 (foot races, Hosea quote).

9. Wilson, *Under the Old Flag*, 2: 254 ("The situation").

10. *OR*, vol. 49, pt. 1, 334 (Canby).

11. Ibid., pt. 2, 1226 ("Impress on Spence"), 1227 ("You had better place," "retain sufficient," "is reported"), 1239 ("will occupy me").

12. Chambers, "My Journal," 369 ("fever"), ("half an inch of candle"); Waters, "Enigmatic Colonel Maury," 17 (clash at Claiborne); *Cincinnati Daily Commercial*, May 21, 1865 (skirmish at Eight Mile Creek).

13. Cameron, "Battles Opposite Mobile," 306.

14. Ibid., 308 (dessert); Smith, *People's City*, 213 ("I am reliably").

15. Rix, *Incidents of Life in a Southern City*, 24.

16. "Civil War Days in Huntsville," 324 (Chadick); Doss, "Every Man Should Consider His Own Conscience," 173–74 (Clay).

17. Doss, "Every Man Should Consider His Own Conscience," 169 (Chadick, *Daily News*), 171 (*Daily Mail*), 173 ("Mr. Abraham").

18. McGee, *History of the Seventy-Second Infantry*, 580; Misulia, *Columbus, Georgia, 1865*, 22 (swamp).

19. McGee, *History of the Seventy-Second Infantry*, 580 ("a most beautiful"), 579 ("men, women, and children"); Misulia, *Columbus, Georgia, 1865*, 24 ("It is one of the finest," "flower garden," "fine homes, beautiful lawns"); Jones, *Yankee Blitzkrieg*, 120 ("yankeefied").

20. McGee, *History of the Seventy-Second Infantry*, 581.

21. Misulia, *Columbus, Georgia, 1865*, 120 ("at once"), 121 ("leaving a fiery"), 149 ("Rally!"); Wilson, *Under the Old Flag*, 2: 262 ("more noisy"); McGee, *History of the Seventy-Second Infantry*, 581 (trophies); *New York Times*, May 4, 1865.

22. Martin, "L. F. Hubbard," 70–71 (Union celebration); Works Progress Administration, *Slave Narratives*, vol. 1, *Alabama*, 17 (Askew).

23. Wood, *History of the Ninety-Fifth Illinois*, 185–86; "Civil Wars Days in Huntsville," 333 (Chadick); Clayton, *White and Black*, 150–51.

24. O'Brien, *Mobile, 1865*, 217–19.

25. *OR*, vol. 49, pt. 2, 1287 (Maury), 1289–90 (Forrest); *OR*, vol. 49, pt. 1, 319 (Gibson).

26. Scharf, *History of the Confederate States Navy*, 596 (on the parole); *ORN*, vol. 22, 180 (surrender); Waterman, "Afield, Afloat, Afield," 27; Cameron, "Battles Opposite Mobile," 308 ("I know that I found").

27. Interview with Robert Bradley, February 16, 2016 (casualties); *Montgomery Daily Advertiser*, April 18, 1865; Rogers et al., *Alabama: The History of a Deep South State*, 229 (Clarke County); Keenan, "Wilson's Selma Raid," 44 ("who have the air"); Doss, "Every Man Should Consider His Own Conscience," 173 ("A'ter").

## Epilogue

1. Delaney and Kearley, *Deep South*, n.p. (entry for "Tait Plantation").

2. "Tait-Starr Home," http://www.ruralswalabama.org/attraction/the-starr-home-white-columns-late-1850s/ (accessed January 20, 2016).

3. Ouida Starr Woodson e-mail, January 13, 2016.

# Bibliography

## Archival Sources

John W. Henley et al. to Governor Moore, January 19, 1861. Alabama Department of Archives and History (ADAH), Confederate Regimental History Files, Box #SG024929.

"Letter of Walter Chapman, Second Lieutenant, Fifty-First Regiment, Second Brigade, First Division, United States Colored Troops." Historic Mobile Preservation Society (HMPS).

Martin, N. B. "L. F. Hubbard and the Fifth Minnesota: Letters of a Union Volunteer 1862–1866." Unpublished manuscript. HMPS.

Mrs. P. E. Collins to Gov. John Gill Shorter, April 5, 1862. ADAH, Admin. Files, Box #RSG00252.

Nerdahl, Miriam Crawford Smith, Genevieve Smith Edington, Rebecca Alice Smith Lapehin, eds. "Samuel Crawford, Private, Co. E., 20th Iowa Volunteer Infantry, 3rd Brig., 2nd. Div. XIII Corps, 11 August 1862–8 July 1865, Civil War and Family Letters." Unpublished manuscript. HMPS.

Phillips, Sarah Ellen. "Reminiscences of War and Episode of Wilson's Raid near Selma." ADAH, Box #SPR7.

Psychological Test by Dr. Julian Pennington of Dallas, Texas, Vocational Clinic on Mrs. C. W. Wyn. Author's collection.

US Bureau of the Census. *Eighth Census of the United States, 1860.* Manufactures. Alabama.

Wilkinson, Joseph. "Diary of the Siege of Fort Morgan." ADAH.

Woods, Marion Jane Thomas. "The Battle of Selma." Unpublished manuscript. Selma-Dallas County Public Library (SDPL).

Worthington Family Letters. Private papers of Miranda Fisk, Shelburne, Vermont.

## Newspapers

*Boston Weekly Transcript*
*Chattanooga Daily Rebel*
*Cincinnati Daily Commercial*
*Daily Ohio Statesman*
*Frank Leslie's Illustrated Newspaper*
*Harper's Weekly*
*Mobile Daily Advertiser*
*Mobile Daily Advertiser and Register*
*Mobile Register*
*Mobile Telegraph*
*Montgomery Daily Advertiser*
*Montgomery Weekly Advertiser*

*New Orleans Bee*
*New York Times*
*Selma Times-Journal*
*Tuscaloosa News*

## Books, Articles, and Other Sources

Amos, Harriet. *Cotton City: Urban Development in Antebellum Mobile.* Tuscaloosa: University of Alabama Press, 1985.

Andrews, C. C. *History of the Campaign of Mobile; Including the Cooperative Operations of Gen. Wilson's Cavalry in Alabama.* New York: D. Van Nostrand, 1889.

Armes, Ethel. *The Story of Coal and Iron in Alabama.* Birmingham, AL: Chamber of Commerce, 1910.

Arnold, J. Barto, III. *The Denbigh's Civilian Imports: Customs Records of a Civil War Blockade Runner between Mobile and Havana.* College Station, TX: Institute of Nautical Archaeology, 2011.

"Astronomical Observatories in the United States." *Harper's New Monthly Magazine* 13, no. 73 (1856): 25–52.

Ayto, John, and John Simpson, eds. *The Oxford Dictionary of Modern Slang.* Oxford: Oxford University Press, 2010.

Bak, Richard. *The CSS* Hunley: *The Greatest Undersea Adventure of the Civil War.* Dallas: Taylor Publishing, 1999.

Baldwin, Thomas, and J. Thomas. *A New and Complete Gazetteer of the United States.* Philadelphia: Lippincott, Grambo, 1854.

Barclay, Hugh G. "Reminiscences of Rousseau's Raid." *Confederate Veteran* 30, no. 6 (1922): 208–9.

Bearss, Edwin C. "Colonel Streight Drives for the Western and Atlantic Railroad." *Alabama Historical Quarterly* 26 (Summer 1964): 133–86.

Beatty, John. *The Citizen Soldier; or, Memoirs of a Volunteer.* Cincinnati: Wilstach/Baldwin, 1879.

Belknap, George E. *Letters of Captain George Hamilton Perkins.* Concord, NH: Rumford Press, 1901.

Benners, Augustus. *Disunion, War, Defeat, and Recovery in Alabama: The Journal of Augustus Benners, 1850–1885.* Macon, GA: Mercer University Press, 2007.

Bergeron, Arthur W., Jr. *Confederate Mobile.* Baton Rouge: Louisiana State University Press, 1991.

Besson, J. A. B. *History of Eufaula, Alabama, The Bluff City of the Chattahoochee.* Atlanta: Jas. P. Harrison, 1875.

Bevier, Robert S. *History of the First and Second Confederate Missouri Cavalry Brigades.* Saint Louis, MO: Bryan, Brand, 1879.

Black, Patti Carr. *Art in Mississippi, 1720–1980.* Jackson: University Press of Mississippi, 1998.

Black, Robert C. *The Railroads of the Confederacy*. Chapel Hill: University of North Carolina Press, 1952.

Bradley, George C., and Richard L. Dahlen. *From Conciliation to Conquest: The Sack of Athens and the Court-Martial of Colonel John B. Turchin*. Tuscaloosa: University of Alabama Press, 2006.

Bradley, Robert. "Tattered Banners: Alabama's Civil War Flags." *Alabama Heritage* (Spring 2010): 10–21.

Brannon, Peter. "The Stars and Bars." *Alabama Historical Quarterly* 18 (Winter 1956): 427–42.

Brewer, Willis. *Alabama: Her History, Resources, War Record, and Public Men, from 1540–1872*. Montgomery, AL: Barrett and Brown, 1872.

Browne, J. M. "Forrest's Last Exploit." *Confederate Veteran* 25, no. 11 (1917): 491–92.

Browning, Robert M., Jr. *Lincoln's Trident: The West Gulf Blockading Squadron during the Civil War*. Tuscaloosa: University of Alabama Press, 2015.

Bryant, William O. *Cahaba Prison and the Sultana Disaster*. Tuscaloosa: University of Alabama Press, 1990.

Bulloch, James D. *The Secret Service of the Confederate States in Europe; or, How the Confederate Cruisers Were Equipped*. Vol. 1. New York: G. P. Putnam's Sons, 1884.

Bunn, Mike. *Civil War Eufaula*. Charleston, SC: History Press, 2013.

Burlingame, Michael. *Abraham Lincoln: A Life*. Vol. 2. Baltimore: Johns Hopkins University Press, 2008.

Burnett, Edmund Cody. "Letters of the Lightfoot Brothers." *Georgia Historical Quarterly* (December 1941): 371–400.

Burnett, Lonnie A. *The Pen Makes a Good Sword: John Forsyth of the Mobile Register*. Tuscaloosa: University of Alabama Press, 2006.

Cameron, William Lochiel. "The Battles Opposite Mobile." *Confederate Veteran* 23, no. 7 (1915): 305–8.

Capers, Henry D. *The Life and Times of C. G. Memminger*. Richmond, VA: Everett Waddey, 1893.

Catton, Bruce. *The Civil War*. New York: Doubleday, 1960.

Center, Clark E. "The Burning of the University of Alabama." *Alabama Heritage* 16 (Spring 1990): 30–45.

Chaffin, Tom. *The H. L. Hunley: The Secret Hope of the Confederacy*. New York: Hill and Wang, 2008.

Chambers, William Pitt. "My Journal." *Publications of the Mississippi Historical Society* 5 (1925): 225–386.

Childress, David T. "Mount Vernon Barracks: The Blue, The Gray, and The Red." *Alabama Review* 42, no. 2 (1989): 125–35.

"Civil War Days in Huntsville: A Diary by Mrs. W. D. Chadick." *Alabama Historical Quarterly* 9 (Summer 1947): 195–333.

Clayton, Victoria. *White and Black under the Old Regime.* Milwaukee: Young Churchman, 1899.

Cline, Wayne. *Alabama Railroads.* Tuscaloosa: University of Alabama Press, 1997.

Cloud, Noah B. "A Day with Daniel Pratt, at Prattville." *American Cotton Planter* 1, no. 5 (1857): 156–57.

Cook, James F. "The 1863 Raid of Abel D. Streight: Why It Failed." *Alabama Review* 22, no. 4 (1969): 254–69.

Corsan, W. C. *Two Months in the Confederate States: An Englishman's Travels through the South.* Baton Rouge: Louisiana State University Press, 1996.

Cox, Benjamin B. "Mobile in the War between the States." *Confederate Veteran* 24, no. 5 (1916): 209–13.

Cumming, Kate. *Gleanings from Southland: Sketches of Life and Manners of the People of the South before, during and after the War of Secession, with Extracts from the Author's Journal.* Birmingham, AL: Roberts and Son, 1895.

Cutrer, Thomas W. *Oh, What a Loansome Time I Had: The Civil War Letters of Major William Morel Moxley, Eighteenth Alabama Infantry, and Emily Beck Moxley.* Tuscaloosa: University of Alabama Press, 2002.

Danielson, Joseph W. *War's Desolating Scourge: The Union Occupation of North Alabama.* Lawrence: University Press of Kansas, 2012.

DeBow, J. D. B. "The American States—Alabama, Part 1." *DeBow's Review* 18, no. 1 (1855): 21–28.

———. "The American States—Alabama, Part 2." *DeBow's Review* 18, no. 2 (1855): 154–59.

———. "The Forests and Timber of South Alabama." *DeBow's Review* 19, no. 5 (1855): 611–13.

———. "Montgomery, Alabama." *DeBow's Review* 26, no. 1 (1859): 117.

———. "Natural Curiosities of Alabama." *DeBow's Review* 26, no. 4 (1859): 468–69.

———. "Railroads of the United States." *DeBow's Review* 26, no. 3 (1859): 342–43.

Delaney, Caldwell. *Confederate Mobile.* Mobile, AL: Haunted Book Shop, 1971.

Delaney, Caldwell, and Frank Kearley. *Deep South.* Mobile, AL: Haunted Book Shop, 1942.

De Leon, T. C. *Four Years in Rebel Capitals: An Inside View of Life in the Southern Confederacy from Birth to Death.* Mobile, AL: Gossip, 1890.

Denman, Clarence Phillips. *The Secession Movement in Alabama.* Montgomery: Alabama State Department of Archives and History, 1933.

Doss, Harriet Amos. "Every Man Should Consider His Own Conscience: Black and White Alabamians' Reaction to the Assassination of Abraham Lincoln." In *The Yellowhammer War: The Civil War and Reconstruction in Alabama,* edited by Kenneth W. Noe, 165–76. Tuscaloosa: University of Alabama Press, 2013.

Duncan, Richard R. "The Storming of Mobile Bay." *Alabama Historical Quarterly* 40, nos. 1 and 2 (1978): 6–19.

Evans, David. *Sherman's Horsemen: Union Cavalry Operations in the Atlanta Campaign.* Bloomington: Indiana University Press, 1996.

Farragut, Loyall. *The Life of David Glasgow Farragut, First Admiral of the United States Navy.* New York: D. Appleton, 1879.

Faulkner, William. *Flags in the Dust.* New York: Vintage, 1973.

Fitzgerald, Edward, trans. *Rubaiyat of Omar Khayyam.* New York: Dodge, 1916.

Fletcher, Henry. "A Run through the Southern States." *Cornhill Magazine* 7 (April 1863): 495–515.

Folmar, John Kent. "The War Comes to Central Alabama: Ebenezer Church, April 1, 1865." *Alabama Historical Quarterly* 26, no. 2 (1964): 187–202.

———, ed. *From That Terrible Field: Civil War Letters of James M. Williams, Twenty-First Alabama Infantry Volunteers.* Tuscaloosa: University of Alabama Press, 1981.

Foote, Shelby. *The Civil War: A Narrative.* 3 vols. New York: Random House, 1974.

Foreman, Amanda. *A World on Fire: Britain's Crucial Role in the American Civil War.* New York: Random House, 2010.

Fretwell, Mark E. "Rousseau's Alabama Raid." *Alabama Historical Quarterly* 18, no. 4 (1956): 526–51.

Friend, Jack. *West Wind, Flood Tide: The Battle of Mobile Bay.* Annapolis, MD: Naval Institute Press, 2004.

Fry, Anna Gayle. "Life in Dallas County during the War." *Confederate Veteran* 24 (May 1916): 216–22.

Gabel, Christopher R. *Rails to Oblivion: The Battle of Confederate Railroads in the Civil War.* Fort Leavenworth, KS: US Army Command and General Staff College Press, 2002.

Gamble, Robert. *The Alabama Catalog: A Guide to the Architecture of the State.* Tuscaloosa: University of Alabama Press, 1987.

Gay, Mary H. *Life in Dixie during the War: 1861-1862-1863-1864-1865.* Atlanta: Charles P. Byrd, 1897.

Gilpin, E. N. "The Last Campaign: A Cavalryman's Journal." *Journal of the United States Cavalry Association* 13 (April 1908): 617–75.

Goodheart, Adam. "Caught Sleeping." *New York Times,* January 3, 2011.

Gosse, Philip Henry. *Letters from Alabama.* London: Morgan and Chase, 1859.

Grant, Ulysses S. *Personal Memoirs of U.S. Grant.* 2 vols. New York: Library of America, 1990.

Griffith, Lucille. *Alabama: A Documentary History to 1900.* Tuscaloosa: University of Alabama Press, 1987.

Grigsby, Melvin. *The Smoked Yank.* Sioux Falls, SD: Dakota Bell Publishing, 1888.

Groom, Winston. *Shiloh 1862.* Washington, DC: National Geographic Society, 2012.

Hague, Parthenia. *A Blockaded Family: Life in Southern Alabama during the Civil War.* New York: Houghton, Mifflin, 1888.

Hamilton, William Douglas. *Recollections of a Cavalryman of the Civil War after Fifty Years, 1861–1865.* Columbus, OH: F. J. Heer, 1915.

Hatch, Carl E. *Dearest Susie: A Civil War Infantryman's Letters to His Sweetheart.* New York: Exposition Press, 1971.

Hawes, Jesse. *Cahaba: A Story of the Captive Boys in Blue*. New York: Burr Printing House, 1888.

Hearn, Chester G. *Admiral David Glasgow Farragut: The Civil War Years*. Annapolis, MD: Naval Institute Press, 1998.

Holt, Thad, ed. *Miss Waring's Journal, 1863 and 1865*. Chicago: Wyvern Press, 1964.

Homestead, Melissa. "The Publishing History of Augusta Jane Evans's Novel *Macaria*: Unwriting Some Lost Cause Myths." *Mississippi Quarterly: The Journal of Southern Cultures* 28, no. 3–4 (2005): 665–702.

Hoole, William Stanley, ed. *Four Years in the Confederate Navy: The Career of Captain John Low*. 1964; rpt. Athens: University of Georgia Press, 2012.

Horrall, S. F. *History of the Forty-Second Indiana Volunteer Infantry*. Chicago: Donohue and Henneberry, 1892.

Hosea, Lewis M. "The Campaign of Selma." *Sketches of War History, 1861–1865, Read before the Ohio Commandery of the Military Order of the Loyal Legion of the United States*. Cincinnati: Peter G. Thompson, 1883.

———. "Some Side Lights on the War for the Union." *Papers Read before the Ohio Commandery of the Military Order of the Loyal Legion of the United States*. Cleveland, 1912, 1–20.

Hoskins, Patricia A. "'The Best Southern Patriots': Jews in Alabama during the Civil War." In *The Yellowhammer War: The Civil War and Reconstruction in Alabama*, edited by Kenneth W. Noe, 149–64. Tuscaloosa: University of Alabama Press, 2013.

Hotze, Henry. *Three Months in the Confederate Army*. Edited by Richard B. Harwell. Tuscaloosa: University of Alabama Press, 1952.

Hughes, Nathaniel Cheairs, and Roy P. Stonesifer Jr. *The Life and Wars of Gideon J. Pillow*. Chapel Hill: University of North Carolina Press, 1993.

Hutchison, William. "The Bay Fight: A Sketch of the Battle of Mobile Bay." *Personal Narratives of the Battles of the Rebellion* 8 (1879): 7.

John, Samuel Will. "Alabama Corps of Cadets, 1861–1865." *Confederate Veteran* 25 (1917): 12–14.

Johnson, Kenneth R. "Confederate Defenses and Union Gunboats on the Tennessee River: A Federal Raid into Northwest Alabama." *Alabama Historical Quarterly* 30 (Summer 1968): 39–60.

Jones, James Pickett. *Yankee Blitzkrieg: Wilson's Raid through Alabama and Georgia*. Athens: University of Georgia Press, 1976.

Jones, J. B. *A Rebel War Clerk's Diary at the Confederate States Capital*. Vol. 1. Philadelphia: J. B. Lippincott, 1866.

Jones, Jenkins Lloyd. *An Artilleryman's Diary*. Madison: Wisconsin History Commission, 1914.

Jones, Thomas B. *History of the 46th Illinois Volunteer Infantry*. Freeport, IL: W. H. Wagner, 1907.

Jones, Virginia, ed. "A Contemporary Account of the Inauguration of Jefferson Davis." *Alabama Historical Quarterly* 23 (Fall–Winter 1961): 273–77.

———. "The Journals of Sarah G. Follansbee." *Alabama Historical Quarterly* 27 (Fall–Winter 1965): 213–28.

———. "Letters of W. H. Mitchell, Jan. 1861." *Alabama Historical Quarterly* 23 (Spring 1961): 180–87.

Jordan, Weymouth T. *Antebellum Alabama: Town and Country.* 1957; rpt. Tuscaloosa: University of Alabama Press, 1987.

Katcher, Philip. *American Civil War Artillery.* Vol. 2, *Heavy Artillery.* Oxford: Osprey Publishing, 2001.

Keenan, Jerry. "Wilson's Selma Raid." *Civil War Times Illustrated* 1, no. 9 (1963): 37–46.

Keller, Mark. "Alabama Plantation Life in 1860—Governor Benjamin Fitzpatrick's 'Oak Grove.'" *Alabama Historical Quarterly* 38 (Fall 1976): 218–27.

Kinney, John Coddington. "Farragut at Mobile Bay." In *Battles and Leaders of the Civil War,* edited by Robert U. Johnson and Clarence C. Buel. New York: Castle Books, 1956.

Knight, James R. *The Battle of Fort Donelson: No Terms but Unconditional Surrender.* Charleston, SC: History Press, 2011.

Konstam, Angus. *Mississippi River Gunboats of the American Civil War, 1861–65.* Oxford: Osprey Publishing, 2002.

Lane, Mills. *Architecture of the Old South: Mississippi and Alabama.* Savannah, GA: Beehive Press, 1989.

Langella, Dale. *Haunted Alabama Battlefields.* Charleston, SC: History Press, 2013.

Lawler, Peter Augustine, and Robert Martin Schaefer, eds. *American Political Rhetoric: A Reader.* Lanham, MD: Rowman and Littlefield, 2005.

Letford, William, and Allen W. Jones. "Military and Naval Activities in Alabama from 1861–1865." *Alabama Historical Quarterly* 23 (Spring 1961): 189–206.

Little, George, and James R. Maxwell. *A History of Lumsden's Battery C.S.A.* Tuscaloosa, AL: United Daughters of the Confederacy, 1905.

Longacre, Edward G., ed. "To Tuscaloosa and Beyond: A Union Cavalry Raider in Alabama, March-April 1865." *Alabama Historical Quarterly* 44 (Spring–Summer 1982): 109–22.

Maffitt, Emma Martin. *The Life and Services of John Newland Maffitt.* New York: Neale Publishing, 1906.

"Manufactures in Southern States." *Hunt's Merchants' Magazine* 38 (1858): 509.

Matthews, Tennie, Jr. "Running the Blockade." *Jefferson City* (MO) *Tribune,*? 1875.

Maxwell, Jerry H. *The Perfect Lion: The Life and Death of Confederate Artillerist John Pelham.* Tuscaloosa: University of Alabama Press, 2011.

McGee, Benjamin F. *History of the Seventy-Second Indiana Infantry of the Mounted Lightning Brigade.* Lafayette, IN: S. Vater, 1882.

McIlwain, Christopher Lyle. *Civil War Alabama.* Tuscaloosa: University of Alabama Press, 2016.

McMillan, Malcom C., ed. *The Alabama Confederate Reader.* Tuscaloosa: University of Alabama Press, 1963.

Meriwether, Colyer, ed. "'A Southern Traveler's Diary in 1840' by William Wills." *Publications of the Southern History Association* 8 (1904): 129–38.

Milner, John T. *Alabama: As It Was, As It Is, and As It Will Be*. Montgomery: Barrett and Brown, 1876.

Misulia, Charles A. *Columbus, Georgia, 1865*. Tuscaloosa: University of Alabama Press, 2010.

Mitchell, C. A. "How Forrest Won Over Streight." *Confederate Veteran* 20, no. 8 (1912): 380–91.

Montgomery, Frank Alexander. *Reminiscences of a Mississippian in Peace and War*. Cincinnati: Robert Clarke Co. Press, 1901.

Moore, Frank, ed. "Expedition to Florence, ALA." In *The Rebellion Record: A Diary of American Events*. New York: D. Van Nostrand, 1865.

———. "General Rousseau's Expedition." In *The Rebellion Record: A Diary of American Events*. New York: Van Nostrand, 1868.

———. "Streight's Raid." In *The Rebellion Record: A Diary of American Events*. New York: D. Van Nostrand, 1866.

Neeley, Mary Ann, ed. *The Works of Matthew Blue, Montgomery's First Historian*. Montgomery, AL: New South Books, 2010.

Nelson, William Cowper. *The Hour of Our Nation's Agony: The Civil War Letters of Lt. William Cowper Nelson of Mississippi*. Edited by Jennifer W. Ford. Knoxville: University of Tennessee Press, 2007.

Newton, James K. "The Siege of Mobile." *Alabama Historical Quarterly* 20, no. 4 (1958): 595–600.

Noe, Kenneth W., ed. *The Yellowhammer War: The Civil War and Reconstruction in Alabama*. Tuscaloosa: University of Alabama Press, 2013.

Novick, Sheldon M. *Honorable Justice: The Life of Oliver Wendell Holmes*. New York: Dell Publishing, 1990.

O'Brien, Sean Michael. *Mobile, 1865: Last Stand of the Confederacy*. Westport, CT: Praeger, 2001.

Oldmixon, John W. *Transatlantic Wanderings*. London: George Routledge, 1855.

Olmsted, Frederick Law. *The Cotton Kingdom*. 2 vols. New York: Mason Bros., 1861.

———. *A Journey in the Seaboard Slave States*. London: Sampson Low, and Son, 1856.

Ormond, John J, Arthur P. Bagby, and George Goldthwaite. *The Code of Alabama*. Montgomery, AL: Brittan and De Wolf, 1852.

Owen, Marie Bankhead. "Raising the First Confederate Flag." *Confederate Veteran* 24, no. 1 (1916): 199.

Owsley, Frank Lawrence, Jr. *The CSS* Florida: *Her Building and Operations*. 1965; rpt. Tuscaloosa: University of Alabama Press, 1987.

Page, R. L. "The Defense of Fort Morgan." In *Battles and Leaders of the Civil War*. Edited by Robert U. Johnson and Clarence C. Buel. New York: Castle Books, 1956.

Patillo, Edward. *Carolina Planters on the Alabama Frontier*. Montgomery, AL: New South Books, 2011.

Perry, Milton F. *Infernal Machines: The Story of Confederate Submarine and Mine Warfare*. Baton Rouge: Louisiana State University Press, 1965.

Phillips, U. B. *Plantation and Frontier Documents: 1649–1863*. Vol. 1. Cleveland: Arthur Clark, 1909.

Pinckney, T. F. "At the Fall of Selma, Ala." *Confederate Veteran* 40, no. 2 (1932): 62–64.

Porter, David D. *The Naval History of the Civil War*. New York: Sherman Publishing, 1886.

Preble, George Henry. *The Chase of the Rebel Steamer of War* Oreto, *Commander J. N. Maffitt, C.S.N. into the Bay of Mobile, by the United States Steam Sloop* Oneida, *Commander Geo. Henry Preble, U.S.N.* Cambridge, MA: Private pamphlet, 1862.

Rix, William. *Incidents of Life in a Southern City during the War: A Series of Sketches Written for the Rutland Herald by a Vermont Gentleman, Who Was for Many Years a Prominent Merchant in Mobile*. Privately printed, 1880. Mobile Public Library.

Roach, A. C. *The Prisoner of War and How Treated*. Indianapolis: Railroad City Publishing House, 1865.

Rogers, William Warren. *Confederate Home Front: Montgomery during the Civil War*. Tuscaloosa: University of Alabama Press, 2009.

Rogers, William Warren, Robert David Ward, Leah Rawls Atkins, and Wayne Flint. *Alabama: The History of a Deep South State*. Tuscaloosa: University of Alabama Press, 1994.

Ross, Fitzgerald. *A Visit to the Cities and Camps of the Confederate States*. Edinburgh: William Blackwood and Sons, 1865.

Royall, Anne Newport. *Letters from Alabama on Various Subjects*. Washington, DC: N.p., 1830.

Russell, William Howard. *My Diary North and South*. Vol. 1. London: Bradbury and Evans, 1863.

Saunders, Ellen Virginia. "War-Time Journal of a 'Little Rebel.'" *Confederate Veteran* 27, no. 12 (1919): 451–52.

Scharf, J. Thomas. *History of the Confederate States Navy from Its Organization to the Surrender of Its Last Vessel*. Albany, NY: Joseph McDonough, 1894.

Scheliha, Victor Ernst Karl Rudolf von. *Treatise on Coast Defence: Based on Experience Gained by Officers of the Corps of Engineers of the Army of the Confederate States, and Compiled from Official Reports of Officers of the Navy of the United States, Made during the Late South American War from 1861 to 1865*. London: E. and F. N. Spon, 1868.

Severance, Ben H. *Portraits of Conflict: A Photographic History of Alabama in the Civil War*. Fayetteville: University of Arkansas Press, 2012.

Sexton, Rebecca Grant, ed. *A Southern Woman of Letters: The Correspondence of Augusta Jane Evans Wilson*. Columbia: University of South Carolina Press, 2002.

Sherman, William T. *Memoirs of General William T. Sherman*. 2 vols. New York: D. Appleton, 1876.

Shingleton, Royce. *High Seas Confederate: The Life and Times of John Newland Maffitt*. Columbia: University of South Carolina Press, 1994.

Shippee, Lester B., ed. *Bishop Whipple's Southern Diary, 1843–1844*. New York: Da Capo Press, 1968.

Sinclair, G. Terry. "The Eventful Cruise of the *Florida*." *Century Magazine* 56 (1898): 421.

Slagle, Jay. *Ironclad Captain: Seth Ledyard Phelps and the U.S. Navy, 1841–1864*. Kent, OH: Kent State University Press, 1996.

Sledge, John Sturdivant. *The Mobile River*. Columbia: University of South Carolina Press, 2015.

———. "Summerfield, Alabama: Historic Preservation in a Rural Context." Master's thesis, Middle Tennessee State University, 1982.

Smith, Winston. *The People's City: The Glory and the Grief of an Alabama Town, 1850–1874*. Demopolis, AL: Marengo County Historical Society, 2003.

Stephen, Walter W. "The Brooke Guns from Selma." *Alabama Historical Quarterly* 20, no. 2 (1958): 462–75.

Stephenson, Philip D. "Defense of Spanish Fort." *Southern Historical Society Papers* 39 (1914): 118–29.

Sterling, Ada, ed. *A Belle of the Fifties: Memoirs of Mrs. Clay of Alabama*. New York: Doubleday, 1905.

Stevenson, William G. *Thirteen Months in the Rebel Army: Being a Narrative of Personal Adventures in the Infantry, Ordnance, Cavalry, Courier, and Hospital Services; With an Exhibition of the Power, Purposes, Earnestness, Military Despotism, and Demoralization of the South*. New York: A. S. Barnes and Burr, 1862.

Still, William N., Jr. "The Confederate States Navy at Mobile, 1861 to August, 1864." *Alabama Historical Quarterly* 30 (Fall–Winter 1968): 127–44.

Symonds, Craig L. *Confederate Admiral: The Life and Wars of Franklin Buchanan*. Annapolis: Naval Institute Press, 1999.

Tenney, W. J. *The Military and Naval History of the Rebellion in the United States*. New York: D. Appleton, 1867.

Thomas, J. J. *Fifty Years on the Rail*. New York: Knickerbocker Press, 1912.

Thomas, William G. *The Iron Way: Railroads, the Civil War, and the Making of Modern America*. New Haven, CT: Yale University Press, 2011.

Thornton, J. Mills. *Politics and Power in a Slave Society: Alabama, 1800–1860*. 1978; rpt. Baton Rouge: Louisiana State University Press, 2014.

Trickey, E. Bruce, Nicholas H. Holmes Jr., and Janet R. Clute. "Archaeological and Historical Investigations at Pinto Battery or Battery Gladden, Site 1Mb17, Mobile Bay, Alabama." *Journal of Alabama Archaeology* 32 (June 1986): 40–62.

Tucker, Phillip Thomas. "The First Missouri Confederate Brigade's Last Stand at Fort Blakeley on Mobile Bay." *Alabama Review* 42 (October 1989): 270–91.

Tucker, Spencer C., ed. *The Civil War Naval Encyclopedia*. 2 vols. Santa Barbara, CA: ABC-CLIO, 2011.

United Confederate Veterans. *Confederate Women of Arkansas in the Civil War 1861–'65: Memorial Reminiscences*. Little Rock, AR: J. Kellogg, 1907.

US War Department. *War of the Rebellion: Official Records of Union and Confederate Armies*. 128 parts in 70 vols. Washington, DC: US Government Printing Office, 1880–1901.

———. *War of the Rebellion: Official Records of Union and Confederate Navies.* 30 vols. Washington, DC: US Government Printing Office, 1894–1922.

Wallace, John William. *Cases Argued and Adjudged in the Supreme Court of the United States, December Term, 1866.* Vol. 5. Washington, DC: W. H. and O. H. Morrison, 1870.

Walther, Eric H. *William Lowndes Yancey and the Coming of the Civil War.* Chapel Hill: University of North Carolina Press, 2006.

Waterman, George S. "Afloat, Afield, Afloat." *Confederate Veteran* 9, no. 1 (1901): 24–29.

Waters, Zack. "The Enigmatic Colonel Maury of the Fifteenth Confederate Cavalry." *Alabama Heritage* (Fall 2010): 8–17.

———. "General Philip D. Roddey: 'Defender of North Alabama.'" *Alabama Heritage* (Fall 2013): 24–33.

Watkins, James Lawrence. *King Cotton: A Historical and Statistical Review, 1790–1908.* New York: James L. Watkins and Sons, 1908.

Webb, Samuel L., and Margaret E. Armbrester, eds. *Alabama Governors: A Political History of the State.* Tuscaloosa: University of Alabama Press, 2014.

Whitsitt, W. H. "A Year with Forrest." *Confederate Veteran* 25, no. 8 (1917): 357–62.

Wills, Brian Steel. "The Confederate Sun Sets on Selma: Nathan Bedford Forrest and the Defense of Alabama in 1865." In *The Yellowhammer War: The Civil War and Reconstruction in Alabama,* edited by Kenneth W. Noe, 71–89. Tuscaloosa: University of Alabama Press, 2013.

Wiggins, Sarah Woolfolk. *From Civil War to Civil Rights—Alabama, 1860–1960.* Tuscaloosa: University of Alabama Press, 1987.

Willett, Robert L. *The Lightning Mule Brigade: Abel Streight's 1863 Raid into Alabama.* Carmel, IN: Guild Press, 1999.

Wilson, Harold S. *Confederate Industry Manufacturers and Quartermasters in the Civil War.* Jackson: University Press of Mississippi, 2002.

Wilson, James Grant, and Titus Munson Coan, eds. *Personal Recollections of the War of the Rebellion: Addresses Delivered before the New York Commandery of the Loyal Legion of the United States, 1883–1891.* New York: The Commandery, 1891.

Wilson, James Harrison. *Under the Old Flag.* 2 vols. New York: D. Appleton, 1912.

Windham, Kathryn Tucker. *Alabama: One Big Front Porch.* Montgomery, AL: New South Books, 2007.

———. *Odd Egg Editor.* Jackson: University Press of Mississippi, 1990.

Wood, Wales W. *A History of the Ninety-Fifth Regiment Illinois Infantry Volunteers.* Chicago: Tribune, 1865.

Woodward, C. Vann, and Elisabeth Muhlenfeld. *The Private Mary Chesnut: The Unpublished Civil War Diaries.* Oxford: Oxford University Press, 1984.

Works Progress Administration. *Slave Narratives.* Vol. 1, *Alabama.* Washington, DC: Library of Congress, 1941.

Young, J. P. *The Seventh Tennessee Cavalry, Confederate, A History.* Nashville: M. E. Church South, 1890.

## Internet Sources

"Encyclopedia of Alabama." http://encyclopediaofalabama.org/. Various access dates.

"New Georgia Encyclopedia." http://www.georgiaencyclopedia.org/. Accessed August 29, 2015.

"Tait-Starr Home." http://www.ruralswalabama.org/attraction/the-starr-home-white-columns -late-1850s/. Accessed January 13, 2016.

# Index